BREAD
AND
RICE

Also by Doris Macauley

What Time Is It in China?

The Lady with Binoculars

Happy Hour

BREAD
AND
RICE

An American Woman's Fight to Survive
in the Jungles and Prison Camps
of the WWII Philippines

Doris Macauley

THE LYONS PRESS
Guilford, Connecticut
An imprint of The Globe Pequot Press

The Lyons Press is an imprint of The Globe Pequot Press.

Originally published in 1947 as *Bread and Rice* by Doris Rubens by Thurston Macauley Associates.

Printed in the United States of America

10   9   8   7   6   5   4   3   2   1

Designed by Kirsten Livingston

ISBN 1-59228-413-2

Library of Congress Cataloging-in-Publication Data is available on file.

To T. M.
For his faith and understanding

CONTENTS

FOREWORD

Bread and Rice is a strangely moving story of heroism and fortitude. Written with warm sympathy and deep sincerity, it recreates in memorable fashion the painful experiences of an American couple in the Philippines during the Japanese occupation of the islands. Though it deals with wartime events, it is in no sense a "dated" book. Americans will read it with satisfaction and profit—those Americans especially who are so easily inclined to forget with what courage the Filipino people and their own countrymen in the Philippines suffered and fought out of shared loyalty to the cause of freedom. As a Filipino, I am especially gratified to meet in the pages of this book the humble yet heroic figure of Fabian, who typifies the nameless thousands who risked or lost their lives befriending and sheltering the Americans in their midst. The book is a kind of stimulating "refresher" course in comradeship that Americans and Filipinos should read with great benefit to their future relations of mutual respect and understanding.

Carlos P. Romulo
Permanent Philippine Delegate to the United Nations
New York, 1947

Bread and Rice . . . Rice and Bread . . . I have eaten the Bread of the West and the Rice of the East . . . I have known two worlds the dynamic outwardness of the Occident and the passive inwardness of the Orient and for a moment in Time I saw the two become one . . . from the throbbing aliveness of America with its volcanic cities erupting into space its wide level prairies and desiccated deserts stretching to gargantuan masses of mountains and rocky canyons from the golden wheatfields and the lush grass and fatted deep uddered cattle from the alchemy of the wheat magically transmuted into Bread a loaf of Bread sweetsmelling lifegiving sex-impelling the root of the life of the West . . . to China and Malaya with their terraced ricefields ploughed up by the coolie the tao the ox the carabao carefully cultivated to produce the beloved Rice white shining grains sustaining the life of the East with its exotic cultures timeless replicas of the past changeless and static . . . I felt the stirring of this ancient life I saw the awakening of the dragon at last I saw China's armies marching and the people quickening to resistance and I too became part of that resistance there and in the Philippines where we fought against the common enemy . . . and it was there I became one with the East living and suffering with its people and eating Rice . . .

DUNGEON IN MALOLOS

THE IRON-BARRED DOOR OF OUR DUNGEON CELL clanged and we
were left in the stone-walled clammy prison. I looked at Ron in
horror, but what I saw on his face made me look desperately through
the bars onto the courtyard of the jail where the bulky Filipino with
his huge ring of iron keys was disappearing behind the mechanical
strut of the Japanese officer.

Dazed by the darkness after the blinding tropical sunshine, we
stood leaning against the iron bars. With a dry mouth, I said at last:

"Did you hear me ask that Jap when we'd get out of here?"

"What did he say?

"Tomorrow."

Ron glanced at me then, but he turned his head away so quickly I
could not see this time the expression on his face.

"Did he really say that?" he asked.

"Yes. He smiled in that sneaky way and said, 'Tomorrow you go.'
Do you believe it?"

"I don't know what to believe anymore. We were supposed to be
taken to Santo Tomas and now look where they've brought us—a

medieval dungeon—" He pressed his head against the bars as if to beat out the desperation he felt. Staring at him, there suddenly flashed through my mind the picture of the wild bird who was kept tied with a rope by the little boy in the mountains . . .

The mountains . . . my little grass house and the bamboo bed . . . the clear sparkling mountain stream where I bathed and the great river where the Negritos would dive and spear the fish . . .

I tore my eyes away from the pallid sunlight of the prison square outside our dungeon and slowly turned to the damp fetid darkness of our narrow cell. Mechanically I went to the corner where Ron had dumped the precious brown sack holding all our earthly possessions, everything we had clung to for almost two years in the mountains . . . Good old sack . . . lucky the Japs let Ron carry it through. Quickly I began to pull out the few rags on top—some old cotton dresses the Filipino women had given me, Ron's faded white-gray jacket, a pair of khaki trousers, our ragged mosquito net, and then at last, buried under all of these, my two precious books, *Shelley's Poems* and John Cowper Powys' *Philosophy of Solitude.* I turned the pages lovingly—torn, bruised, and bent, it was a miracle they were still intact and even legible. We were lucky. Now if I ever needed anything, I needed these books. In the mountains I had practically memorized Shelley's poems, there where they seemed to me to express so perfectly the spirit and beauty of the place. But now I wanted something that would keep me in this terrible moment, something I remembered reading years ago that Powys had written:

> *A man is in a prison, say in the midst of a vast city . . . There are horrors not far from him; and maybe sounds and sights within his reach which will not bear thinking on . . .*

I glanced up for a moment and suddenly my eyes were glued to the strange figure peering at us from behind the outer bars. At first I thought the creature was a woman, poised as it was in the striking pose of a flirt, head flung back and graceful body arched and swaying its narrow hips, as it ran a comb through its lovely, Pan-like curls. Unmistakably it was ogling and leering at Ron, whose head was still bent, trying to attract his attention. A woman? Was this faun-like creature a woman? Were there women then in this jail also? I stared with horrible fascination . . . but no, it had the lean muscular legs of a boy. I nudged Ron and pointed. He looked up, startled out of his trance . . .

"What's that?" I whispered, curious. "Girl or boy?"

He glanced through the bars for an instant and then turned his back.

"Don't pay any attention. Hermaphrodite—surely you've heard of them in the islands. Well, that's one."

The faun-like creature, obviously disappointed at the lack of response, began wriggling away with many an arch look over its shoulder, but it was soon replaced by a group of vicious-looking prisoners with shaven heads, gaping at the Americanos through the bars.

"Damn it all—if only we could close this door," Ron muttered. "Staring at us as if we were animals in a cage."

Horrors not far from us, I thought . . . and I went on reading:

I am in a hospital, in a prison, in a madhouse and it is the same thing! I stretch out my spirit to these walls, to that window, to that square of blueness, of yellowness, of grayness, of blackness, which is the window of this place. These inanimate substances, this inanimate space, this air, this light, this darkness is my universe, the world into which I—this living self—have been flung by an inscrutable destiny . . . It is in my power to satisfy my senses upon them and to feel . . . that I am defying the whole material world.

Having realized the miracle of his being . . . the next thing he does is to ponder on the inevitability of death.

The inevitability of death . . . I stared up again at the sunlight streaked by the bars . . . sun and life . . . darkness and death . . . Death, perhaps, but torture, no, no! . . . Don't think of it, don't think . . . Abruptly I got up—we were still together. . .

"Let's try to close the door and stretch out . . . I'm so tired."

Ron swung the ponderous stone door so that the other prisoners could not see us. I folded our blanket on the floor and we lay down together . . . And then, once again, there was the miracle of our oneness obliterating the outer world . . . the horror vanishing—the dungeon, the Japs, the iron bars, the fear, and torture, the vicious faces . . . Powys had written and it was true: "Ecstasy even while one knows that there are unthinkable things going on around one . . ." Suddenly we heard shuffling feet, the jingle of keys. Quickly we sprang up and Ron pushed back the stone door.

A huge, muscular Filipino clothed only in striped bathing trunks loomed genie-like in front of the bars. He was holding a stick in his hands, and for a moment in that dim light, I had the wild idea that it was a whip, and that he had come to beat us. . . . I stared at him terrified. He leered and said in a broken English:

"I am José, the keeper of the jail. . . . I have brought you something." He handed us a small brown paper bag and waved his stick toward the outer jail. "The other prisoners have sent this to you."

I laughed a little hysterically . . . the stick . . . the whip. . . . Was I going mad already? I must pull myself together—this thing was only beginning. It wasn't so bad—we weren't alone . . . even these Filipinos were our friends. I opened the bag quickly—cigarettes and bananas. . . . We thanked him many times.

Ron asked José about a toilet and a place to wash up for me.

"Yes. . . . Come now and I will show you." José inserted one of the huge keys in the iron lock and swung open our door.

The joy of stepping out of the prison cell rushed through me, the joy of walking again, even if it was only through the outer prison and into the courtyard. I was conscious of a million eyes watching us from behind bars, but I was not afraid. These people were Filipinos, and even if they were thieves or murderers, they were one with us against the Japanese.

José pointed to a big wooden screen in the extreme right-hand corner of the courtyard and said to Ron:

"That is yours. Your wife come with me."

He led me to the left into the main building of the prison and into a tiny room containing a filthy toilet. Afterwards he showed us an open faucet in the courtyard where we could wash. I wanted to lie under it, to be washed clean of this foul place, and again with a nostalgia that was almost pain, I remembered my sparkling stream in the mountains. . . .

"When do you think we leave here?" Ron asked José, as he was locking us in again.

"Americanos who were here before stay two weeks."

"Two weeks! Americans here before—" Dazed we repeated his words. "Who were the Americans?"

"Soldiers. One Spanish mestiza. Very smart." José grinned. "Make believe he is very sick and Japs take him to hospital. Think he will surely die." And with that, José left us.

We looked at each other. . . . Two weeks—and that lying Jap had said tomorrow. . . . Tomorrow and tomorrow. . . . Two weeks, two weeks, two weeks. . . . I could never stand it, I would go mad, I would die.

Die, inevitable death. I stared at Ron, but his face was averted. . . . What could he say?

At that moment we heard the bell, followed by such a cacophony of wild unearthly shouting and rattling of cans, that we thought all hell had broken loose.

The prisoners were rushing about like wild animals escaped from their cages, shrieking and yelling and banging on their tin plates and cups, and pushing in a mad scramble to get in line. It was mealtime. A moment later, a Filipino woman and a man appeared from the inner building carrying a huge vat of steaming rice and meat. The woman began to dole out the portions to the outstretched hands. . . . I watched her avidly and hungrily—if only I could talk to her . . . maybe we could contact the guerrillas. But I was mad, how could she risk coming into the dungeon where we were, even if she wished? When the prisoners had been fed, I saw her glance in our direction and say a few words to her companion. I knew then that the bamboo wireless had been operating. Of course the woman had known all along that we were there—the whole town of Malolos probably knew by now—but it was a town heavily concentrated with the Japanese military and an attempt to free us would be foolhardy. A few moments later, José appeared with two plates of rice and pig meat.

"Hurry to eat this—Japs will come soon." We devoured it ravenously. Not since the mountain people had cooked for us had we tasted such dry well-cooked rice. The Japanese do not know how to cook rice. Theirs is always too wet or too sticky. I smiled gratefully through the bars at the woman.

After their meal, the prisoners stood around chatting and smoking and laughing. Among them were murderers, thieves, and God only knows what else in this abyss, and dressed in their rags, they looked a wretched, pitiful lot. But as I watched them, enjoying an interlude of freedom we no longer had, perhaps would never possess, I felt a strange mingling of pity, friendliness, and envy . . .

There was a sharp whistle and the clanging of a gate. The prisoners vanished, and in the empty courtyard now appeared the Filipino warden followed by two Japanese soldiers, carrying army mess gear. They glanced suspiciously around the yard and then motioned to the warden to unlock the gate leading to our dungeon. The Japs stood staring at us insolently, then one of them pointed to me and nudged the other. They said something in their own language and laughed hilariously. Suddenly one of them said to us, in English:

"Kiss . . ." And he made the motions for Ron and me to come together.

I felt as though I were turning to stone. I pretended not to notice, and looked down. Ron just stood there, very pale.

"Kiss!" the soldier shouted louder. "No kiss, no chow," he yelled.

It was crazy . . . like some fantastic scene in a weird world that had never existed: in a dungeon, behind bars, before two Jap buffoons.

Ron turned to me in desperation.

"They're clowning now—I don't think they mean any harm . . . but they might get nasty." Swiftly he stooped down and kissed me.

Their hilarious laughter was still ringing in my ears as they pushed the food in through the bars. . . . I turned sick when I saw it—a sloppy, watery mess of rice and fishy greens. Even worse than this morning. We pretended to eat as they stood watching us, jabbering their gibberish. Finally Ron handed back the kits and the soldiers grunted and swaggered out. José gave us some water in a tin cup and I washed out the foul taste of that awful mess.

Dusk had fallen and an eerie silence shrouded the jail, broken only by a mournful singing and a low murmur of voices. We squatted in the darkness of our cell, smoking the cigarettes the Filipinos had sent us. The tobacco burned away the slimy, fishy taste of the food and the light of the cigarette made a warm glow in the dark. I smoked and stared at the last patch of blue light arching the prison courtyard, reluctant for it to fade into the darkness—I was afraid to think of the night to come.

José suddenly appeared again like the genie in Aladdin's lamp, and asked whether we would like to go out into the courtyard for a quick walk before sleeping. Now that it was dark, it was safe—no Japs were here in the jail. Once again, he unlocked the door, and as we stepped out we both had the same thought. If there were only some way to get to the mountains again . . . there in the woods we were always safe. But it was hopeless even to think of it and we knew it.

Later, while I struck matches for light, Ron unrolled our blanket and then fitted the mosquito net over it like a tent, with two ends tied to the iron bars. At last we crawled in, glad just to lie down, glad even for the darkness that shut out everything around us. . . . We must have fallen off then for the next thing I remembered after that was a sudden blinding glare, a ghastly rattling of the iron bars, and shouting. I jerked up in a panic and then mechanically turned to shake Ron.

The next instant I instinctively shielded my face with my hands as the powerful glare of a light was focused on us from the outside of our cell. I heard a piercing shriek:

"Stand up!"

As I fumbled up, half-grasping at Ron's arm, I tried to see into the darkness outside. Dimly I made out the bulky figure of the warden grasping a ring of keys and an officer with gleaming sword and shining boots. I saw black slits for eyes and a deadly cruel mouth, now opening to shout:

"That is woman here!" He played the light up and down my figure. "American man and woman—why are they together?"

"Husband and wife—" I heard the warden mumble.

"Americans!" screamed the hysterical officer contemptuously. "American prisoners! Separate them—"

Then I thought my heart had stopped. Never in the terrible days after the Japanese had taken Manila, nor in the months stretching into years in the mountains when we had been hunted, never until this night had we been separated, even for a night. This was it, this then was what I had been fearing all along, this had been the meaning of my nightmares? Together no longer. . . .

The monstrous keys grinding in the gigantic lock of the dungeon door, the stone door swinging open, and his bare feet stumbling past the iron bars, and then the utter darkness closed upon me, walling me in . . .

THE CAPTURE

I WAS ALONE IN THE DARKNESS OF THE DUNGEON . . . the heavy thud of boots grew fainter and fainter and then died in the silence of the night. . . . Slowly the icy fear released its grip on my trembling body and I lay numb on the cold floor . . . aeons passed in the black void that was the present. Suddenly I remembered the strange dream I had once had, seven years ago, before I had first sailed for the Far East. . . . It was only a figment that rose from my subconscious mind, and it was this: I was surrounded by a semicircle of dark eyes, cruel, sinister eyes, staring at me—

My mind groped in the darkness and then in a flash I knew. . . . Last night that prophetic dream had become a terrible reality . . . last night we had been captured by the Japs, and I had looked into a semicircle of dark, cruel-veiled eyes, lit with the glint of their gleaming swords—the eyes of the Jap soldiers who surrounded us . . .

Last night we had been captured after hiding in the mountains of the Philippines for a year and a half. We had planned on holding out for the duration, but when the news came that they had taken Fabian, our faithful Filipino guide, and thrown his whole family into jail and threatened to kill them all, then we knew it was all over. The officer in command,

Captain Tanaka, sent Fabian to tell us that we would be transferred immediately to Santo Tomas if we surrendered peacefully. Of course, we did not believe that—but what could we do? Fabian knew where we were hiding, and the Japs knew that Fabian knew—and besides, we could not see the Filipino who had stuck by us for a year, and his family too, shot for us. We had no choice. So late on the afternoon of April 13, 1943, we made the weary trek down from the hills to Fabian's father's house in the little town of Montalban, about thirty kilometers east of Manila. The Japs were to pick us up the next morning . . .

It was midnight. We were lying in bed, too nervous to sleep, thinking that this was our last night of freedom, wondering about the days to come. . . . I had placed a black drill suit (black seemed the only fitting color for the occasion), the remains of a once elegant Manila wardrobe, at the foot of my bed, to wear the following morning. . . . Suddenly we heard the rumble of trucks coming nearer and nearer until they seemed almost on top of us and then they stopped. We heard Fabian shouting: "The Japs!" And I had just time to pull on my black suit when I heard them stamping into the adjoining room. And as the Jap detail swarmed in, armed with fixed bayonets and gleaming swords, it seemed as if the whole Japanese army in the Philippines had been ordered to capture the two of us.

Flanked by a cordon of soldiers, Captain Tanaka stepped forward to stare at us, and in the eerie light of the candle, I looked into a semicircle of cruel, sinister eyes—Jap eyes. . . . I began to tremble—my nightmare . . .

A clipped, harsh voice cut the dark silence. It was the voice of Captain Tanaka—and the grueling inquest began. He shot question after question at us: Where have you been? Why did you hide out in the mountains? Why did you not surrender before this? Why did you leave Manila? Were you not making propaganda in the hills?

Anti-Japanese propaganda—the Japs were rabid about that—and that was our Achilles heel. It was exactly what we had been doing—

we had been in constant touch with the guerrillas up to the very end. I prayed that my face would not betray the fear creeping over me like a clammy hand.

Ron pointed to the map Captain Tanaka had spread in front of him on the table. He pointed to the Sierra Madre range of mountains leading to the east coast of Luzon, and said slowly:

"Here we lived with the wild people of the mountains. They are called the Negritos, and they speak a strange dialect, not even Tagalog. We cannot speak their language. How could we make propaganda among them?"

Captain Tanaka looked at us blankly for a moment. Then slyly: "Negritos? They live in those mountains? What do they look like?"

"They are very small people with curly hair—they wear very little clothing and do much hunting and fishing," Ron replied.

"They hunt with poison arrows," I suddenly heard myself saying. I could have bitten off my tongue the next moment, when for the first time that night the Captain stared directly at me through his thick-lensed glasses. Up to now he had addressed himself only to Ron, ignoring me completely. I remembered then that a woman does not count with the Japs—and at this moment, it was far, far better that way.

"You are a woman," he said in his clipped icy singsong. "Were you not afraid to hide in these mountains?"

"Yes . . ." I was surprised to hear my own voice saying. "But we heard so many stories in Manila—"

"Anti-Japanese propaganda!" the Captain shouted vehemently. "All anti-Japanese stories . . ." He glared at me with hatred, then cried: "What did you do before the war?"

"I was a teacher of English at the University of the Philippines." Again I silently cursed myself for telling him this. Better, far better to be merely a housewife, as all good Japanese women are supposed to be, otherwise you are suspect for the "Dangerous Thought" police . . .

"You know Yay Panilio?"

It hit me with the impact of a bullet and for a split second I thought I would faint or scream hysterically at those cruel eyes boring relentlessly through me. Who was it that answered in that darkness with my voice, instinctively guarding me?

"No . . . who is that?"

Only too well I knew who "that" was—the famous woman guerrilla leader now in the hills where we had once lived, now at this moment with Marking's guerrillas fighting it out with the Japs. Even last week, we had sent her a letter and some money. We had been close friends before the war when she had been writing for the *Herald* in Manila.

The Captain glared at me and the inquisition bored on until the semicircle of eyes became a circle and slowly began to spin and whirl in that strange nightmare where I was held to reality only by the cold, steely voice, relentlessly questioning, questioning. . . . It was a circle ringed by the cordon of Jap soldiers with their gleaming swords and their bayonets, fixed, pointed at us . . .

Then suddenly it was over. Captain Tanaka got up so abruptly that his chair toppled over with a crash that shook me out of my trauma. He shouted an order for the soldiers who jumped to attention and started filing down the stairs. The Captain turned to us:

"Now come with me. Get ready quick."

Ron was about to hoist our sack over his shoulders, when the Captain stopped him with a motion of his hand. I held my breath while he eyed the sack suspiciously. Then he said something in Japanese to the two soldiers who had remained and they began to examine it disdainfully, as if they expected a hand grenade to pop out. They shook our dirty mosquito net, tossed aside my clothes contemptuously, and pounced upon a pair of khaki trousers and my two books. The trousers had been given to Ron by one of the guerrillas who must have gotten them from some American soldier.

Captain Tanaka looked significantly from the trousers to Ron.

"Soldier pants—you soldier, hiding perhaps, yes?" He smiled cunningly. The Japanese had a big price for American escaped soldiers in the hills. A civilian still had a chance.

Wearily Ron repeated that he was a civilian civil service employee for the Navy in Manila, but the Captain looked as if he were only weighing up all the evidence that would spell our doom. Then slowly he began to turn the pages of the books. The word "Poems" of Shelly seemed to strike some lost chord in him, for I saw him glance at us curiously for a moment, before he leafed the torn pages of the *Philosophy*. It was the first intimation I had that gave me anything like a feeling of hope, that all was not entirely lost. I thought he had looked at us in that moment as though he judged us to be an impractical poetical couple who liked adventure and philosophy. But his expression was stony and inscrutable when he finally handed the books over to the two soldiers who stuffed them back into the sack.

"Okay—go now," he shot out. Ron quickly swung the sack over his shoulder and motioned me to follow him.

The soldiers were already piled into the two trucks when we came down to the deserted street of the little town. I remember there was a light somewhere—I think it was the flashlight of one of Tanaka's guards—and it lit up that street for me like some unforgettable painting. Real houses where there were beds and where people slept. I would have given anything that night to sleep without fear, to be human again. . . . Tanaka told us to get in front of one of the trucks with him, shouted something, and we were off. After driving for about ten minutes, we stopped abruptly before a big house with a wooden fence around it. I heard the other truck behind us roar to a sudden stop with a screeching of brakes. The Captain jumped out and we followed him, and stood uncertainly near the fence, waiting for the next order.

Do you remember Dostoyevsky's immortal description of his feelings as he faced the firing squad in *House of the Dead*? For what happened to me in the next five minutes by some strange trick of my mind and imagination was just that. I think it is a kind of hysteria that seizes one in times of great emotional strain. At any rate, as I heard Tanaka scream out an order, and the Japanese soldiers lined up in front of us with their guns fixed, on that lonely deserted street in the middle of the night, I had the terrible panicky feeling that we were about to be shot. . . . I saw the guns moving and in a wild impulse I flung myself at Ron, hiding my face, and in that moment a kaleidoscopic flash of my whole life up to that time seemed to converge with the present, and I felt as though I could see everything with a terrible clarity. . . . It was just an instant—then I looked up dazed and saw that the soldiers were filing back into the trucks and we were alone with Tanaka in front of the house. We followed him into the house and he led us upstairs and across a wide room to another smaller one in which there were two beds. He pointed to one and said:

"You both sleep here." Then he pointed to the other: "I sleep here." Abruptly he turned and left. We heard him say something to the two guards who remained in the outer room, directly outside our door.

Slowly Ron swung his sack in the corner of the room near our bed and stared at me.

"What the hell does he mean—'you both sleep here and I sleep here'. . . . Damn him, if he—"

"It doesn't mean anything . . ." I tried to make my voice sound convincing. "Look, he hasn't separated us—that's something anyway . . . and he let us keep those books—maybe he's educated—and trying to protect us from the soldiers. Anyway we better get in before he comes back."

There was a mosquito net on a ring at the head of the bed and I quickly rolled it down. We crawled in, just as we were.

It must have been about three or four in the morning—we had about two more hours of torture before dawn, sleep being impossible to our taut nerves. Suddenly we heard footsteps and a flashlight shone full upon us. We lay rigid as though dead. . . . Just when I thought the light would sear through me, it was snapped off and I heard a shuffling to the other side of the room. I opened my eyes and was barely able to make out the outline of the figure getting into the other bed: Captain Tanaka, satisfied that his prisoners were still here, could now sleep.

For the next hour I kept my eyes glued to Tanaka's inert form, waiting for the slightest move. I felt as though I were waiting for a bomb to explode, and it was with a terrible relief that I finally saw the first blessed streaks of light creep into the room. They lit up the still prostrate figure of Tanaka sleeping in the full regalia of his uniform under his net—only his boots lay on the floor beside the bed. After that I must have fallen off from sheer exhaustion, for the next thing I recall was starting up at a loud knocking at the door. We both sat up, tense and waiting. Then one of the guards entered noisily and Captain Tanaka stirred and muttered something and opened his eyes.

There was much bowing and scraping, and then some sort of pow-wow in Japanese. It must have been important, for as soon as the guards reared out of the room, Tanaka jerked himself sleepily up from the bed, pulled on his boots, adjusted his sword, and without so much as a glance in our direction, left the room. That was the cue we had been waiting for, and we sprang up hurriedly, rolled back the net, and sat down to await the next move. Whatever it would be, we did not want to take it lying down. . . . It was then that we noticed the door behind Tanaka's bed, in the farther right corner, and as Ron went over to investigate, I hoped it would be what I wanted. And when he made a quick gesture for me to come over, I knew that it was. Apparently, Tanaka had chosen the best room in the house for himself, with a private toilet and luxury of luxuries, even a little washstand with a mirror. The cold water was electric to my taut, tired face and hair, and after powdering my nose, I felt almost able to face things again. I suppose no amount of water could tone down Ron's shaggy beard, but he made a go at it anyway, and looked a little less ferocious.

A few minutes later the guards entered again, carrying two army mess kits, and with a grunt handed them to us. One of them contained rice and the other a soupy concoction with soya bean curds and fish bones floating around in it. My stomach turned at the fishy smell and I felt a wave of nausea—so this was the Japanese breakfast. The guards watched us with wooden expressions. Ron scooped a little rice in his hands and then gave me the kit.

"Better eat some rice—force yourself," he murmured.

I managed to gulp down some rice and then to the guards made the motions of wanting a drink. One of them took the kits and came back with a cup of water, which we shared. After awhile the guard returned and motioned for us to follow him into the next room.

Captain Tanaka was seated at a round table littered with papers and among them I saw our passports (how glad I was we had had to change our old passports for new ones in Manila just before the outbreak of war; my old red one with the Chinese visas was safe in the High Commissioner's vault) that had been taken from us last night. . . . Last night . . . already an eternity seemed to have passed since last night, an abyss that separated us from freedom, and now we were prisoners of this sinister little Jap in a crumpled uniform. . . . He waved us to chairs. The guard had taken up an immobile position at the door, his fixed bayonet erect, poised.

Captain Tanaka leaned back and stared at us for a moment with a curious mixture of cunning and cruelty, as though about to lure us into a trap. I felt jittery and unnerved and jumped at the question he fired at Ron:

"You know American—Mr. Spalding—yes?"

I knew by the way Ron blanched that he would fumble that. The Jap had caught him unprepared and since he had last night denied knowing any Americans in the hills he had to continue the lie. Whatever happened, I knew he would never mention any names.

"No . . ." replied Ron in a low voice.

"No?" Tanaka repeated in mock surprise. "Mr. Spalding also hiding in hills?"

"I don't know . . ."

The cruel eyes glittered behind the spectacles and for an instant I thought he would spring at Ron and slap him as his hand suddenly jerked upward. Abruptly he shifted his myopic gaze to me.

"You—American woman—teach at university, yes?"

"Yes . . ."

"Who started war?" he suddenly demanded.

I stared at him in amazement. Was this another trap? Why this sudden veering off into politics? It was a tricky question—he was writing down all our answers and it would all be held against us. What could I say? . . . Instinctively I decided on evasion.

"I am a woman. I know nothing of such things . . ."

He smiled craftily. "*Sodeska* (so that's it) . . . but you teach at university . . . surely you have opinion?" His singsong voice rose to a querulous and insistent treble.

I shook my head. "In the mountains I did not think," I answered slowly. "I only cooked rice . . . and lived with the mountain people . . ."

He looked baffled for a moment and then resumed. "But you read much in mountains, yes? You have books . . ."

He had remembered the books in our sack, my Shelley and Powys. "Yes . . ." I murmured.

"You like philosophy?"

It was incredible: at that moment the Jap looked almost human, like a bookish little Oriental engaged in a discussion. But I distrusted him.

"Chinese philosophy very interesting, yes?" He smiled mockingly. "I study Chinese philosophy at Tokyo University—before war . . ."

I shall never know where this curious talk might have led, for just then a soldier entered, bowed, and said something in Japanese to Tanaka. The Captain glared sternly at us and then spoke to the soldier, who bowed again and left the room.

"Mr. Spalding downstairs," Tanaka told us. "He come here . . ."

Ron and I looked at each other. What was Spalding doing here reporting to a Jap? The last we had heard of him was that he had surrendered to the Japanese, it was true, but why was he not a prisoner as we were?

I could hardly recognize the smooth-shaven, well-dressed man who then came into the room and bowed expertly to Captain Tanaka. I still had the picture of him as we had last seen him in the mountains: gaunt, thin, and trembling with malaria, dirty and unkempt . . . only the weak chin was unchanged. . . . He did not seem surprised to see us. On the contrary, it was as though he had expected to find us. He grinned sheepishly, one eye on Tanaka, who was watching us fixedly, and said:

"Hello—everything OK?" He shuffled uneasily. I looked down at his army boots and remembered the pale, limp feet, hanging over the bamboo bed in the mountains, inert and helpless . . . he had never had shoes then . . .

"No use hiding anything, Johnston." He looked at Tanaka. "He knows everything. . . . Been pretty good to me, taking care of my family, and giving me plenty of liberty to see them."

Ron's eyes were hard with contempt. I think that only Tanaka's presence kept him from hitting Spalding, who looked away, embarrassed. Tanaka interrupted in a sharp voice:

"OK, Spalding—go now. Your pass?" he demanded.

Spalding took out a small card and handed it to him. Tanaka flashed it before us. There was a rising sun emblem on it and it bore Spalding's picture and his name in Japanese characters. Tanaka smiled at Ron.

"Very good—go any place. You also like pass? Only one thing— must go with Japanese officer to tell Americans hiding in hills how good is Japanese army. Or maybe you like working here, yes?"

Ron said nothing and Captain Tanaka's eyes grew cold and hard. Angrily he handed the pass back to Spalding and snapped at him: "Go!"

Spalding glanced at us mutely and shuffled out and as I watched his strangely defeated figure receding through the door, I felt a flash of pity for him.

For a moment after Spalding had gone, the Captain stood glaring at us with a look of baffled anger and frustration. Then he picked up our passports and handed them to Ron. "Get ready—we go." Tanaka shouted at the guard.

Ron slung the sack over his shoulder and we followed Tanaka and his soldiers into the street. . . . We were in the square of the little town of Montalban, shining in the hot noonday sun. Young Filipino girls were clattering past on their painted *bakias* (clogs) and youths in *pina* blouses were carrying birds under their arms for the cock-fights and children were running about . . . then in the shadow of the doorway of a shop I caught sight of Fabian and Ponciano, watching us. . . . I wanted to smile at them but was afraid. . . . The Japs led us across the square, past the church, to a large low wooden building with the word *Escuela* (School) painted on it. We entered a bare room along the walls of which some Filipinos lay as if asleep. At our entrance they stood up and bowed from the waist. Tanaka turned to us and said sharply: "You sleep here." Then he marched out.

The Filipinos there were unmistakably guerrilla suspects and we recognized among them at least one familiar face—a member of the guerrilla band that had visited us. But we knew he would not talk, though Tanaka was dreaded for his infamous methods of torture. . . . A hundred or so Japanese soldiers were quartered in improvised barracks adjoining the school: They were the soldiers who were being sent up into the hills and mountains to wipe out the guerrillas and we could see them piling into trucks, armed to the teeth. Some of the trucks never returned . . .

There was nothing in that bare room, no place to sit, no place to sleep, no place to wash—worst of all, no toilet. There was only the one outside used by the soldiers. When Tanaka came back at chow time

I asked permission for a soldier to take me to a house in town. It was obvious that having a woman prisoner was a matter for which no rules had as yet been drawn up and he consented.

After eating the meal of rice and fish soup, I set out on my unique journey and we must have made a strange picture to the people of the town who turned to stare as we passed: a rough-looking Japanese soldier with rifle striding ahead, followed by a slim woman with long black hair, clad in a black suit and wearing worn sandals. Going by the pillbox in the square, the soldier stopped and bowed to the sentry. I watched politely and was about to go on when the soldier grunted and motioned for me to bow too. Awkwardly I imitated him and the sentry looked at me as if he were a god gazing at a miserable mortal.

The soldier stopped in front of a rather spacious house and loudly rattled the gate and an old Filipino man and a boy ran out. They led us in the house and upstairs to an old Filipino woman, who bowed when she saw the soldier and stared at me with great sympathy in her eyes. Like Tanaka's quarters, the house presumably belonged to some rich Filipino, for it was well furnished. I heard the soldier saying *"Benjo, benjo"* to the Filipinos and he pointed to me. The woman smiled and motioned for me to follow her. In the corner of the room I caught sight of a piano. A piano . . . it was as if the earth itself had opened up and whirled me back to the other side of the world . . . my world: the world I had lost and nearly forgotten, the world of music and song, the world of peace and beauty and of freedom from fear and violence . . . and I forgot the Jap soldier, forgot the Filipinos, forgot that I was a prisoner of the Japs, forgot everything but that here was a piano, which I had not seen for so long . . . and I sat down and played Bach's English Suite in D Minor and the music dropped from my fingers as if it had been waiting in me all these months to be born and I wanted to weep as I played. . . . I stopped and remembered suddenly where I was—I jumped up in fear and whirled around: The soldier stood leaning on his rifle, his head cocked to one side while the Filipinos stared at him open-mouthed as if they expected him to take aim and shoot me. . . . The Jap grinned and pointed to the other room: Apparently, he wanted me to understand that the concert was over and now I could go to the *benjo*.

That night we slept on the floor of the school. At dawn the next morning we were roused by the sound of a truck jamming to a stop outside. Then Captain Tanaka strode into the room. We stood up, facing him. He barked at us:

"You go now—truck waiting."

I stifled a sudden impulse to ask him whether we were going to Santo Tomas. Intuitively the cruel imperturbability of his face told me the story, and I felt a chill spreading through me as of some impending disaster while we followed him into the street. Vaguely I was aware of some Filipinos staring at me as we climbed into the back of the truck already loaded with soldiers armed with rifles and fixed bayonets. I sank down on our sack, and Ron stood as close as he could to me to act as a kind of shield from the soldiers. But I was hardly conscious of them—only of the question pounding through me: Where were we going?

The truck swung at a break-neck speed through the narrow dusty streets of the little town of Montalban—that same friendly little town through which we had driven eighteen months ago, heading for the mountains beyond, running away from the Japanese. . . . Well, they had finally caught up with us—and what now? We had left Montalban behind and were driving though flat open country. I held up my face to the sun and the wind and said a silent farewell to the mountains that had protected us for so long. We drove on through the deserted, desiccated countryside; occasionally we saw a Filipino farmer driving his carabao through the rice paddies, but for the most part everything looked desolate and destroyed. We detoured past blown-up bridges and piles of debris of what had once been houses—nothing had been rebuilt.

We must have been driving for about two hours when we entered a fairly large-sized town, certainly bigger than Montalban. I watched intently to catch its name on any of the shops we passed. Finally Ron nudged me and whispered: "Malolos!" Malolos—I had never heard of it before, but I knew this much: that it was not on the road to Manila, for we had driven many times before the war on the roads branching out of Manila.

"Where are we?" I whispered to Ron.

He shrugged his shoulders. "Don't know exactly. But I've heard of Malolos—it's the capital of Bulacan province."

The truck had left the center of the town and had veered off on some side road that ran parallel to the railroad tracks. We crossed the tracks and drove into the grounds of what appeared to be some government enclosure, in which was a group of imposing buildings. We noticed a Japanese flag flying from the tallest of the buildings. "Probably central Jap headquarters of the province," Ron whispered.

Our truck stopped with a jerk and the soldiers began to pile out. One of Tanaka's guards who had sat in front with the driver, now came up to us and motioned for us to get off. I jumped down stiffly, and stared uneasily around. We saw a few Japanese officers coming down the steps and others going into the buildings. Through the windows we could see Japanese clerks with pencils behind their ears working at desks. Our guard had taken some papers out of his pocket, and after telling a soldier to watch us, was hurrying off into the central building—to get his orders, I supposed. For a moment the official look of the place reassured me—perhaps we were merely being checked here before being sent on to Santo Tomas. . . . Santo Tomas suddenly seemed like heaven on earth—the thought of being under American protection, where there were other Americans, including women, appeared incredibly wonderful . . .

The guard was coming back . . . he was coming nearer . . . I saw that he was smiling, and it was a cruel mocking smile, and again that cold chill spread over me.

"Okay—now. You follow."

He led the way to the right, until we reached a low rectangular stone building. Directly in front of it stood two Jap guards with fixed bayonets. As they examined our papers they stared at us insolently and then motioned for us to pass.

We passed through a dark archway, and for no accountable reason the words ran through my mind: "Abandon hope all ye who enter here." The next moment I stared at a bulky Filipino with a huge ring of keys who suddenly loomed before an iron gate. He smiled and bowed to the guard and glanced significantly at us. Then he proceeded to unlock the great iron-barred gate and lead us across the prison courtyard to our dungeon cell . . .

I was aroused from my numbed semi-conscious torpor by the sound of footsteps and rattling keys. Instinctively I shrank as far back as I could against the wall. A few weak streaks of a pallid dawn came creeping in through the bars and lit up the two ghost-like figures peering into the darkness of my cell. Then I heard José's familiar voice.

"Do not be afraid, Missus. . . . No Japs here now. Here is some hot tea and cakes for you."

"José!" I sprang up in hysterical relief. "José, tell me—what have they done with my husband? Where have they taken him?"

"Don't worry—he is not far from you. They only put him in another room—alone—" He waved his hand vaguely towards the other end of the dungeon corridor. "You will see him at mealtimes."

Weakly I leaned against the bars for support and reached for the tea and cake the other man was holding out to me. Hot strong tea and the sweetness of a cake that was not rice. I began to feel human again. I held out my cup and watched the vendor pour the golden liquid from his kettle . . . nectar and ambrosia—tea and cakes . . .

Then José asked if I would like to go out now to wash up.

"You will see him as you go," he whispered as soon as the vendor had left. "We will bring him tea."

Ron had been thrown into solitary confinement at the other end of the corridor. He was lying on the stone floor of his cell, and he started up fearfully when I cried out to him. His face looked like a ghost in the early morning light—pale and worn, and I thought I could see some ugly red marks across his forehead.

"What did they do to you? Did they beat you or anything?"

He looked at me steadily for a moment and then said quietly:

"Nothing—don't worry about me. I'm all right—you can see. . . . And you, are you all right? This is a terrible mess we've gotten into. You will try to be brave, won't you? No matter what?"

●

For the next seven days and nights I was alone in my cell, and there were moments when I fought with all my inner strength against going mad. The days were not so bad—there was that soothing and terrible monotony of prison routine that bound all of us behind these bars, and then there were the times I could see Ron. And as the days wore on, the prisoners began to accept us as one of themselves, and share with us the little things that made their life tolerable—cigarettes, cakes, candy, or any other delicacies brought or smuggled in to them by their friends or relatives. We learned to know a few of them by name and their stories: Juan, the recognized leader among the prisoners, tall, muscular, vicious-looking, who seemed to be the favorite of Aphrodite, the nymph-like creature who so startled me the first day.

Juan was just an incorrigible jailbird—he was always bouncing in and out of prison; he was no sooner released than he was right in again with some other crime to his credit. At first convicted of some petty larceny, he had ended up knifing someone for his money, and now he was in for life. You could see that Aphrodite just adored him the way he followed him around all day, forever arching his body, and coquet-tishly combing his Pan-like curls. After that first unsuccessful attempt, he had given up trying to make Ron, or Juan might have had a serious rival. But now he was prancing around the prison courtyard after Juan just as merrily as ever. I began to develop a real affection for José, the prison-keeper—my genie, as I thought of him—for it was he who would take me to Ron whenever he could and do all sorts of little favors for me. It was with somewhat of a shock that I learned that he had been serving a ten-year sentence for murdering his wife's lover, but had been recommended for leniency for good behavior and might soon be leaving the jail. As for the other prisoners, I gradually lost my fear of them completely and grew quite accustomed to seeing them knotted in a group outside my cell staring at me through the bars; after a while, I even began to try to talk to them in the little Tagalog I knew, just to relieve the monotony.

I was afraid of only two things then—the Japs and the darkness of the nights alone in my cell. Ever since the traumatic shock of that first night when the Japanese officer had separated us, I lived in fear of what might happen the next night. As soon as I was locked in for the night within those black walls a terrible wave of hysterical foreboding would seize me and I would have an overwhelming desire to scream out in the darkness, to throw myself at the iron bars and break them so that I could run out and be free. Finally in despair, I would throw myself down on the floor, cover my head with my blanket, and try to blot out the ghastly pictures moving kaleidoscopically through my mind . . .

There was that one dream that haunted me with the fixity of an obsession—the dream I had remembered the first night alone: that pic-ture of being surrounded by a semicircle of eyes, cruel Jap eyes. . . . I could not escape the feeling that even before the night of our capture, somewhere this dream had been a sinister reality . . .

I began to relive my past, subconsciously seeking for the memory that would be the clue to the strange pattern of events that had

3

JOURNEY INTO CHINA

L IKE THE EVER-RECURRENT MOTIF of a symphony, this dream of being surrounded by a semicircle of Japanese eyes obsessed me. . . . And I lay in the jail night after night thinking about the dream going back into Time, to a point in time when the dream had first become a reality for me. . . . And I remembered: The night before I had left America on my first journey to China, a journey to the end of night curving to this very moment as I lay in the darkness now a prisoner of the Japanese, I had dreamed that dream. It was as though in some cryptic way my subconscious mind in a blinding flash of prescient awareness of my fate would have warned me. Yet nothing could stop my going. Was it not Heraclitus who said: "A man's character is his fate"? And I suppose that was also true of a woman's.

My life up to the time I left for China had been the full, absorbing pattern of the American girl student. I was rather precocious, graduating from college at nineteen, dabbling in writing, in life, not wanting to miss anything. After receiving my B.A., I started to work in a psychological clinic dealing with children, meanwhile studying at night for my master's degree and later for a doctorate. But the year I was to get my Ph.D. was 1938—the year of Spain—and soon I found myself more absorbed in the forces that were shaping our world than in the mind. A remark of my brilliant professor of neuro-anatomy at the Rockefeller Foundation where I was studying seemed to epitomize my feelings. We were watching him delicately dissecting a human brain, when he said: "This must be the brain of a Nazi—it is so tough." It was this same professor who later, when I told him I was leaving for China, looked at me with a curious expression and said lightly that he wished he were young enough to go with me on this adventure.

Adventure, I thought ironically, lying in the dungeon, what had apparently started as an adventure of an American girl reporter in China shaped itself into a kind of pragmatic philosophy that was to determine my life for the next eight years.

It was the year of the Fascist tidal wave in Spain and China. Anyone even remotely aware of what was really happening could see that the Japanese in China, like Franco in Spain, were only part of that wave that threatened to engulf us all. If you wanted to fight it, you could take your choice—Spain or China—or even right here in America, except that the bombs and the shooting had actually started over there. I became more and more interested in the social and political forces in China as part of this whole world picture. I began to read everything I could on China—her history, her economics, her women, but I think the books that influenced me most of all (and perhaps were really responsible for my going to China) were Vincent Sheean's *Personal History* and Edgar Snow's *Red Star Over China*. Both these books eventually became reality for me. Anyone who has ever read *Personal History* will remember Sheean's description of those two remarkable women—Madame Sun Yat-sen and Rhayna Prohme. I became obsessed with the idea of meeting Sun Chingling (Madame Sun); somehow she seemed to symbolize China's revolution and China's struggle today.

I had always been interested in writing and journalism, but had shunned the fashion and society niches usually the lot of the girl reporter in America. I had taken journalism courses at Columbia, but had been most discouraged when I applied for my first job on a New York paper. The editor had not taken my youthful ambitions very seriously; instead, he asked me out to a nightclub to discuss the matter and in the taxi proposed running away to the South Seas. This incident cold-douched any more journalistic inspirations for the time being and I concentrated my efforts to make a living in the psychological field.

After four years of it, I felt suddenly confined, limited to the narrow world of the child's mind. Not only did I begin to feel the need of knowing a wider world, but I felt it was important—the most important thing at that time—for each of us to contribute something towards the shaping of that world. I was influenced more than I ever realized by *Personal History*. From a passive philosophy of enjoyment and mere living, I jumped to an active, more aggressive one. I felt that I was leaving my Ivory Tower, and throwing my weight on the right side of the scales in the tenuous balance of Democracy and Fascism. I think those men and women who went to Spain must have felt that intensely at that time.

It happened to be China for me. In America some of us could see that certain groups were supplying Japan with the materials for bombing China, thus indirectly helping in that sinister and far-reaching blueprint to conquer the world by stages—first China, then America. I joined organizations protesting the shipment of scrap iron to Japan and boycotting silk stockings and raising money for China. I remember once taking fifty children from Chinatown to a great rally at Madison Square Garden where Luise Rainer (who had starred in The *Good Earth* film) pleaded on behalf of China. It was during this period that I learned to know such people as Haru Matsui, author of *Restless Wave,* that lovely young Japanese girl who had risked all to write and speak against her own country, and Jack Chen, brilliant leftist artist, son of Eugene Chen—China's foreign minister of 1927—and Jack's sister, Si-lan, the dancer.

Events were moving swiftly: Franco was gaining in Spain, the Japanese had been bombing Shanghai, and their armies were wiping out town after town in the interior. In New York, the pattern of my thoughts suddenly crystallized. I decided to change worlds—to plunge into the vortex. My plans were vague, inchoate: I had money enough to reach China but had no idea how I would ever get back—I just left that to Kismet. I now realize that I must have been slightly touched with the China fever or I would never have gone off so bravely. If I had not been so young, a million fears and rationalizations would probably have arisen to keep me from going. When I mentioned the idea to my friends they would invariably look at me as if I had suddenly gone mad (but a look that had an unmistakable tinge of envy) and say: "But there's a war going on in China. Aren't you afraid? And what about all those strange Oriental diseases—choler, typhus, bubonic plague, dysentery?"

In retrospect, I see that some fears, which I would never admit consciously, must have crept into my mind. The Japs in China—the rape of Nanking—what would they do to a white woman if they caught her? But I was young and I knew only one thing—to be able to say: "I have seen China"—and perhaps even more: "I have tried to help China."

I could not foresee that setting off as I did from the relative peace of a psychological clinic to the turbulent chaos of the Orient, would only be the beginning, the first thread of the pattern of my life for the next decade until this very moment in the Japanese jail. . . . Only that dream warned me, but it faded (though I never forgot it) when I awoke that morning in May of 1939 to start so gaily on my adventure, eager to be off, to shed my old world, to leave the America I had never left before.

I booked passage on the Norwegian freighter *Tancred* from Los Angeles to Kobe, where I would have to continue on to Shanghai and Hongkong, my destination. I still do not know why I picked Hongkong and not Shanghai as my final port—perhaps it was the subconscious feeling that from there I might be able more easily to go into the interior of China, or perhaps it was the musical euphony of that fascinating name. Most likely it was because I had heard Madame Sun Yat-sen was living there.

At sea I discovered ironically that the *Tancred* was carrying a shipload of scrap iron to Japan—the very thing I had been fighting in New York. It made me more than ever aware that my journey was not merely a romantic trip to a mysterious Orient of singsong girls and chopsticks, but to see and work in a country that was fighting for its life against a Fascist aggressor. I had arranged before I left to write for various newspapers and magazines on a freelance basis, and I spent a great deal of time aboard ship reading up on the political background of China. Donald Davies, the brother of John Davies, American vice consul in Hankow, whom I was to know well later, was also on the *Tancred,* and we spent many hours discussing the Chinese situation. Don, the son of a missionary doctor, had been born in a remote town in the interior and there spent his childhood, before being sent to America for his education. He was on a freelance assignment to photograph the war areas in devastated China. The other four passengers were bound for Manila—a honeymoon couple who planned to settle on a sugar plantation and a mother and son. The latter pair I was to meet again years later in the Japanese internment camp at Santo Tomas. But Manila then held little significance for me, compared to my intense preoccupation with China, and nothing on that sunny journey could ever have warned me that almost a decade later I would be a prisoner of the Japanese in that very city. . . . Three weeks later, we were in Japan.

Japan . . . dark furry islands humped on the horizon . . . Japan . . . backdrop of the Oriental stage of that great drama in which even I was destined to play a small part. . . . *Your insolent soldiers who hold me captive now. . . . I have seen you and I know your roots. . . . I have seen the flimsiness of your country, your feudal hierarchy, the abyss yawning between your poverty and your wealth . . .*

Japan . . . stepping ashore at Kobe, I have the sudden fleeting feeling of standing upside down on the other side of the globe. I am fascinated by the Japanese girls click-swishing by on wooden shoes, dressed in flowered kimonos, under parasols . . . precisely garbed, compact gentlemen under huge umbrellas . . . crowds of peasant women with babies slung on their backs plodding through the streets . . . bewildering traffic: rickshaws, bicycles, primitive carts, automobiles fly in all directions . . . the City—a toy miniature replica of our cities . . . tiny shops with familiar signs like Singer Sewing Machine. . . . I wander through the Motimachi, the main shopping district of Kobe . . . stalls with colorful wares gleaming in the sun. . . . I wander on and on through crowded streets until I come to the "coolie" section, rows and rows of little straw houses on stilts overflowing with hostile eyes peering at me. . . . I hurry back to the City . . . everywhere I see squads of young soldiers, marching, marching, marching off to China.

China. . . . I too was on my way to China. . . . I left Japan on the P & O liner *Ranchi* and passing through the Inland Sea of Japan saw the last of the island, volcanic green-covered points rising erect from the sea, then on through the Korea Straits, headed for Shanghai.

On July 4th we approached Shanghai, steaming up the Whangpoo alive with its motley armada of junks and sampans and other native craft of all sizes and shapes, their sails arched in the wind, picturesquely patched with varying colors, and steered by a woman or girl with a long pole. The modern skyline of Shanghai burst incongruously upon this scene—a strange juxtaposition of the West superimposed upon the East. And as I stepped from the gangplank to the Bund teeming with Chinese and westerners, I suddenly felt utterly bewildered, utterly lost . . . Lying in the jail now and remembering that lost feeling I had in Shanghai, I laugh. . . . For no longer do I feel I belong to the West as I did then. . . . No, I have eaten Rice too long and lived like the Oriental women, stared into the faces of their Oriental men, suffered with the Chinese people and the Filipino people . . . and most of all I have forgotten the taste of Bread . . .

After the first moment, I was no longer lost in Shanghai, but soon became part of the vast sea of humanity in that strange, exciting city; with its coolies panting before their yoked burdens and rickshaw boys bearing their human cargo, Shanghai always has been like an open wound to me, its suffering, disease, and horror bared to the eye.

But I saw nothing of that then. I had only one day in Shanghai. I had to be back aboard the *Ranchi* at midnight to sail for Hongkong and I decided to make the most of it. I had an introduction to one of the best-informed Americans on China—Randall Gould, editor of the *Shanghai Evening Post* and *Mercury*. He was very cordial and immediately took charge of my day. After tiffin—my first lunch in China—he arranged a tour of the bombed Chapei area, usually impossible to see without a special newspaper pass and which was most carefully scrutinized by Japanese sentries guarding the entrance to that No Man's Land.

The Chapei area was my introduction to the real China—not the romantic China. It remained with me as a kind of panoramic waste-land, a graphic symbol of Fascist destruction, and a foreshadowing of the bombings I was to see in China, in Europe, and in the Philippines. It was the nucleus of the picture that was Shanghai to me then; the rest was filled in with the dynamic movement of its throbbing life: Nanking and Bubbling Wells Roads thronged with heterogeneous Chinese types—students, merchants, coolies, beggars, whores, and the lame, the aged, the diseased . . . and at night the city coming to life in gay dancing spots with singsong girls and White Russian prostitutes.

Hongkong looked deceptively peaceful, a dream island rising from the sea, its jagged peaks shimmering in the tropical dawn, as the *Ranchi* docked across the harbor at Kowloon. Actually Hongkong with its luxurious hotels, department stores, theaters, and banks on one hand and its picturesque Chinese quarters on the other was a strange and fantastic blend of the modern and the old, the West and the East. On its steep rocky incline, wealthy foreigners had built splendid villas, while below in the twisting narrow lanes of the Chinese section, the sidewalks swarmed with half-naked beggars, women with babies, whining children, and pompous merchants in sedan chairs. And even in the staid British section of the city, Eurasians and Sikhs mingled with impeccably attired English, as the side streets overflowed with the thousands of Chinese refugees fleeing from Japanese bombs.

For the next two months, I worked in Hongkong for its leading British newspapers, the *South China Morning Post* and the *Hongkong Herald.* In a few days I lost my illusions about the placidity of the island. That summer of 1938, Hongkong was a city of intrigue, international espionage, and political ferment. The Japanese were preparing for their main push into the heart of China and meanwhile were busy sending emissaries to ferret out the main arteries of supplies going into China from the coast. Under British control, in supposedly neutral territory like the International Settlement of Shanghai, Hongkong was the springboard for diplomats, correspondents, and royalty with real or spurious titles of all nationalities bound for the interior.

My immediate assignment was to cover ships arriving from all parts of the world and interview important visitors. When the day's passenger lists looked dull, I would go to the Hongkong Hotel and wait for possible tips on interesting people coming from the interior of China or French Indo-China. My first real scoop was about the ordeal of a New Zealand woman, Iris Wilkinson, who had been caught by the Japanese as she fled from the captured city of Hsuchow; she had been attacked and found half dead by missionaries, who brought her to Hongkong. After treatment in the British Hospital on the Peak, she left for England, and I subsequently heard with sorrow that this brave and talented woman had committed suicide in London. Later, when I myself was preparing to go into the interior, the story of Iris Wilkinson was held up to me by old China hands as a terrible example of what happened to women who attempted to go into China then.

But I was beginning to tire of both Hongkong and its old China hands who beat their Chinese servants and thought anyone who tried to help the poor Chinese either a Red or a missionary. I interviewed Edgar Snow on his arrival from the interior and obtained two stories: one for *The Hongkong Herald* on China's determination to resist the Japanese in the threatened Hankow offensive; the other on the Chinese Cooperatives for a New York paper. Snow also gave me a spectacular story on the International Brigade then being formed in Hankow.

The growth of China's great Cooperative movement after the Japanese destroyed most of her factories in the coastal cities has become a saga in China's terrible struggle for survival. Snow was one who believed that in this economic experiment lay China's hope in the years to come. He had known and worked with Rewi Alley, the famous Australian who had been so indefatigable in organizing the Cooperatives, which were even then beginning to produce China's vital necessities by hand or with primitive machinery laboriously carried into the vast hinterland. Snow himself was a most modest person, but he welcomed any publicity that might reach the States on the Cooperatives, which so desperately needed support and money to keep alive. I think it was mainly due to the fact that he learned I also was interested in getting help for this project that he arranged an interview for me with Madame Sun Yat-sen, then living in seclusion in Hongkong.

He telephoned one morning to tell me I was to meet Madame Sun that afternoon at three. I was tremendously excited; since I had first heard and read about Ching-ling Soong, she had always seemed to me to epitomize in her person a greatness that transcended national boundaries. She is one of those great women who belong to no specific country or time. Undoubtedly my feelings about her were strongly colored by Vincent Sheean's portrait of her in *Personal History*. There was hardly a detail of this story—of her friendship with Rhayna Prohme, their work in Hankow in 1927, their flight to Moscow after the debacle of the Revolutionary government—that was not etched irrevocably in my mind. After that terrible period, Madame Sun's decision to stay out of politics and concentrate on relief work was well known. During that summer she was directing work in China and abroad of the China Defense League, now the China Welfare Fund.

On August 23 I wrote in my diary: "I cannot wait until I meet Madame Sun—it is as though I have come to China for this alone. I want to work with her—only with her do I feel I will get the true feeling of the work I have been waiting to do . . ." I took a taxi to the address Edgar Snow had given for the house of Mrs. Ching (the name Madame Sun had assumed), a tiny stone house overlooking the harbor. Trembling slightly, I knocked at the door, which was opened by a lovely Chinese girl. In the few moments I waited for Madame Sun, everything in that simply furnished room with its modern furniture and cool yellow curtains seemed to take on an almost symbolic significance, as though somehow everything in my life had been moving irresistibly to that moment and was to have the greatest importance in shaping my life thereafter. . . . I heard footsteps, quick and sure, and the next instant I looked up into the face of Madame Sun.

Lying in the jail, I remember that face now with a joy that is almost pain, for to me her face has become the face of all China, the face that had all the beauty, all the wisdom, and all the suffering I was to feel and see for the next year in China. In that instant I looked into her face I knew it all and I remember it with a terrible joy and sadness and I am no longer afraid because I am a prisoner of the Japanese. . . . So it was decreed that afternoon in Hongkong five years earlier when I saw Madame Sun Yat-sen.

I have never fully agreed with the epithet "fragile beauty" that has been applied innumerable times to Madame Sun. To me she was beautiful, yes, exquisitely so, with her jet-black hair drawn straight back from a wide forehead, her large expressive eyes, and her fine white skin, but certainly not fragile—there was nothing weak or crushable about her. On the contrary, she gave me an instantaneous impression of extraordinary strength that seemed to radiate from within, permeating her entire person and accentuating her every gesture. You sensed at once that here was one who would not be swerved from a path once taken, and all of Madame Sun's life since the death of her great husband—her refusal to deviate from his principles or to compromise with a government that repudiated those doctrines—has been motivated by that same inner strength and fidelity to an ideal.

But she is also the charming hostess, tastefully dressed in a close-fitting simple dark gown, smiling and serene, tactfully putting you at your ease. We talked about Rhayna Prohme and Vincent Sheean and she remarked, smiling almost mischievously, I thought: "But I expected to see someone much older than you—you are like a gypsy!"

In Hongkong, since her so-called retirement from politics, she has been concerned mainly with relief activities for war refugees and orphans and the all-important Cooperatives, which she regards as one very important solution to China's economic problems. Since the Japanese have destroyed most of the country's coastal industrial production, the Cooperatives have been producing the vital necessities. Madame Sun was concerned lest the Cooperatives be stifled by the profiteers and monopolists of the reactionary Koumintang elements—as they were later on. Even during the war, profits were being made by ruthless speculators who would not hesitate to destroy any movement that interfered with their gains.

There was no discussion of politics—her politics—in my interview with Madame Sun. Actually her only politics have been her steadfast belief in the principles of Dr. Sun Yat-sen—Nationalism, Democracy, and Socialism—which carried out literally would involve a program of land reforms and a coalition government with Communists and other parties participating.

Only when she feels it necessary at some sharp crisis in China's affairs to remind the Koumintang that it is not carrying out Dr. Sun's principles, does she voluntarily come out of her retirement. Such was her 1946 broadcast to America, when she denounced civil war, called for a coalition government, and pointed out that the presence of American military forces in China were hindering rather than helping the peace.

That summer of 1938, I had a unique opportunity to be present at another of those rare moments when she emerged in public. It was a critical period in China's struggle: The Japanese had been victorious on all fronts and were forcing the retreat of Chinese armies far into the interior; Canton was being bombed mercilessly in efforts to undermine the people's morale, and reports were beginning to circulate about the possibility of a Koumintang sellout to the Japanese. It was also the time of the anti-Japanese United Front of the Communists and the Koumintang, a marriage of convenience that the Japanese were desperately trying to split. As a great gesture of defiance to the enemy, a huge torchlight procession was held in Canton and Madame Sun left her retreat to march in the demonstration. I shall never forget that night when I marched side by side with Madame Sun Yat-sen in a great column of humanity representing every stratum of the Chinese people—coolies, peasants, students, merchants, landlords, intellectuals.

Before I finally left Hongkong for the interior, I met Madame H. H. Kung (Ei-ling Soong), different in so many ways from her older sister, Madame Sun—in background, in temperament, in politics, even in appearance. Where Madame Sun lived modestly and simply in a small house with one servant, Madame Kung occupied a huge dwelling, decorated in traditional Chinese splendor, overlooking Repulse Bay. Several servants bowed me into a formidable room full of vases and screens and bric-a-brac, and there I waited uncomfortably at least half an hour before I was formally received by Madame Kung, a small, serious, rather stern-faced woman who did not relax during our interview. She impressed me as being shrewd, practical, and positive. Her talk revolved mainly around China's finances and she underscored China's great need for financial aid from abroad. Before I left, she asked curiously if I had met Madame Sun in Hongkong. When I replied in the affirmative, she rose, and with a parting stereotyped phrase about the need for unity against the common enemy, Madame Kung indicated that the interview was at an end. The fact that Madame Sun had received me was enough to tell her exactly where my sympathies lay. Much later, when I was in Hankow, it was significant to me to learn that the three sisters, including Madame Chiang, the youngest, whom I was also to meet, had thrown overboard at least on the surface political differences and antagonisms to present a united front appearance.

Already I was preparing to leave Hongkong. The limitations of working on British newspapers, where everything was so carefully slanted to suit His Majesty's imperialistic pattern in the Orient, were becoming more irksome every day.

I began to feel my apprenticeship in Hongkong was drawing to a close; it was time to try to reach China proper. By a happy coincidence, Jack Chen was in Hongkong at the time, just back from a tour of Eighth Route Army areas where he had completed a vivid series of sketches for various magazines and papers. Since he was also planning to go to Canton before returning to America, we decided to make the trip together, and one evening at dusk we took the famous Hongkong-Canton railway.

Canton that summer was the most bombed city in the world, but after a week even I, like the Chinese, began to take the Japanese raids fatalistically. And I never ceased to marvel at the resiliency with which these stoical people snapped from a frozen immobility, looking like Chinese idols squatting in the searing sun of those afternoons, to quick smiling movement and life. Later in Hankow, in Paris, in Manila, I remembered my first experience of air raids in Canton—the city that smelled of corpses and smoking ruins.

It was in Canton that I met a party of five Indian doctors who were proceeding to Hankow and Yenan in a few days. After much negotiation, I finally obtained the necessary permits and visas to accompany them. Our entourage was composed of a fleet of five Red Cross trucks laden with medical supplies for the Chinese Red Cross in Changsha, which was to be our first stop.

Lying in the jail, I saw once again that countryside of China unrolling before my eyes like a Chinese scroll. The road wound through precipitous inclines, terraced hills topped with an occasional pagoda, cultivated rice paddies, with solitary Chinese farmers under wide coolie hats staring at us as we roared past. We were passing through the steep mountainous country of Kwantung Province and I thought: this is China . . . this is the *real* China!

It was barely daylight but already I could dimly see peasants at work in the fields. I saw at times men with yokes across their shoulders from which swung two heavy wooden water buckets, laboriously transporting the water to rice fields on higher ground. We climbed higher and higher, until at last we could see the blue of the Nan-ling Mountains, the boundary between Kwantung and Hunan Provinces. At the foothills of those mountains we halted at noon to eat the food the Indian doctors had prepared for the journey, boiled chicken and rice and hot tea. Nearby was a cool mountain stream, from which I was very tempted to drink but sternly forbidden to do so by the doctors, so I contented myself merely with washing my face and hands. From the crest of the mountains I looked back at the sloping terraced rice fields, the bright green of tea plants, and an isolated pagoda etched against the deep blue of the sky, to seal it forever in my mind.

Changsha, capital of Kwantung Province and the largest city we had seen since Canton, was then headquarters of the Chinese Red Cross under the brilliant leadership of Dr. Robert Lim. With a limited staff and medical supplies he had achieved miracles in training young Chinese doctors and organizing base hospitals behind the lines. But in the face of his almost superhuman task, he sometimes despaired, and the Indian doctors, who brought both supplies and their services, were enthusiastically welcomed. During raids we were given steel helmets and led to the shelters—a long line of caves in the hillside that had been utilized formerly by the Communists in their fighting against the Chiang forces in 1927, and perhaps may still be used again in the civil war threatening China today. . . . Three days later we were once more on our way and as we drove off a squad of Chinese women soldiers sang the stirring *"Cheelai,"* the March of the Volunteers:

Cheelai! Boo yuan tzo noo lee-dee run men,
Bah wo-men dee shueh ro tzo chen wo-men sin dee chang chung!
Joong hwa ming joo dow liow tzuay way shien dee shur hoe,
May guh ren bay po jo fah choo tzuay hoe dee hoe shun:
Cheelai! Cheelai! Cheelai!
Wo-men wan joong ee sing,
Mow jo dee run dee pow ho, Chien jing!
Mow jo dee run dee pow ho,
Chien jing! Chien jing! Chien jing! Jing!
(Arise, you who refuse to be bond slaves,
Let's stand up and fight for liberty and true democracy.
All our world is facing the chains of the tyrants;
Everyone who works for freedom now is crying:
Arise! Arise! Arise!
All of us with one heart,
With the torch of freedom, March on!
With the torch of freedom,
March on! March on! March on and on!)

On the road our Chinese drivers were always on the watch for Japanese bombers—actually we were bombed only once that day, late in the afternoon just before we reached Hankow. We drove into the town past fresh smoking debris where the Chinese were pitifully dragging out bodies.

From Changsha to Hankow we were closer to the front lines and could hear the intermittent booming of the guns. Miles of road, which had been recently bombed and then hastily repaired by the Chinese, were little more than stones over which we barely could crawl. Several times we had to stop and scurry into the fields for cover.

On the last stretch we saw long lines of wounded soldiers, refugees carrying their belongings, old women hobbling along on "lily feet," children and old men lying down to die . . . all headed for Hankow.

WINTER IN HANKOW

HANKOW IN THE OCTOBER OF 1938 WHEN I ARRIVED, was a dying city, feverishly and desperately preparing for the evacuation before the Japanese marched in. But like a person who knows he is doomed to die and is determined to have his final fling, so this strange city writhed in the last spasms of suffering and gaiety. The Bund along the Yangtze was crowded with wounded soldiers and refugees fleeting from the Japanese, but the nightclubs in the French concession glittered with scintillating entertainment and the one cinema did a riotous business. Then, as rumors grew of the coming of the Japanese "dwarfs" (*yat pun yai*), as the Chinese called them, the great exodus of the civilian population commenced. By rickshaw, by carriage, by car, by wheelbarrow, and on foot, the people started streaming out of the city, leaving behind them only the aged and the sick to meet the invaders.

But when I arrived that late afternoon in October, Hankow was still the capital of China and both the Generalissimo and Madame Chiang were still there. I drove down the seething Bund through this city that looked like a miniature Shanghai with its foreign buildings and international concessions. The eyes of the world were on Hankow then; the war with Spain was finished and correspondents from all parts of the globe were waiting to report the fate of Hankow. The great question was: Would the Chinese defend the city or would they evacuate it? At the Lutheran Mission in the ex-Russian Concession where most of the correspondents were living, I met Agnes Smedley, who was tireless in her efforts to get me a room. By an odd coincidence, it was the room of Freda Utley, the author of *Japan's Feet of Clay,* who was leaving that day for the front.

I awoke the next morning and stared out at the Yangtze gleaming a dull silver in the distance, and I wrote in my diary: "I feel as though I am present at an important time in China's history and a joy filled me at the thought that I might be of some help to the Chinese people. After the trip from Canton and Changsha, somehow I felt, that by sharing their suffering and hardships, I had become one of them. . . . Last night I met Agnes Smedley. I liked immediately her frank direct manner and I think she possesses a certain quality of greatness." In the exciting days that followed, I learned to know and admire more and more this strong-looking woman with the mannish haircut who seemed possessed of an inexhaustible reservoir of energy as she dashed about Hankow on her multifarious activities in behalf of the Chinese. Occasionally I would see her picking up a wounded soldier lying on the Bund, help him into her rickshaw, and bring him to the improvised hospital of the Eighth Route Army headquarters.

Madame Chiang was then engaged in training Chinese girls in first aid and nurses' duties to work in base hospitals. I was very fortunate in securing an interview with her through George Shepherd, a missionary friend of hers for many years. Since I had already met Madame Sun and Madame Kung, I welcomed the opportunity of completing my picture of the three Soong sisters.

I met Madame Chiang in a building on the Bund that had been temporarily converted into barracks for the Chinese Women's Soldier

Corps. Dressed simply but in excellent taste, Madame Chiang struck me at once as being an extraordinarily dynamic woman. Her English was perfect and she spoke in a direct if somewhat dramatic manner about the important role of the Chinese women in the war and how much the New Life movement was contributing to it. That this was a pet project of the Chiang government was well known, and Madame Chiang emphasized this still further by talking at length about the marvelous strides being made in eradicating the old habits of laziness, slothfulness, and uncleanliness. And as she talked, I could not help thinking of the wounded soldiers lying even at that moment, perhaps dying, not far away. . . . A revealing incident in that interview remained with me: As we walked around the barracks watching the girls at their various functions, Madame Chiang suddenly stopped in front of a girl bending over her work. She pointed dramatically to a hole in the girl's black stocking and then stooped and said something to the girl, who hurriedly left the room. "This girl must mend her stocking at once," Madame Chiang said to me. "In this way she will really learn the precepts of the New Life movement."

Soon after my arrival I joined the staff of the United Press bureau, situated conveniently in the Lutheran Mission. With the capture of Hankow imminent, the agency thought a "woman's angle" would be useful, but aside from that, there was plenty to write about. Everywhere in the streets there was life and death: beggars lying with outstretched arms and clutching at you as you passed; a dwarf woman with bare breast crouching beside her child; a girl panting with fever on the pavement; children with ghastly sores; a boy swollen with elephantiasis.

I began to attend the press conferences in the Chinese city presided over by Hollington Tong, where I met one day the famous Chinese Communist leader Chou En-lai, a dark man with an unusually alert, intelligent face and a small pointed beard. That noted leader's presence in the Chinese capital reflected the current anti-Japanese

United Front line agreed upon between the Communists and the Chiang elements—a unity that was then more important than ever, in the face of the Japanese advance.

One of the most brilliant men in Hankow at that time was the American vice consul, John Davies, whom Freda Utley has described so vividly in her book *China At War*. He was a gracious, cultured, and witty host, always at home to tired correspondents who would often gather in his charming apartment to relax, let off steam, or listen to music.

The tension in the city was mounting daily as rumors seeped in that the Japanese were coming nearer and nearer. Raids grew more frequent and we could often hear the booming of guns in the stillness of an early dawn. It was also increasingly evident that the Generalissimo was not planning to defend the city to the last ditch, as had been expected earlier, but rather was preparing to move everything possible deep into the interior—from the iron gratings in the gutters over the sewers to doorknobs; they were piled on rickshaws and carts and on the backs of coolies and the great exodus began. One morning we awoke to find that practically all the rickshaws had vanished overnight, commandeered by the government. That afternoon Generalissimo and Madame Chiang left secretly by plane for Chungking.

Three days later—on Wednesday, October 26, I watched the Japanese troops march into Hankow, bedraggled, mud-stained, and limp, looking more like a defeated army than victorious invaders. They were met by Father Jacquinot, that astute one-armed Jesuit priest, and other representatives of Hankow's International Settlement, who led them through the city in the hope of averting another rape of Nanking. But in the Chinese sections, the Japanese committed the usual atrocities, and although we correspondents reported them conscientiously, they were hush-hushed by home offices feeding a public already weary of rape stories—especially Jap rapes.

Correspondents were going home. The United Press asked me to take charge of their Hankow bureau. I should have thought twice about the implications and responsibility of remaining in a Japanese-occupied city, but naively I jumped at what I thought would be a real chance at last to help the Chinese by reporting the truth. Nor could I foresee that this would inevitably mean being blacklisted as an enemy correspondent whom the Japanese would not hesitate to get rid of if they could. . . . And lying in the jail now, I wonder: How much of my China past did the Japanese Intelligence Office in Manila know from their Tokyo files; how much did they know of my winter in Hankow?

Remembering that winter in Hankow, I think of black crows—the black crows that came with the Japanese, hovered over the stinking captive city, over the rotting corpses in the Chinese city, clustering in the trees, and eternally cawing, cawing, cawing. . . . How long, how long, how long, they seemed to say. . . . The Japanese roared insolently through the desolate streets in yellow military trucks and in the wake of the army came the Japanese merchants and *ronin* or notorious gangsters, with their opium dens and "comfort houses," as they called their brothels.

Towards the foreigners or third-party nationals left in Hankow, the Japanese revealed the blueprint of their strategy—a strategy that had its climax at Pearl Harbor. They stopped all foreign shipping in the Yangtze, allowing only Japanese transports carrying home products from Japan to come up that river. Foreign trade in the Yangtze Valley became zero. The Japanese took immediate control of the foreign concessions with the exception of the French, which they took over by a more gradual process.

Suspecting that guerrillas were hiding out there, the Japanese launched an all-out campaign to eliminate them. They would swoop down at any time of the day or night, block off whole streets, and make a house-to-house search. At last they decided to starve the Chinese into surrendering the suspects by imposing a stringent food blockade. On the Bund, at the barbed-wire entrance to the French concession, every Chinese person was rigorously searched before entering and not infrequently the sentries would net such prizes as eggs and fish carefully extracted from the trousers of a Chinese woman who was stripped right in the open. Another tactic was the stopping of the water supply so that thousands would be queued up at all hours of the day or night at the Yangtze, carrying water in pails yoked to their shoulders. This went on for a few weeks until the Japanese finally rounded up some groups of Chinese whom they promptly shot. But the guerrilla activity continued: Chinese "puppets" working for the Japs were murdered, lines of communication were sabotaged, and truckloads of soldiers ambushed, until the Japs began to burn entire villages in retaliation.

I was the only American correspondent in the city; three others, Valiev of the Soviet Tass agency and correspondents of the British Reuter's and German Transocean had also been left by their bureaus. We began to attend the Japanese press conferences, but only as a matter of form, for actually there was hardly any point to sending the stereotyped Japanese-angled communiqués given us by the military spokesman, Colonel Nagoya. It was a farce and we all knew it—all except the Transocean man, a big-boned German with drooping mustaches, who was meticulously polite, to the point of servility, to Nagoya at all times.

Since I was nominally the correspondent of a "third power," my dispatches were not subject to censorship. The American gunboat *Oahu* was anchored off the Bund and I arranged with its commander for my dispatches to be picked up by an American sailor at specified times. This was an invaluable service since it eliminated the necessity of passing the Japanese sentries, which was a ceremony in itself. My pass was stamped "U.P." and for some reason the sentries found this uproariously funny. After a while, when they recognized me, they would call out *"Upee! Upee!"* as I approached.

It did not take the Japanese in Hankow long to learn of my pro-Chinese dispatches. Actually, I was only reporting truthfully what the Japanese soldiers were doing in the Chinese city. It was not difficult to get these stories from relatives of victims who occasionally escaped into the foreign concessions—stories of young girls raped and burned alive, of the torturing of guerrilla suspects—the old, old stories, still happening. I was young and idealistic enough to think I could report the truth about Hankow. No sooner did the Japanese become aware of my pro-Chinese tendencies than they embarked on a subtle campaign to win me over. I realized it had begun when tall, handsome Colonel Nagoya himself called, sending his aide-de-camp first to say he was waiting, to take me to an important Japanese dinner. Driving through the streets in his car, Nagoya asked if I would like to broadcast to Tokyo on the "peaceful occupation by the Imperial Japanese Army." When I politely refused with the pretext that my voice was not suitable for short-wave broadcasting, I saw an unpleasant glint in his eye as he bowed slightly and murmured: "*Sodeska* . . ."

The next overture came with the advent of Daisy Adams into my life in Hankow. I was still in the Lutheran Mission, for I did not like to break that link with the former life before the Japanese came; besides, it was the most convenient place and the most protected too, since it was still run by missionaries. And somehow Daisy Adams in her well-cut Japanese army uniform with shiny black boots and smart cap looked very much out of place in my room. Daisy might almost have looked beguiling until you saw the hard face with the cruel eyes. . . . In nearly perfect English, Daisy introduced herself, saying she had just arrived and since she was planning to stay some time was sure she could be of great service to me, give me much information on Japanese activities. In the next few months that Daisy trailed me, hoping to discover that I was a spy left behind by the Chinese government, she revealed more about herself than she could ever find out about me. I was merely an idealistic young American girl reporter, who did not then realize that as a reporter it is impossible to take sides. The fact was that Daisy soon disclosed, woman-like, that she hated the "Japanese man" even though compelled by patriotic reasons to serve them in many ways. It seems she had been treated very badly in Japan before she went to live in California, where she met many "nice" American sailors. About a year before Pearl Harbor she returned to Japan for a visit and had been there when war broke out. Her knowledge of English and American ways made her indispensable to the Japanese Army and she was put in charge of the Comfort Corps, the prostitutes that followed in the wake of the Nipponese military wherever it went. I had seen these little painted ladies riding under parasols to various assigned houses.

But Daisy's job was more than merely being a madam and attending herself to high-ranking officers. It was well known on the American gunboat, where she "called" on several occasions, that she was a spy from way back, now promoted to spying on officers, but to no avail. They were *au courant* with her, and an evening with Daisy was an amusing lesson in the crudity and naiveté of Japanese women spies. She also did her best to sell me the Japanese occupation of Hankow, but it was equally futile for her. When the Japs began to use their all-out tactics of exterminating Chinese guerrillas, Daisy, involuntarily and naively boasting about the prowess of the Japanese Army, told how the Japs had caught a Chinese girl with a shaven head posing as a man and had punished her by burning her alive with her male companions—a story I promptly filed.

Whether it was that story or the fact that the Japanese were beginning to see the hopelessness of converting me, John Davies called one morning to inform me Nagoya had asked the Consulate to use efforts to have me removed. Davies retaliated with a speech about American freedom of the press, but told me privately that the Japanese could be very nasty and that I should be most careful . . . they had been known to "remove" a blacklisted correspondent by a careless "accident."

Suddenly I began to be afraid. The first snow, which fell on Christmas day, brought with it nostalgic memories of America that seemed ineffably peaceful compared to that horrifying medieval city. But the snow could not hide the unspeakable bloodstained filth of death and corruption around me. I spent sleepless nights, when I would lie awake listening to the groans and shrieks of tortured Chinese.

As the spring approached and I wanted more than ever to escape from that sinister city of the black crows, I began to feel that if I did not get out soon I would never leave Hankow alive. The Japanese then did not even bother to veil their antagonism; Colonel Nagoya was sarcastic or openly hostile. At last, on March 21, the first day of spring, a wire came from Shanghai saying the office was trying to arrange my transport out by Japanese plane. That was what I wanted least of all—it would be so easy to arrange an "accident." But I need not have worried, the Japanese were not too anxious to oblige with transport of any sort; as far as they were concerned, I could rot in Hankow. And if Admiral Yarnell had not come up at that time on his yacht *Isobel,* I probably never would have left. Reports of the increasing hostility of the Japanese towards all third-party nationals had their effect, and it was planned to evacuate all foreigners who wished to leave.

On the occasion I met Admiral Yarnell in Hankow, at a party in his honor at the American consulate, I found him to be one of the most charming, considerate, and intelligent of men. Not only did he arrange to have me leave on his yacht, but he also gave me permission to wire my office from it. Perhaps he was thinking of another *Panay* incident, as I was. He had also arranged for the evacuation of Valiev of Tass as well as the entire Soviet consulate staff. The Russian consul and his wife were guests with me on the *Isobel,* while the rest traveled on one of the two gunboats evacuating other foreigners. As I strolled across the deck chatting with the Admiral, he made a remark about this Soviet evacuation that I never forgot: "We never know when we might be needing their help." . . . And lying here in the jail, I think of Russia fighting side by side with America and Britain against the common enemy.

If I had thought of another great scoop like the sinking of the *Panay,* I was quite mistaken. Our trip down the Yangtze was uneventful—we were not bombed or machine-gunned—and yet for me it was everything. Slowly, as the yacht left Hankow, I felt myself coming to life again, and I could have caressed it all—the smooth yellow water, the green-terraced landscape with its peaked hills in the far distance. Once again I was seeing China—but it was a China that lay utterly destroyed and barren. We passed Nanking, but could see only crumbling walls around which stretched the scorched earth with a few straw huts sticking up like mushrooms. Two days later, we reached Shanghai.

As the modern skyline of Shanghai once again rose on my horizon, I could not help remembering the wonder and the mystery I had felt almost a year earlier when I had first come from America to that Paris of the East. Yet even on that first day when I had toured the devastated areas of Chapei with Randall Gould, I had known that I was not coming to China only to be a passive spectator. I had wanted to see it all, to understand what the Japanese were doing in China, to know what the Chinese people were suffering. And I had seen it all, and like them was then no longer a third-party national but an enemy of the Japanese. I found myself suddenly famous in Shanghai; reporters were on dock to meet me, and I was photographed with the Soviet consul and his wife. But the U.P. office in Shanghai warned me against releasing any stories about Hankow; the Japanese were sufficiently angry at me already and could make it miserable for me even there. As it was, I found a little Jap spy waiting in my hotel room with a huge bouquet of flowers; but, unlike Daisy Adams, she was dressed demurely in civilian clothes (Shanghai was still under international control): Would I like to write some articles for the *Asahi*

Shimbun, a local Japanese paper? (Would the Japanese never give up trying to convert me?)

What I did write in Shanghai was a series of articles on Hankow for J. B. Powell's magazine the *China Weekly Review* under the pseudonym "Observer." Whether the fact that those articles happened to appear just after my arrival in Shanghai made the Japanese suspect I was the author, I never really knew, but I know they did retaliate by printing an article about me in their paper blacklisting me officially as an "unfriendly" correspondent and fabricating a mass of lies about my career. And so, although I had been basking in the civilized atmosphere of Shanghai after the barbarousness of Hankow under the Japanese, I soon realized that I could not remain much longer where the Japs were growing stronger every day.

It was the beginning of the summer of 1939 and fierce fighting broke out between the Russians and the Japanese on the Manchurian border, to culminate in the battle of Nomanhan where the Japanese were so ignominiously defeated. Meanwhile, the news agencies were fuming because correspondents were cooling their heels on the border, *persona non grata* to both sides. John Morris, U.P. Far Eastern manager, suddenly had an idea that the Russians might allow a woman correspondent behind their lines to cover the fighting or even into Outer Mongolia. He wired Moscow accordingly.

When the answer finally came back in the negative, I was not too disappointed. I was tired of war, tired of the Japanese, even tired for the time being of China. I had seen too much horror and suffering. I had an offer from Hollington Tong to broadcast to America from Chung-king, but I felt I did not have the strength to cope with the hardships of another trip into the interior. I felt the need of a complete change, to be able to breathe freely again without fear of Japanese spies, and to be where I would not have the festering open wound of China constantly before my eyes. I wanted to live again for a while, and I decided on a holiday in Paris, which I had never seen. Nor had

I seen Europe, so I planned to go via the Trans-Siberian Railway: In that way I would fulfill another dream I had had—to see Russia. I applied for a Soviet visa and it came about a month later. Valiev meanwhile was also leaving for Russia from Hongkong and when I wrote him I was going through Russia he wrote back: "I am disappointed that you are planning to see my country through the window of a wagon-lit. You will see nothing. Why don't you go when you will be able to stay?"

I was both sad and happy to leave China: Sad because I knew that in the year I had lived and suffered there, I was bound to her forever and that always I would want to return to continue the struggle; sad because I knew that in that year when I had come close to death so many times, I had lost the lightheartedness and youth I had had when I left America. I knew that I could never be the same again—I had seen and lived in that other world, the world of terror and destruction, of starvation and death. I had stepped back into the centuries and lived in a city where men were slaves and beasts of burden and where unspeakable barbarism ruled and cruelties were condoned. But by sharing China's suffering she had become an irrevocable part of me, and Japan was also my enemy, and I knew, lying in the jail a prisoner of the Japanese, that it was a natural sequence in the pattern of my life. I had eaten Rice . . .

I was glad to leave China, glad to escape so miraculously the vortex of destruction, eager to breathe again the air of the West, to go from the passive timelessness of the Orient to the active dynamic awareness of the Occident, to hear stirring vital music, to feel the throbbing pulse of culture in the not-yet-destroyed cities of Europe. . . . I wanted to eat Bread again.

In early August I left Shanghai, panting in its ghastly heat, by Japanese boat to Tsingtao, and thence by train to Harbin and Manchuli, which was like the roof of the world—desolate, windswept, bleak. We stood waiting at the station for the Soviet train to arrive, staring out at the blizzard that raged there in August and watching groups of wounded Japanese soldiers arriving in trucks from the front.

My Chinese luck had held still on all that trip by Japanese boat and train—I had been afraid only one moment when a Japanese military inspector had examined my Chinese visa a little longer than was necessary and then looked at me curiously but let it pass. In the blacked-out train from Harbin to Manchuli I had been lucky in meeting three other foreigners who were also planning to take the Trans-Siberian train—a New Zealand nurse who had been working in Shanghai during the war; a rather elegant and cultured Norwegian on furlough; and a most voluble Frenchman, an engineer who had complained vehemently and steadily about the vile Japanese food on the train, rolling his eyes and throwing up his hands. He could hardly wait to get to Paris to eat again, and I must admit I heartily agreed with him; whether it was out of fear that never left me until I felt myself safely on the Russian train, or the really bad food, I had had spasms of nervous indigestion on the journey from Shanghai to Manchuli.

At last we saw the Russian train pulling in, and the Russian characters on the cars seemed at that moment magic symbols spelling the freedom that was to take me away from the Japanese at last. . . . Aboard the train we found all four of us were traveling tourist or "hard" and so we were able to share a compartment.

Lying in the jail, I wanted once more to be on that Russian train speeding across the great plains of Siberia, traveling through the mountainous country of the Lake Baikal region, and on towards Moscow. Great sprawling Russia has one foot in Asia and the other in Europe, as though she bridged that yawning gulf between East and West. And it is impossible to understand her without realizing this duality. I saw it on that train in the strange mixture of races mingling freely together—the Outer Mongolian faces, the Caucasians, the Khirgiz, the Slavs . . . these are also the Russians.

Remembering that journey on the Russian train, I remember most of all the atmosphere of friendliness, of conviviality, the absence of servility on the part of those who served us. I sensed no hostility in the attitude of the Russians at any time. Many tried to talk to us, but when they found we could speak no Russian, simply smiled for the rest of the trip. There was a samovar at the end of our car always filled with steaming hot *chai* (tea) and our steward would bring us tea at all hours of the day, or even night. The meals in the dining car were magnificent to me, who had been trying to exist on the Japanese slop for so long: steak, black bread with quantities of butter, borscht, eggs *spiegelein* (served fried in the pan), and black caviar and vodka. And if you wanted it— extra. I ate with a gusto I did not recall having since I had left America—there was something in that cool Siberian wind. . . . Our group had been assigned an Intourist guide, a rather shy young man who spoke good English and told me he was a student in Moscow and had taken the job for the summer. He answered all our questions about the cooperative farms and the cities we passed fully and without hesitation.

As usual it is the little things one remembers in reliving the past: I never forgot the Russian who stood beside me as I stared out at the collective farms. He turned to look at me, smiled, made a wide arc with his arm to embrace the sweep of land, and said something in Russian. I shook my head uncomprehendingly. Then he said, this time in German: *"Alles ist unseres"* and looked at me significantly as though to see if I could possibly understand the depths of meaning behind his simple words.

It was true I was seeing Russia only through the windows of a wagon-lit train. Valiev was right—what could I possibly learn of his country? But it was enough at that moment only to "see" Russia—to see its greatness, its wide distances, its tremendous potentialities. Siberia reminded me of our West—but it was the West of the pioneering days when we were building America. Everywhere you saw things being built: houses, factories, stores . . . everywhere Russia gave you the impression of being in motion. Nothing was static, least of all her people, for in the stations at which we stopped, Irkutsk, Omsk, or Tomsk, everywhere crowds of people with children and their bundles were waiting to go somewhere. And everywhere also was the Red Army, well-dressed, well-fed, with intelligent faces, and the inevitable reticence—police, smiling, but never talking. We were able to buy fruit and milk and candy at our various stops, but we never halted long enough to really see a village, to see more than its façade—a few buildings scattered beyond the station, and perhaps a market place.

We reached Moscow on the morning of August 25—a most significant day, though we did not realize it until we crossed the border into Poland. It was the day of the signing of the Soviet-Nazi pact but since we did not read the Russian papers (and I do not know whether it was announced or not), we had no way of knowing about it. . . . Lying in the jail, and remembering the strange impressions and bewildering events of that day, two things that might have given us an intimation of the war that came so swiftly, flashed through my mind. One was that two armed guards had barred the entry to Lenin's Tomb, which is usually open to the public, and the other was the news circulated at the Hotel Metropole that all foreigners were being asked to leave Russia immediately.

Otherwise, I think I might have asked for an extension of my tourist visa to remain in Moscow a while longer, for suddenly it seemed to me, of all the cities I had seen, the most fascinating and wonderful city on earth. It was as though I had dropped from another planet onto this city I had read about in Tolstoy, in Dostoyevsky, in Gorky, and I felt that the silhouetted line of the Kremlin against the morning sky was as familiar to me as my own name, and that I had lived there always.

What could one do in one day in Moscow? We could have gone on an organized tour, I supposed, but that seemed too tame. The New Zealand nurse and I decided to explore Moscow for ourselves—to absorb all the impressions we possibly could by wandering around as though we lived there—just mingle with the people. And that was just what we did—and nobody followed us, nobody molested us, nobody questioned us. We roamed in the vicinity of the Kremlin, went into what looked like a church but had been converted into a museum where they charged you a few kopeks to look at the ikons and other trappings; in Lenin's Museum I found myself more interested in the strange conglomeration of people being led around by young Russian women who stopped before pictures and gave lengthy discourses—all kinds of people, from old women in peasant dress to Mongolian tribesmen.

That night at dusk we had to be aboard the train to take us to the Polish frontier, where we would change to go on to Warsaw. We changed trains at midnight and sat up all night riding through Poland, and it was then that our Frenchman, who had gotten into conversation with a passenger, told us very excitedly about the signing of the pact between Russia and Germany. All of us were stunned and shocked—we knew that somehow it meant war, but how soon?

I saw Warsaw, its beauty and elegance gleaming in the early morning sunshine, a beauty that was to be utterly destroyed a few days later. At Berlin, where we stopped at noon, again to change trains, we saw marching troops everywhere, troops going aboard trains—and they were the Wehrmacht men who marched into Poland the following day. We reached Paris on the very last train to cross the frontier. My luck had still held.

Britain and France declared war against Germany a week later. I had run away from one war to run straight into another. The Paris I had come to see was blacked out, and every night I had to go down into the *abri* of my Montparnasse pension because of the German raids. . . . The United Press wanted me to stay in Paris for the European war, but stubbornly I longed for peace. I left Paris one morning in late September and a few weeks later was in America.

I thought I had come home to peace, and for awhile it was indeed a semblance of peace. Marriage in Virginia, honeymoon in Washington, an apartment in New York. But I had married a writer and a newspaperman. That spring, Ron got an assignment to do a series of articles for the *Christian Science Monitor* on the Near East and Dutch East Indies . . . French Indochina and then Manila. He wired for me to join him and once again I was on my way back to the Far East, ten months before Pearl Harbor.

ESCAPE FROM MANILA

M Y WHEEL OF DESTINY WAS INEXORABLY COMPLETING its circle, and
I returned to the Far East, as though drawn there by forces over
which I no longer had any control. While Ron worked for the Navy, I
began broadcasting my own program over Radio Manila, called
"World Scene and the Far East," directed primarily against the Japanese. This was in addition to my teaching English and American litera-
ture at the University of the Philippines.

I still remember how pathetically my students tried to keep their
minds on the poetry I was reading to them on the morning of December 8, when we heard the news that the Japanese had attacked Pearl
Harbor. We knew that Manila would be bombed that morning and it
was exactly at noon that day we heard the first air-raid siren. My students scattered, some to their native provinces and an uncertain fate
at the hands of the Japs; others were young ROTC boys whom I was
to meet later in the hills as guerrilla warriors. . . . A few days later, I
was broadcasting for the government office of publicity and propaganda to the women of the Philippines, those same women who were
to teach us immortal lessons in bravery, many of whom fought in

the hills during the following three years: Courage, courage, remember the women of China, of Spain. . . . Brigadier General Carlos Romulo, whom I had known as the brilliant editor of the *Philippine Herald,* was also broadcasting for the government then, before he was called to Bataan.

Then came the news that the Japs were closing in, were about to enter Manila, and we decided to take to the hills and stick it out there for a month or so until MacArthur came back. We knew of a little town east of Manila where we had driven for weekend parties. It was called Montalban—literally meaning mountain—and beyond it stretched the chain of the Sierra Madre range reaching to the east coast of Luzon. And if the worst came to the worst, we thought we could head for the coast and contact a submarine to take us to Australia. This was the mirage that buoyed us up in many of the terrible days to come until our capture almost two years later.

In Montalban, we knew of the summer house of an American mestiza friend where we had often spent weekends. It has a magnificent view of the whole Mariquina Valley—that same country where three years later our own American forces were to fight the Japanese, making a last stand from the caves and woods. We stayed in that house for a new nights, getting the lay of the land, and waiting for news—the news that would tell us we could go back to Manila.

The old caretaker, Luis, and his wife and boy were very friendly and helpful to us, despite their fear of the Japanese. They had another son in the ROTC now in Bataan, and helping some Americans would be a very real and good thing to them. And without them, we certainly would not have been able to start on our journey into the hills. It is true the Americanos were rich and offered plenty of money—luckily we had taken about 1,000 pesos ($500) with us, but I like to think Luis and his little boy offered to be our cargodores for other reasons; and we allowed him to oversee a few more boys he thought could be trusted. We had come out with our car loaded with all kinds of canned foodstuffs and supplies we figured would be sufficient to last us six months—if we took it easy—but naturally we never thought it would be more than a month at the most. I had crammed three suitcases full of clothes and books and precious feminine things like cold cream, Kotex, and a hairbrush. Since we could not possibly take everything out at once, we cached the typewriter and a suitcase and some food in the house. We never saw them again—soon afterwards the Japanese raided the house and took everything. Luckily Luis had been warned and fled to the hills with his family. . . . We loaded as much as the cargodores would take the first day, and that night at dusk—I think it was the night of January 4—we set out for the hills beyond Montalban.

Luis had told us of a tiny barrio about ten kilometers away, and we headed in that general direction. I remember the full moon was just coming up and bathed the valley with a luminous glow, and in spite of my anxiety, I felt a strange sense of adventure. We began to climb the steep trail leading to the crest of the huge hill looming in front of us. The footpath, winding around innumerable curves on the edge of the hill, became more narrow and precipitous as we climbed, and at last, when I felt I could almost touch the sky with my hands, we were on top. All around us was lush, tall, razor-edged grass which the Filipinos call "cogon," and we decided it would make an excellent shelter and bed for the night. I spread out a blanket, threw a coat over us, and we lay smoking and staring at the star-studded tropical sky. It was my first experience sleeping out in the open, and the fragrance of the sweet-smelling grass and the earth in the velvet warmth of the night intoxicated me.

But all my exhilaration evaporated the next morning as we wearily followed the cargodores in the fierce searing heat through the choking jungle underbrush of the bamboo woods. It seemed that Luis had seen some refugees trudging past us early that morning, running to the hills away from the Japanese—the same old story I had seen in China, only now we were a part of it. But he was not taking any chances on our being seen and decided to beat out a new trail to the barrio through the woods, and not a few times did I sink down exhausted, too weary to move another step. I could not help thinking that our stay in the Orient, where you are so carefully shielded from the slightest physical hardship, especially walking, had certainly not fitted us for that kind of life. I felt somewhat better at noon after a hot lunch of pork and beans, good American coffee, and bread and butter. The cargodores cooked their rice of course, but we had not yet reached the Rice Stage—as I called it—and as long as I had a crust of bread or crackers left, we would avoid it.

We reached Barrio Labug late that afternoon, and as we came down the steep trail and saw it lying there in the hollow of the valley, a tiny cluster of little bamboo huts, I felt a strange sense of uneasiness. It had a desolate and forlorn look about it—like a ghost town—and as we came right into it, we could see why. Not a soul was to be seen anywhere. The cargodores threw down their loads and stared about uneasily—even the people in this remote little barrio had taken to the hills, running from the Japanese. . . . Only Luis and his little boy Hernandez stayed with us that night; we could not bribe the others with any amount of money.

I shall never forget that night in Barrio Labug—my first night on a bamboo bed. It was like sleeping on a medieval torture rack; the hard bamboo slats dug into my flesh like iron rails. I was like the Princess and the Pea: No matter how much clothes I put under me it was the same agony. The strange noises of the tropical night alive with the cries of the birds and animals echoed through the empty barrio, and as I lay tense and unnerved any sound that was not a bird cry seemed to us to be strange footsteps approaching and I would start up in terror. I had the uneasy feeling that we were being watched from the surrounding hills—after all, those cargodores knew where we were—and I felt that we might be attacked and caught at any moment. At last, in despair, I gave up the thought of trying to sleep and I crept over to the open doorway where I could see the comforting light of the full moon as it sailed serene and remote through the white-blue sky, until I saw the first streaks of the dawn.

We decided not to risk any more nights like that, and after a good breakfast, we started on an arduous trek through the hills behind the barrio. We had no definite plan yet, except that of getting to some spot not too far from Manila, and pitching camp there for about a month or so until the Americans got back. We headed vaguely in the direction that Luis said led eastward to the coast, for we still had the idea that as a last resort we might try to make it to Infanta and then Australia.

I paused for a moment to catch my breath in the long climb, and stared at the wide expanse of rolling country we had left behind. In the far distance gleamed the blue of Manila Bay, and I wondered when I would see it again. All around us stretched fields of waving green cogon grass, and as the wind played over its swaying surface, it looked like a sea of cogon. Suddenly I smelled burning grass on the wind and turning in that direction I saw that to our right in the distance, the fields of cogon were a mass of roaring orange flames. It was a startlingly beautiful picture, yet terrible in its implications: Were the Japanese burning some barrio over there? They had done that in China, I remembered, trying to exterminate the guerrillas. We seemed too close to Barrio Labug for comfort.

We hurried on, and soon left the cogon fields behind us and reached a new broad level spot near a huge rock, beyond which the ground sloped directly down to a dense stretch of woods. Panting and hot after the stiff climb, we sank down under a tree near the rock. I made a quick lunch of crackers and cheese, which we washed down with the tepid water from our canteen. Water—that was going to be our chief problem in finding a suitable place. . . . I saw Ron staring speculatively on that wood in the distance, and after lunch he and Luis left me with Hernandez to explore its possibilities. About an hour later they returned and Ron said he had found a stream there about a kilometer or so deep in the woods. It was not much, but it would do for a temporary camp.

Those woods . . . from the Bald Rock where we spent the night, they loomed in the distance, remote and mysterious, as though they had a secret, lugubrious life of their own. And the next morning, as I stepped into their misty dimness from the blinding tropical sunlight, I felt as though they were swallowing me into their gloomy depths. They were not like our woods at home, not friendly or warm; they were jungle woods, full of twisting choking vines and treacherous under-brush, where you expected the hooded head of a snake to suddenly spring at you. Luis had to slice his way through the hanging vines with his bolo, and this despite the fact that he and Ron had tried to make a trail yesterday afternoon, but it seemed to have vanished overnight. We had stumbled along for more than a kilometer when suddenly the eerie stillness of the forest was broken by the sound of trickling water and we climbed down a steep embankment and saw a large pool gleaming in the still green light. Here at last was our oasis in this trop-ical desert and we decided to make our camp somewhere in these woods, close to the stream.

We lived in those woods for a month, and I grew to hate them more every day with a horror and fear. To this day, I cannot enter a wood without the feeling of being watched by unseen eyes, and hunted like an animal. I was afraid of the sudden stillness of the late afternoons when you could hear with a terrible distinctness the falling of a single bamboo leaf and where every sound would take on a sinister meaning. There must have been wild animals somewhere in those woods—the natives used to hunt for wild pig and deer, according to Luis—but they must have smelled us and they gave us a wide berth. Ron had an excellent rifle given to him by the Philip-pine Constabulary before we left, but I hoped he would never have to use it, even though he did keep it gleaming and polished with my cold cream.

I remember one night when the moon lit up the woods with a ghostly silver light that made me think of *A Midsummer Night's Dream*, we suddenly heard a prolonged unearthly shriek that sounded half-human in its frenzy. I sat up in alarm—never had I heard anything so anguished; it was like a wild cry torn from the bowels of the earth itself. Ron, half-asleep, automatically grabbed his rifle and a bolo and was all for exploring the surrounding woods. But I finally dissuaded him with the argument that in the dark he would not have a chance against the werewolf or gorilla or whatever it was. We decided to make a fire and sit it out, waiting for something to happen—but nothing did. The terrible cry was repeated a few more times, making me shiver in its banshee-like reverberations, and than at last it faded into the night. The next day when Luis came up we described it to him, and he said it was either a wildcat or a deer, but I have always felt that it was something stranger even than that . . .

We still had no definite plans, just living from day to day, still hoping to hear the news that MacArthur had come back, and we could return to Manila. The result was that we did not even attempt to build a house but simply cleared a space in the woods and put up three stones for a fireplace. Luckily enough it was the beginning of the dry season here and up to now it had not rained at all. At night we just spread our blanket on the ground and used all our clothes for cover, all of which would have been fine if it had not been for the fleas. Those fleas tormented me for a month until I thought I should go mad. They seemed to like only my flesh, for they boycotted Ron, concentrating on me with a vengeance as soon as dusk fell, until my body was a mass of red welts. After a frantic night of itching and tossing, I would welcome the dawn with almost hysterical relief.

Morning was the only bearable time to me in those woods, even though it did mean wrestling with the fire with wood still wet from the dew. There was always that sense of anticipation, the feeling that perhaps this might be the day when we would be going back and this nightmare would be over. And it was always cool and fresh, and as I made my way through the woods down to the stream for water, for a few moments I shed my anxiety, my tension, the discomfort . . . the hushed stillness of the forest pool and the green foliage lit with the gleaming gold of the sun's first rays made me feel suddenly glad just to be alive and awake to all this beauty.

But as the days slipped by with no sign from the American forces, our life began to take on a curiously dream-like aspect, and I could not escape the feeling that I would wake up some morning in my luxurious Manila apartment and ring for the servants to bring my coffee. But alas, there were no servants here to do the dirty work anymore, and these Americanos got their first dash of bitter reality in the daily struggle for survival. Luis came up every few days, or sent little Hernandez, to chop wood and carry water for us, but in the meantime, all those chores had to be divided between Ron and myself. A year later, when these tasks had become routine, I recalled ironically how desperately I had struggled with simple things like making the fire, cooking rice, and washing clothes. I literally went through the tortures of the damned trying to prove to Ron that I was not completely useless, mastering little things like not using up a whole box of precious matches to start a fire in the damp morning. I would blow and blow and fan frantically at the sparks until the smoke choked me and tears streamed down my face. Or washing greasy dishes in icy cold water or scrubbing dirty clothes hopelessly, because I had not learned the native way of beating them on the rocks. I had never washed or cooked in my life, and now I had to take it. The nail polish began to chip off my carefully manicured fingernails and my hands were cut with bamboo splinters. I was so tired at night that I no more thought of creaming my face or brushing my hair than of flying to the moon. But my one stick of lipstick and box of face powder I treasured and hoarded carefully— somehow I think it is instinctive to modern women to feel that they can face almost anything with a dash of lipstick. And when the Japs captured us almost two years later, I still had a tiny sliver of lipstick left in my case. As for clothes, I practically lived and slept in the two pairs of slacks I had brought along and used most of the rest of the dresses, housecoats, and evening gowns either as covers or mattresses.

Some afternoons Ron would go down to Barrio Labug to forage for bananas or squash or any other vegetables growing wild. Those times he thought it too risky for me to be seen down there just in case any of the natives returned, the idea being that the less it was known that an American woman was hiding in the hills, so much the better. And so I would be left alone and would spend a few agonizing hours wrestling with my imagination that pictured every sudden sound as a prelude to a Japanese attack.

It was on one of these afternoons that I made the acquaintance of my ichthyosaurus—"Iccy" I called him later when he became quite a pet of the camp. I had been trying fruitlessly to lose myself in one of Shelley's poems, when I heard a rustling sound that seemed unmistakably to my hypersensitive ears like a foot stealthily approaching, nearer, nearer. . . . And then, just as I was ready to scream in terror, I saw a pointed head like a snake's emerging from the bush. I stared fascinated at the red tongue darting out fang-like and then at the long green body shaped like a miniature ichthyosaurus. I stood up and seized a stick . . . the creature vanished. Luis told me later that it was only an iguana—Philippine lizard—which is quite harmless and often treated as a household pet by the Filipinos. After that I let him forage around my fire, and even began to amuse myself by watching his movements. As for snakes, the only times in those woods I ever seemed to run into them was when I was taking my bath down at the pool—water snakes, I guessed. But it invariably happened that no sooner was I naked and ready to step into the cool delicious water, when I detected an almost imperceptible movement, and I would turn hurriedly to see a snake gliding through the underbrush.

One afternoon toward the end of the month, old Luis came staggering up with the story that the Japanese had visited Wa-Wa Dam—that dam on the river into which our little stream drained. We could easily reach it by following our steam for about five kilometers down to its source, according to the terrified Luis, who was sure the Japs would find us the next morning. So we decided to look for another spot. And that is how I finally emerged from the darkness of the woods at last into the sunlight and from our camp to a real house with a real bed of my own.

The house that Luis built for us was situated somewhere between the woods and the Bald Rock, and it was precisely because it was just "somewhere" that we were able to live there for five months before the Japanese attacked us. There were no obvious trails leading to it, and unless you knew exactly how to get there, you just could not find it. And this despite the fact that it was not in the woods, but in the open on a small hill overlooking a wide expanse of country stretching to the blue line that was Manila Bay. The secret of the location was what we like to think of as "camouflage." Our tiny bamboo house was not in the woods but it was set up directly against a wood, with a few trees around it, so that unless you came very close you could not distinguish it very well. The forest behind us had no trail that we knew of yet, but we gradually made one, in case we had to escape in a hurry.

Meanwhile, I felt like a prisoner suddenly released from jail, as we made our way late one afternoon from the dim woods into the glaring sunshine of our new place. I felt as though I had been blind and just regained my sight as I blinked at the radiant splash of brilliant colors of the tropical sunset, and it was sheer joy that night to look up again at the wide, star-lit sky. I was enchanted with my new grass house with its shaggy roof of cogon and positively luxuriated in my bamboo bed. A month of sleeping on the hard ground now made me utterly impervious to the hardness of bamboo slats—in fact, I was ecstatic at being at last removed from the fleas.

The next month—March—was the most peaceful we knew since we left Manila, and the most peaceful we were to know in the hectic months to follow. Inspired no doubt by our new little house, both Ron and myself began to grow positively domestic, and we both discovered hitherto unsuspected talents for homebuilding. From split bamboo and rattan, Ron made a bamboo table and chairs, and a fencing for our precious sacks of rice and sugar, which Luis had bought for us in town and transported up there. As for me, I blossomed out as an expert in making hotcakes in the mornings, for we still had a can of flour and made syrup of the brown sugar. This period was what I call our "intermediate Bread-Rice stage"—we had hotcakes for breakfast, but the staple of the remaining two meals was rice, and willy-nilly, I had to literally swallow my former scornful attitude about rice and begin to try to like it. But I still could not, or would not, dare to think of what it would be like to get up in the morning and have nothing but rice for breakfast—the Americans must be back in Manila by the time we used up our can of flour!

Meanwhile, I began to experiment in the Art of Making Hotcakes . . . first the fire: there had to be an absolutely raging inferno under them or they just would not do. And that meant that Ron had to spend hours chopping good dry wood. Next there were the ingredients: flour, a little milk (we still had a few cans of condensed milk left), a little sugar and salt, and most important for the perfect hotcakes—eggs. And that is where Gabriel entered our life at that time. For it was Gabriel who brought us the chickens—five pullets, a laying hen, and a Rhode Island Red rooster—that laid the eggs that cooked our hotcakes . . .

Strange how I always remember Gabriel as I first saw him that morning when Luis brought him up to us—a dressed-up dandy replete with shoes and necktie, incongruously clutching the squawking hen. Perhaps it was just that very ludicrous incongruity that saved him, for although I never completely trusted Gabriel, I also knew that he would never betray us.

Luis had brought Gabriel up to us because it was becoming more and more dangerous for him to leave his family to make that surreptitious long trip to the Americanos. Gabriel had a common-law wife, a beauty from Barrio Labug, but he told us with a sly grin that he was not married to her—and later we could see that in his grandiose aspirations of the scheme of things, she just did not count. Gabriel was the barrio slicker out for big game: the Americanos who at that time represented a gold mine to him, enough to justify any risks. And he always played that up—to jack up the price. He would roll his eyes and click his tongue and slice his head off with his forefinger, just to make it more vivid what the Japs would do to him if they caught him bringing supplies to the Americanos in hiding. But as I say, maybe it was the chickens that Gabriel brought us—for a stiff price of course—but I had the feeling that as long as we could pay Gabriel more than the Japanese could, he would stick with us.

The situation was getting worse instead of better. All day from our hill we could hear the guns booming on Bataan—and then one day they stopped . . . and the silence was pregnant with ominous foreboding. Gabriel brought us the news that the Japs were really on the warpath now for escaped soldiers or civilians in hiding, all of who could plant the fertile seeds of guerrilla resistance. And they had enlisted the aid of that fifth column outfit of the islands—the Sakdals—an illiterate gang of hoodlums who would act as the eyes and ears of the Japanese and for a price of course, lead them to the Americans. The Japs were offering a reward of one hundred pesos per head for every American captured alive or dead.

After that, our illusory fragile peace was shattered. Gabriel kept bringing increasingly alarming rumors of Americans being caught and how they were being tied up in the sun in the public square as punishment and a warning. God only knows what the Japs were doing to them secretly . . .

The beginning of May, I think it was, we decided to prepare for the worst, and began to make plans in case of an attack by the Japanese. Ron built a cache in the woods behind us and hid some foodstuffs we might need in an emergency and for about a week after that we made daily trips to the cache, each time by another route so as not to make an obvious trail. We carried our two suitcases, and as much supplies as we possibly could, leaving in our little house only enough for daily necessity. Meanwhile we began to talk to Gabriel about the possibility of moving on towards the coast, and offered him more and more money to guide us out of this place. But he was evasive with that typical native *mañana,* and kept postponing it from day to day, saying he was looking around for cargodores he could trust, and finding the easiest route.

I think the truth was that he was just plain scared at the thought of going into that unexplored country beyond the mountains he knew. Still, he did not want to say no entirely because he was so much tempted by the money. Of course to us at that time, the important thing was to keep Gabriel coming to us, for without him we knew we were lost. We did not know the country or the language or the people. Gabriel at least spoke some English, bad as it was. He had been raised in the town and had gone to grade school where he had been taught English, and that explained some of his grandiose aspirations as far as Americanos were concerned. So we kept offering money desperately to Gabriel, hoping the Japanese would not offer him more to betray us. And Gabriel did keep coming, though less and less often as time wore on. Then one day he told us that two Sakdals had been to Barrio Labug looking for us—they had heard that we were somewhere in the vicinity, but did not know exactly where.

That night, after Gabriel left, we decided to build a makeshift house in the woods and sleep there, while our real house would be merely a decoy. Even Gabriel would not know where it was. Ron made a huge bamboo bed and stuck some leaves and cogon over it in case of rain, in a spot not too far from our cache—the idea being that in case of a raid, we could always grab some supplies from our cache and go deeper into the woods.

Each night, as soon as dusk fell, we packed as much as we could into a small bag, rolled up our blanket, and holding a lantern, we fumbled precariously through the woods to our bed. Sometimes we would spend our days in the woods, and other times we would come back cautiously to our house to meet Gabriel and get the news. . . . So the days and nights crawled forward in ghastly monotony and grueling fear. It was now the peak of the dry season and everything had a withered desiccated look and the parched bamboo cracked ominously under our feet through those silent woods. Even our little water hole began to show signs of drying up, and we were forced to ration water carefully. All in all, I felt as though those days and nights of tense, morbid waiting were approaching some horrible climax, that the stage was being set for something to happen . . . and then . . . like a sudden burst of thunder on a hot dry day, it happened. . . .

Everything that occurred from the last afternoon of May 13 and the terrible twenty-four hours that followed, I remember with a clarity that nothing can ever erase. . . . Gabriel's sudden appearance when we had not expected him that afternoon, panting, chalk-white, and stammering that the Japs had raided Wa-Wa, his barrio, rounded up a lot of suspects, and were now looking for him. It was also rumored that they knew our exact whereabouts through some Sakdal and would raid our place in the morning. Now, as I have said, I never completely trusted Gabriel, but we could see that this was definitely not an act, and even if he were faking and hoped to be rewarded well for his warning to us, we could not afford to take chances. Of course, Gabriel would not sleep with us that night—that was expecting too much of him—if the Japs caught us, there would be no point in their catching him, too. So we arranged that Gabriel should come the following day and call to us in the woods.

As soon as Gabriel left, we grabbed our blanket, lantern, and a few supplies in our little bag, and started on our trek to the woods. But this time we decided not to sleep in our bamboo bed, in case the Japs should decide to search the woods. We knew, however, that this was just a remote possibility, for Gabriel had brought us reports that the Japs were usually afraid to enter the woods where they might be ambushed and wiped out. Anyway, we decided to climb as high as we possibly could and then lose ourselves somewhere on the other side of the big hill. We followed the trail past our cache and climbed steadily until we reached the very top, and then we groped down the sheer incline for about a quarter of a kilometer. We came to a fairly level spot in a tiny bamboo thicket and made our bed for the night. It was dusk by now, and long past our usual suppertime; but tonight, neither of us felt like eating—we were both living on our nerves. My mind was extraordinarily clear, almost clairvoyant, though my knees and legs felt wobbly from the long climb. I felt like one who has been sentenced to die the following morning. Sleep was impossible of course, and we just lay there smoking and talking . . . subconsciously of course, I was dreading the dawn and what it might bring.

Then about six o'clock or so we heard it: first a rifle shot, then another rifle shot, and then the *rat-a-tat* of machine-gun bullets. We jerked up mechanically and stared at each other incredulously. Suddenly we heard what sounded like an explosion, then the crackling sound of cogon burning. We sprang up and forced our way down the slope of the hill until we came to a deep stretch of woods. It seemed unlikely that the Japanese would search for us as far as this, and we were probably safe for the time being. Moreover, neither of us could really believe that the Japs had actually attacked our place—probably they had been rounding up some Filipino trainees. Still it had sounded a bit too close.

Again began that interminable waiting, waiting, waiting . . . in the still woods where every sound was the footstep of the enemy. The sticky heat was growing more unbearable as the sun climbed, and at last, about noon, Ron decided that he had better go up and see what was what. I would go up as far as the cache with him, and then he would continue on until he reached a spot where he could get a view without being seen.

The palpable, clinging heat enveloped us in a blanket as we slowly retraced our way. At the cache, I sank down on a stone, dazed and hot and hungry, and prepared myself to wait, while Ron went on alone. I sat there in a kind of stupor for a while, then I realized that I could get some cans of peaches or something from our cache. I felt a little better after eating one can and was just about to open another, when I heard a sound of thick, heavy panting, almost a groan. I sat up tense and peered through the dusty green foliage. At last I made out the figure of a man, stumbling up the path . . . and then I saw that it was Ron, looking like a ghost, deadly white, his breath coming in spasms. He grabbed me by the arm and pushed me up the path, as he gasped hoarsely:

"Hurry up—we've got to get out of here fast—they may be fol-lowing us."

I still cannot remember how my legs moved. I felt as though I had been paralyzed by fright and turned into a kind of mechanical robot as we stumbled through those woods and down the hill to the place where we had spent the night. There we both collapsed. I forced Ron to swallow some water from the canteen and eat some peaches, and after that he managed to tell me what he had seen. It was the shock, I think, more than anything else, of seeing nothing but black, charred embers where our little house had stood that had so unnerved him at first. Everything had been slashed and destroyed, our rice and sugar scattered around. But more than that, both of us kept seeing the pic-ture of what would have happened to us had we been asleep in the house when the Japs had attacked that dawn.

What were we to do now? The immediate danger was the possi-bility that the Japs were on the lookout for us to return to the house, so we decided we had best keep away for a while, anyway. We would spend the night here again and then tomorrow steal up quietly and watch for Gabriel . . .

Gabriel—veritably at that moment he seemed to my numbed mind like the Angel Gabriel, who had saved us and would lead us out of this wilderness. . . . The way of the gods is unfathomable—Gabriel had saved the lives of two Americans this morning and would save us once again by leading us out of this inferno to the mountains beyond. And a year later, we remembered those days when we in turn, by some strange trick of Fate, were called upon to decide whether Gabriel was to live or die—to decide his fate, which was in the hands of the guerrillas. And we remembered the morning of May 16, the day after the Japs had machine-gunned and burned our house, that Gabriel did come back, and like the Angel Gabriel, led us out of that wilderness to the mountain people.

Stealthily at night, he led us through the woods by a secret trail to the Mariquina River and past the huge Wa-Wa Dam to the fork in the road which went to the Sierra Madre range of mountains, more than forty kilometers away. It was he who brought us, on the shores of that river, to meet the mountain people (*tao bundok*), that non-Christian tribe of people who had just come down from the mountains to trade their rattan for salt and sugar.

I shall never forget that strange safari, into the deep mountains of the Sierra Madre range stretching to the east coast of the Philippines. The trail we followed led through dense forests and jungle brush and the giant trees towering above us seemed as ancient as the earth itself. I felt as though I were suddenly stepping into a world of the earth's dim past, where giant creatures roamed the forests, and I half expected to see a huge dinosaur or ichthyosaurus emerging from the gloom of some deep cavern.

We had to walk swiftly to keep up with these mountain people who sped through the jungle on their bare feet. Our heavy shoes were clumsy and seemed to weigh a ton, especially when we waded through the innumerable streams and pools of this forest. But when we tried taking them off the stones pierced our tender soles, and so we had to plod along in our sodden heavy shoes.

At first I was conscious of only one sensation—a great relief at leaving behind me the terror of being hunted by the Japanese. No physical hardship could be greater than that terror to me. It was good at last to be among people who were friendly, who had accepted us and were taking us to their far distant home. After about an hour of walking, I began to feel my terrible exhaustion, the fatigue, and hunger of the past week.

Suddenly we heard the rumble of thunder, and a moment later the tropical rain was pouring down. We heard the natives shouting and then an old man turned to wave to us to show that he was making an abrupt turn to the left. A few moments later we were in a large bamboo shed where the mountain people had thrown down their loads and were now squatting comfortably and laughing among themselves while the storm raged around them. They began passing betel nut and the women offered us their sweets and rice-sticks wrapped in bamboo leaves. Out of politeness we did not refuse, but as we sat eating the sweet, gluey concoction, we were thinking of steak and french-fried potatoes. . . . But someone was already preparing the fire for the rice, and as we sat warming ourselves and staring into the leaping gold-blue flames licking the earthen black rice pot, I felt suddenly that this safari with these mountain people was a kind of bridge into a new world for us where we would glimpse that simple primitive life such as our ancestors lived when the earth was young, and that if we came through it alive, it would be an amazing and wonderful experience.

6

THE PLANTING

I WAS LYING IN THE JAIL THINKING ABOUT THAT YEAR we spent in the mountains, and as I lay there in the silence and in the darkness, that year seemed to me like a great painting, full of light and color, the green of the mountains and the blue of the sky, the silver of the little stream and the great gray river, the gold and yellow of the fire and sunlight. And it was also to me like the music of the symphony, the rush of the wind through the forest, the roar of the river and the "Waldeweben" of the woods, the lashing beat of the tropical rains and the steady drone of the life of the fields.

But most of all I remembered the Songs of the Seasons—the Song of the Planting and the Song of the Harvest, the Song of the Winter and the Song of the Summer. And I knew that nothing could take those songs away from me now, for before we were captured by the Japanese, we had lived the full cycle of the year in the mountains through those four seasons, and in that year I had become part of those mountains.

We heard first the Song of the Planting—we heard it from our tiny hut as it reverberated to us from beyond the steep kaingin where the mountain people, the women and children and men, were planting the rice to the rhythm of the guitar. All that day the monotonous chanting and singing and shouting were carried by the wind across the black, charred hills to us as we lay on our bamboo bed exhausted from our journey. And this song seemed to me to embody all the strange mystic intimations of this secret bond of these primitive people to the earth, and the planting of the seed . . .

Sometimes we would see the full-breasted figure of a woman silhouetted against the sky as she paused for a moment to rest from her work, and we did not wonder later when we heard stories they told here that many a child is conceived at such moments on that fertile earth. And then at dusk we saw them as they came down from the kaingins, the dark-skinned heavy women with babies slung on their backs, the lithe young girls of the scarlet mouths, and the youths carrying their guitars, and the old women and the children running after them. And the Song of the Planting ceased for the day.

We had come to the mountains in the spring. The black, charred soil of these hills that arched around us was the "good earth"—the "kaingin" these mountain people called it—that would produce the *palay* that would be pounded into the sweet rice—*beegas*. They had burned wide stretches of these forests to plant the rice in the rich soil fertilized by the ash of the fire. All around us lay the logs and huge stumps of great trees, like wounded and dead on a battlefield. A thick hot vapor arose from the scorched earth and enveloped us in its sticky suffocating heat on that blistering afternoon as we lay in the hut.

The broad river slicing through the mountains sparkled in the early morning sun, and as we followed our guides along its level banks I had a sudden sense of release and joy. For the first time since we had escaped the Japanese army in Labug, I felt safe: We were about fifty kilometers away from town in the heart of the mountains among these primitive people, who had taken us to live with them because they too hated the Japs and remembered the Americans as their friends. *"Americanos mabute tao"* (Americans good people) was what the chief of these strange savage mountain people, who are called the non-Christian tribes, had told Gabriel yesterday, when I had asked him why these people were willing to take us to their mountain home. The Americans had given them schools, doctors, and medicine and were kind to their children. . . . *"Haponese masama"* (Japanese bad people).

It was a significant answer and it was enough: For me it was the answer also to the question as to who would win the war. I knew it with a wonderful certainty that moment as I stood on the bank of a river in the remote mountains of the Philippines listening to a tiny grotesque savage chief of a pagan nomadic tribe, talking of America and the Americans. We would be safe, he assured us, because if the Japanese dared to come up the river, they would shoot them with poison arrows. The enemies of America were also their enemies; had they not also fled from their barrios when the Japs had come to Manila, and migrated to these mountains to plant new rice kaingins? Only when the Americans returned to the islands would they also return to their barrios.

And thus Gabriel had given us to these mountain people, while he returned to town, promising to come up again with the supplies from our cache. The chief of these people also remained on the bank of the river to finish the cutting of the rattan, which would be traded for salt and sugar and rice in the town. He would come back *"bukas"* (tomorrow) and meanwhile he instructed his people to take good care of us. They were to take us first to the house of an American who had been also living in the mountains for many months now.

We reached the house of the American, a Mr. Spalding, at noon that day. It was a dilapidated bamboo shack with a patched cogon grass roof and a forlorn, neglected look. In the doorway we stopped, puzzled for a moment by the group of Filipino women and children lying on the huge bamboo bed and a long figure muffled in a blanket stretched on the earth floor near the fireplace, while another Filipino woman holding a baby squatted by him. I turned to our guides. Was this the wrong house? Where was Mr. Spalding? Suddenly the figure on the floor stirred and a thin, chalky-white face emerged from the blankets and a pair of frightened, watery blue eyes peered out. With a convulsive movement, Mr. Spalding jerked himself up to a sitting position and stared at us as if we were ghosts.

"Hello, who are you?" he gasped finally.

The noon tropical heat beat through the thin roof of the flimsy hut and huge flies buzzed blindly around like bats. We stood there uncertainly. . . . The Filipino women and children seemed transfixed as they stared at us. I think they must have been frightened by Ron's beard and I did not know whether they would quite make out whether I was a man or woman in my slacks.

"Hello yourself. . . . We're the Americans to the rescue," Ron tried to be jocular. He waved his hand around the shack. "What's this setup?"

Spalding's thin face relaxed into a feeble, apologetic smile that lit up his pale eyes and weak chin. "My family," he said.

The Filipino woman with the baby in her arms rose suddenly, scooped rice into two plates, and brought them to us with a shy smile. "*Asin*" she said to one of the children on the bed, who brought us some salt in a bamboo leaf. The inevitable rice and salt. We accepted out of politeness, but only pretended to eat. I felt nauseated and wanted suddenly to get away from this stifling hut to the cool sparkling river.

So this was the mountain Shangri-La we had come to—this miserable desolate scene. We revived Spalding with some hot coffee and he slowly pieced out his grim story: Since he had left Manila with his family—his wife and three children, and her sister and child—he had been wandering from place to place just as we had, evading Sakdals and Japs, until they had run out of supplies. Then they had come up here, hoping to live with these mountain people, who were friendly and eager to help them. But they had come to a barren country. These *tao bundok* were only just beginning to plant their rice kaingins. They too had fled from the Japanese, leaving their fertile barrios of coconuts and bananas and mangoes to come here to plant. Even they were living on their old stocks of rice and corn and a little fish and meat they could get by hunting or trading with the Negritos, the aborigines of these parts. In a few months after the rains and the harvest, food would be plentiful, but now they guarded their rice carefully and would only part with it for money or trinkets, which they dearly loved.

"When we ran out of supplies and money about a month ago, my wife started trading her dresses and any jewelry she had just for rice," Spalding said.

"You mean they would just let you starve if you don't have money?" I asked incredulously.

"Well, look at us—we've been slowly starving for the past month. It's not that they mean to do it—they're friendly enough. Sure, they bring us a little rice now and then when they remember . . . but most of the time we have to beg for it—send the kids out to beg."

I looked at the skinny bodies and listless faces of the two older children on the bed, a girl of about nine and a boy about eleven. Even with their dirty ragged clothes and unkempt hair, you could see they were unusually handsome mestizas. The other little girl about six, had an odd look with her shaven head and ugly face—she looked like a little rat.

"But why do these natives want to take care of Americans if there's no food?"

Spalding puffed away at a native cigarillo and stared at the mountains in the distance. "They're just like kids themselves—these *tao bundok* . . . . For them, living on rice and salt is nothing, and they think we're the same. Why they can even go for days without food, and then make up for it by feasting for a week on a wild pig or deer they've caught. Trouble is we don't ever get to the feasting—"

To make matters worse, Spalding had come down with malarial fever, which had just about done him in.

"Just had an attack when you walked in." He smiled bitterly. "Anyway, looks like my luck is still holding out—I was just about ready to give up . . . couldn't take much more of this."

"No use surrendering," Ron said. "The Japs would only beat us to death. They're riding high now and they're mean and vicious."

"What can we do then—just starve to death here in these mountains?"

"We've got to stick it out—somehow. You won't die. We've still got a little money, and we're waiting for supplies now. After you're stronger maybe we can make it to the coast—and live there on fish and coconuts."

Ron was dreaming again. Infanta—contacting a submarine, maybe getting to Australia. The important thing was getting Spalding on his feet and his family so they could move. We only had a small sack of food supplies with us: a paper kilo of coffee, a little sugar, some mungo beans, a few cans of corned beef. After these ran out, we would have nothing until Gabriel brought up the supplies we had left in our cache at Labug, and when that would be no one could tell. . . . Anyway, we decided to risk it and that night we threw most of what we had into a big mess to feed the starving Spaldings, and it was worth it when we saw the ecstatic faces of the children and Spalding himself looking almost human again as he watched his family eat.

Spalding was so grateful he offered us the bed to sleep on while he and his family slept on the floor by the fire. Although this was a natural thing for Filipinos to do, somehow coming from an American, it shocked us. Of course, we would not hear of it—we found an empty hut nearby with a hole in the roof through which we could see the stars, and fervently hoped it would not rain.

The next few days we used up the rest of our food nursing the Spaldings back to health. Among the nine of us it did not go very far, but we enjoyed it while it lasted, and enjoyed even more the companionship of this strange family—at least during those early days. We were like a Swiss Family Robinson, only the setting was this barren mountain instead of a desert island. I liked especially being with children again, after the terrible loneliness of the past few months: Life suddenly seemed right and normal, as though we were no longer outlaws being hunted. I made friends with Doris and Robert, both of whom spoke English hesitatingly, with a curiously singsong inflection; but the other little rat-like creature would not emerge from her tiny corner unless she was threatened with a stick by her mother, Corinne, a big, slatternly, ugly girl, who obviously hated this illegitimate offspring of some casual dalliance. I soon discovered that sturdy Doris was by far the most enterprising and healthy of the entire Spalding family—it was she who would go off and beg, borrow, or steal among the natives and usually return triumphantly with some delicacy like *panocha* (sugar cake) or a few precious eggs. Robert was more frail and shy, and would often be laid low with malaria attacks like his father; when he was well he would help his mother with the baby. Altogether, it was a queer household. We often asked Spalding why he did not send his family back to Manila and strike out for himself— surely it would be easier than trying to feed several people every day. But he would only shake his head and answer that his wife insisted on sticking it out with him until the end, and she needed her sister to help her. It was a hopeless situation.

At last, after a few days, the Spaldings were stronger and we decided to move to some new houses a few hills beyond, near the rice kaingins. Spalding said the houses were probably better there and we would also be safer, away from the river, which was dangerous as long as the dry season continued. Although you could trust these mountain people, you never knew when the *balita* (news) would reach the Sakdals that some Americans were living up here, and if it did it would probably be exaggerated to the effect that we were an armed camp.

We had to be on the move all the time. Our little safari must have made an odd picture: Spalding staggering along with his rifle over his shoulder; his wife with her baby slung on her back; the children with sacks yoked to their heads native-wise; Ron bent under our sack; I clutching the precious leather portfolio containing his writings; and, finally, a Filipino boy carrying our suitcase. Spalding and Ron and I had to rest about every five minutes and when I looked at Spalding's death-like pallor after a climb, I thought he would never make it.

Our new houses jutted picturesquely enough on the palm of this great hand of mountain ranges stretching to the coast. From our little bamboo bed where we sank exhausted after our trek, we could see the black slope of the kaingins against the wide sweep of the green forests bent against the mountains. Actually these flimsily made shacks were little better than the ones we had left; they were the hastily improvised huts of the mountain people who had been planting rice on the near-by kaingins during the dry season, and had been deserted for bamboo houses that would give them some protection against the heavy rains to come.

We were close to the black-charred rice kaingins now, and there was a smell of burnt wood in the hot sticky vaporous wind, drifting in from the kaingins, presaging the rains. They came every afternoon now as if they were rehearsing for the grand finale of their great per-formance—the rainy season. But now as we lay waiting, listening for the first drops, all the jungle vegetation was torpid, ablaze in that sear-ing heat of the early afternoon, also waiting for the rain.

At last it came with all the fury of the brief tropical storm, and if we had wanted a shower to cool us off, we certainly got it as the rain poured in. Everything was wet—our suitcase, our bed, our floor, and our fireplace (those three stones for the rice pot that these natives call a fireplace) and I was glad I did not have to struggle to make a fire that night. We went up to the Spalding's house, a bigger one with a better roof, and found them all huddled together on the bed as usual, wait-ing for the rain to stop. Mrs. Spalding, like all Filipinos, was adept at making fires whether it rained or not, and she soon had a cheerful

roaring blaze under the rice pot. We had no supplies left so she sent
the children off in a little while to gather *camote* leaves to eat with our
rice. We washed it down with sassafras tea. Altogether it was a melancholy meal, and as we sat afterwards smoking our last cigarettes, looking out on the fading sunset that lit up the hills around us, we thought
gloomily of the days and weeks ahead.

Tomorrow and tomorrow . . . each day we waited in vain for
Gabriel to come up with our supplies from the cache. Meanwhile we
just lived from day to day on rice and *camote* leaves, gingerroot or sassafras tea. The food we had eaten in Labug—during our Bread and
Rice stage—seemed like an incredible dream now: Was it possible we
had actually had hotcakes and eggs and coffee? Coffee . . . coffee was
what we missed most those cold dismal mornings—I think we could
have stood everything better if we had been able to buy a chicken, but
the natives even hoarded their few scrawny chickens for hatching.

One afternoon we had a real bit of luck. A couple of Negritos
came down the trail from the forest beyond our houses carrying a
deer they had shot. Mrs. Spalding negotiated with them with the help
of some mountain people and was able to buy a whole leg for only
five pesos. It was the first time I had seen these little people at close
range and I was struck at once by their beauty. They are small and
extraordinarily handsome with graceful bodies and well-shaped heads
and curly hair. I was fascinated by one of them who had a star tattooed
on his forehead, which seemed to be the mark of a certain clan of
tribes. It is very difficult to understand their language—even Mrs.
Spalding had to get one of the mountain people to interpret for her.
They speak a kind of bird-talk with a rising nasal inflection, a distor-
tion of Tagalog. The *tao bundok* like to imitate and even caricature
them, for they consider themselves far superior to these Negritos.
But just as the townspeople look down upon the mountain people,
the latter consider the Negritos their inferiors, and often make them
work for them.

After that venison feast, we resumed our monotonous starvation diet of rice and salt that soon left us sick with dysentery and fever. The Spaldings in a weakened condition had again succumbed to malaria and for a terrible time, we thought we too had caught that disease. On June 3, I wrote in my diary: "Still ill with dysentery and fever, and we are worried that it may be malaria—everyone else around here seems to have it. The only thing that gives us hope is that we don't seem to have the same attacks as theirs with that terrible chill that makes your teeth rattle . . . but God, how miserable we are. Last night I almost wanted to succumb and just lie down and die. I felt such a wave of futility about this whole impossible situation. What are we going to do? We are in a trap, and we can neither go backwards nor forwards. Will we live through this? Only one thing could put an end to our misery and uncertainty, and that is the end of the war and that is nowhere in sight. We haven't heard any news for weeks now . . ."

Oh Death in Life of that strange existence where we lived on the edge of a terrible danger with only hope to sustain us, I will remember you always, not only for the horror of your days, but also for their wild savage beauty: the weird tropical sky ablaze with riotous color before the rains, the blinding sunshine of the morning carved with the moving silhouettes of the natives climbing the hills to plant their rice, singing their monotonous chant . . .

At last, when we had given up hope of ever seeing him again, Gabriel suddenly appeared one afternoon. But it was a Gabriel we hardly recognized as he strutted up the hill nonchalantly smoking a great cigar, dressed grotesquely in knickerbockers and a snappy straw hat. He looked like a caricature of a village yokel in his Sunday best. Behind him panted two cargodores with packs yoked to their heads, and occasionally Gabriel would turn around to shout something to them in Tagalog. At last Gabriel was the entrepreneur, and no doubt he was expecting fabulous rewards from the Americans for making this long trip to the mountains—we saw that at once when he presented us with the fantastic bill for the meager supplies he had actually brought. No flour, no canned bacon, no American coffee from our cache.

"Where are the supplies we left in our cache?" Ron asked him.

"Sir, they were not there, sir," Gabriel replied with much feeling.

"But where are they then?"

"Sir, I am sure the Sakdals robbed them after the Japs went away."

"But how did they know where the cache was?"

"Sir, Roberto the Sakdal dressed in the Jap uniform who led them to your place must have informed those in the town, sir."

"But I thought the Japs shot Roberto when they did not find us the morning they attacked our place."

"Sir, he must have told his friends before he was shot, sir."

It was hopeless. Much later we found out that Gabriel had sold our supplies at great profit in the town. With Gabriel, you had to take both the good and the bad. The good was that now he had brought us some native coffee, sugar, cigarettes, a few cans of corned beef and pork and beans, some fresh vegetables, cakes, and candy. The children had a party and we had a feast and Gabriel was forgiven for the time being. We could not afford to be angry with him even if we wanted to—at the moment he was our only link with town.

"What's the news in town, Gabriel?" Ron asked as we sat round the fire after supper smoking the black native cigarillos.

"Sir, five hundred Japs in Montalban now, sir," Gabriel said promptly with the usual exaggeration. Anyway, we knew there was an unusually large concentration of Japanese in town.

"How about Sakdals—still many of those rats around with the Japs?"

"Sir, plenty, sir. But they are not favorites with the people, sir, and they do not like the Japs to serve much more because the Japs slap their faces and shoot them easily, sir. It is all bad, sir."

"Do you think any of these Sakdals could get up this far?" I asked.

"*Seguro*" (Perhaps). Gabriel grinned. "Missus—sir, have you not heard the story of Mr. Dugas?" he turned to Spalding expectantly.

Spalding was sitting upright on the bamboo bed with his bare feet hanging limply down, and in the light of the fire, they looked strangely detached as though they could float off in a moment of their own volition, away over the mountains. I stared at them with repulsion.

"Dugas . . ." Spalding rolled a cigarette and licked it meditatively. "Oh yes, Dugas—quite a story in these parts. Don't think these mountain people will ever forget Dugas—great, big, strapping, dark-haired chap. About a month ago, he come up to hide here—lived in a house on that hill over there—" Spalding waved in the direction of the mountains in the distance. "They say he had so much stuff he needed ten cargodores to carry it all, brought up a lot of useless stuff like wires and crates and whatnot—a pity too because the Sakdals got it all."

I felt suddenly frightened.

"Your man, the Sakdals got him?" I asked quickly. "Up here?"

"They not only got him but they beat him up badly before even the Japs could do it. The Japs almost finished him by tying him to a post in the village square under a hot sun for a day. Don't know where he is now—" Spalding's pale thin feet waved helplessly.

"But how did it happen? Didn't these people warn him or something?"

"That was just it. You see, they hated him—called him '*masama tao*' (bad man). Thought he was stingy, wouldn't ever give them anything. Hell, Dugas was so stingy he wouldn't part with an extra grain of rice if he could help it. And that's what these natives hate more than anything— if you get the reputation of being stingy, they'll just let you be and let the Sakdals or Japs get you. Even if you haven't got anything to give, you've got to offer it—that's how it is . . ." Spalding smiled helplessly.

"But there were other reasons, too, they let the Japs get him. The main reason was his wife, I guess. Dugas came up here with the prettiest little thing you'd ever seen, only she was so small she was just about half his size. That was all right, but he'd made the mistake of buying her for about a hundred pesos somewhere in town. These natives didn't like that—God only knows why—they're so damn immoral themselves. Maybe they figured he didn't pay enough for her. And another person didn't like it—her brother. He followed them up here and started spying on them. Then he began asking Dugas for money and things. Dugas told him to get the hell off the place or he'd shoot him dead. Naturally the brother hated Dugas' guts by then, so he began to plot revenge. He knew that the couple used to stay in bed until noon—it was common *balita* among the natives too—so he led the Sakdals up here and got them at just the right moment. They sure caught Dugas with his pants down, all right." Spalding's weak chin was lost in the broad grin that swallowed it.

"What about the mountain people—did they know the Sakdals were coming?"

"Know? Why they saw them on the trail going up to Dugas' place—could've mowed 'em down even with their homemade shotguns or used poison arrows on them if they wanted. But they didn't want to—that's all." Spalding spit into the fire. "They hated Dugas—just let him be captured."

Captured and beaten and hung up in the sun. Then even here we were not safe. . . . Would we ever be safe again? I shivered and drew closer to the fire. . . . Ron's voice broke the stillness.

"How far is it to Infanta from here, Gabriel?"

I saw Gabriel's face stiffen with a sudden fear.

"I am very sorry to say, sir, but it is very, very far, sir."

"How far?"

"Many hundreds of kilometers, sir."

"Could you get any cargodores to take us there?"

There was a pause. Gabriel looked very unhappy.

"Perhaps, sir. I do not know, sir," Gabriel got up to put another stick on the fire. "Mountain people are afraid to go to Infanta. They tell *balita* here that people near Infanta are very wild, sir. When they put on the red handkerchiefs on the heads they attack the white man and eat them." He glanced up to where Mrs. Spalding was squatting on the bed with her baby asleep in her arms. Her face in the flickering firelight looked tense and frightened. *"Hindi ba kayo natatakut?"* (Are you not afraid?), he asked.

"Akoy natalakut—mastado malayo Infanta" (I am afraid—Infanta is very far), she murmured.

In those words I heard the death knell of our dream trip to the coast with the Spaldings. Spalding would never go without his wife and it was clear that Gabriel was afraid to go. He had always been afraid, but he was always procrastinating. We could not go without a guide whom we could trust. Gabriel left the next morning. He had learned that we had very little money left, so he decided to let the mountain people take care of us. We never saw him again, but he never completely left our lives. We heard of him from time to time until that terrible moment almost a year later when Ron had to decide the life or death of Gabriel at the hands of the guerrillas. And whether we wanted to or not, we had to remember that it was also through Gabriel that we met Fabian.

Fabian is the real hero of our mountain story. To me he shall always be the symbol of the fidelity of the simple Filipino people to the Americans and their resistance to the Japanese. Without them we could not have won the war, and without Fabian we could not have held out for the next year against the Japs.

Fabian was the prototype of the Filipino *tao,* the farmer in the rice fields with his carabao; he was the *tao* who was the backbone, the very heart of these tropical islands. He was not a politico or a merchant or an entrepreneur—he was just a simple farmer who had nothing to gain and everything to lose by helping the Americans. If the Japs caught him, he could not buy them off, nor did he know how to compromise. He was not a collaborator. His loyalty to the Americans sprang from sentimental reasons. As a little boy, his father used to tell him stories about the American soldiers who first came to the islands at the turn of the century, how kind they were to the people, how they loved the children, and how lavish and generous they were with money. They were entirely different from the Japanese soldiers who beat the people at the slightest provocation, raped their women, and mortally insulted them by slapping their faces in public. And Fabian belonged to that generation of children who remembered also the first kind American teacher in their little barrio school giving them their first lessons in English and the American way. He grew up with many "bamboo Americans," a number of whom married Filipino women and lived among them. So it was these countless sentimental reasons that bound Fabian and thousands of Filipinos like him irrevocably to the Americans, regardless of economic exploitation by a ruthless clique, and made him fight side by side with the Americans against the Japs when the time came.

Fabian had actually followed Gabriel up into these mountains to "find an American he could help" as he told us naively later on. It seemed that Gabriel had been drinking too much *alak*—native wine—in town one night and had been boasting about the fact that he was "keeping some Americans in the hills." Later he had proved it to Fabian by showing off his wife attired in my evening gown and coats, which he had purloined from my suitcases after the raid in Labug. Fabian had never trusted Gabriel much and he decided to come up to these mountains to see for himself. He joined Gabriel's party on the pretext that he wanted to gamble with the mountain people who loved to play a card game called "monte," which is something like our poker. This game was a vice with them—once they started, they would play for days and nights without stopping. The night Gabriel came up there was a game in session in one of the native huts at the bottom of the hill near the river. Gabriel joined it after he left us and played all night, according to Fabian who slept there. In the morning when Gabriel came to say good-bye, Fabian followed him up to our hut to see the Americanos.

I liked Fabian instantly. I liked his wide handsome honest face that lit up so warmly when he smiled, his strong white teeth, a dazzling white against his dark skin. He was young, somewhere in his twenties he seemed. Unlike Gabriel, there was nothing shifty or dandyish about him—on the contrary, he had a clean look and the powerful rugged physique of a man who has lived his life close to the soil. And I felt at once I could trust him—he had the kind of open face that could not hide any thought or feeling. I knew that when I saw the expression of shock and pity when he came into our miserable little hut with its soggy mud floor and saw us lying pale and thin and listless on our bed that morning.

"Sir, this is Fabian San Juan, the cousin of the Mayor of Montalban," said Gabriel in a voice of importance. And when he saw our startled look he added, smiling: "But sir, he can be trusted, sir. The Mayor is a very good man, sir."

Fabian stood there silently with a look of great pity on his face. Only when Gabriel left did he relax somewhat. I got up and offered to cook some coffee but he shook his head vehemently and said to Ron: "Sir, I would like to be able to help you very much. I have so much pity for your wife, sir. The life is so hard in the mountains, sir."

I told Fabian I had been a teacher of English at the University of the Philippines and that I would like to get a note down to Manila to a friend of mine, an American woman who had also taught there. She was the wife of a Filipino doctor and had probably not been interned by the Japanese. At the mention of the University of the Philippines, Fabian's face lit up.

"But my older brother is also a graduate of the University, Missus," he said. "If you were to also write a letter to him, I am sure he would be happy to go to your friend. Perhaps we will both come up next week and bring an answer to you and also supplies, sir."

It sounded too good to be true: two Filipinos walking fifty kilo-meters with packs without a big reward? Remembering Gabriel, I was skeptical of course, but somehow Fabian looked different. . . . Besides, we were desperate—what could we lose? I wrote the letters: To Mrs. Jaramillo I wrote that I wanted to get to Manila if it were possible, by some kind of disguise, as we were starving in these mountains; I also asked for some quinine, aspirin, and clothes. We watched Fabian until he was out of sight of our rice kaingin, and wondered: Will we ever see him again?

Once again we were alone. The days passed in the monotonous routine of eating or just lying on our bamboo bed in a kind of stupor. Sometimes we would read Shelley, but for the most part we were too tired even to do that. While we still had some cans of meat left, we would have sporadic spurts of energy, but then we relapsed into a weakness and stupor after our endless diet of rice and salt. The moun-tain people were hurrying now to finish their planting before the rainy season began in earnest, and we would watch them climbing gaily up the steep black slopes of the kaingin until they had reached the very top and were silhouetted against the brilliant blue sky before they dis-appeared over the other side. Then the strains of the guitar and the chant of the Song of the Planting would float down to us bringing inti-mations of happy living and the pure primitive joy of life, and sudden-ly I longed to be one of them, full of hope, planting the seed for tomorrow.

The chief of the mountain people came at last to Spalding's house one morning. We had met him on the bank of the river the day we came up to these mountains, but it seemed as if months had already passed since that day, and already we had forgotten what he looked like. He had told us he was coming back *bukas* (tomorrow), but it was a tomorrow that had stretched out into almost a month.

Placido was a small, wizened man with a squint in one eye and blackened stubs of teeth, stained a blood red by betel-nut juice.

Squatting by the fire, in his ragged shorts and torn shirt, he certainly looked less like a chief to us than some of the handsome Negritos we had seen. Only his wide straw hat gave him any dignity. It was hard to believe that this little man ruled all these mountain tribes with great cunning. True, they were all related to him in some way—he had at least three known wives, according to Spalding, and God only knows how many children scattered among them. We knew how important it was to make the right impression, that we were "*mabute tao*" (good people)—not like Dugas—and we had brought out one of our precious cans of pork and beans and now offered it grandiloquently to the chief. Placido smiled broadly and wagged his head delightedly as he accepted this gift offering. We then asked Spalding to ask him how much he would want to build a house for us that would keep out the rain. The mention of money seemed to delight Placido more than ever. He spit a red squirt of betel-nut juice into the fire and held up three fingers: "*Tres pesos. Maganda ding-ding bahay*" (Three pesos for a magnificent house with walls to keep out the wind and the rain).

"He also says he'll build the house for you behind his own house down by the river," Spalding continued to translate. "And if the Japs come he will shoot them himself."

Placido got up excitedly and seized Spalding's rifle. "*Pung! Pung! Pung!*" he shouted.

Ron and I exchanged looks. We had to show proper appreciation of this magnificent gesture with one equally magnificent. I watched Placido's face as Ron took off the black pearl ring he wore—it was a silver ring set with a black pearl he had bought from a Moro in Manila—and presented it to the chief. I felt as though I were looking at some scene in Indian history—the White Man-trading-with-the-Chief-sort-of-thing. Placido looked incredulously at Ron, wagged his head a few times as though he could not think of accepting such a handsome gift, and then promptly put it on. Our friendship was sealed—if not forever, then for the time being at least.

Spalding smiled skeptically after Placido had gone. "Won't believe it until I see the house. He's as unreliable as all these people here with their *mañana* and *bukas*." He scratched his head thoughtfully. "Still you can't tell—he might do it for money. He'd probably want fifty pesos to make one for my brood."

A few days later Placido returned to tell us the house was finished and would be ready to move into the next day. We told Spalding that if this house really kept out the rains, we would see that Placido built one for them also. Actually, we were glad to be moving away from the Spaldings now—it was becoming torture to watch their suffering and not be able to help them, now when we could scarcely help ourselves. Of course Ron would miss his daily talks with Spalding, and I would miss the children, but at least we would not watch them slowly starving to death. We too were now weak and thin from those weeks of sickness and hunger, so weak that we could hardly walk. Ron had to lean on a big stick, and Placido held my hand to keep me from falling as we slid painfully down the steep slippery trail leading through the cogon grass to the river. Bleak little bamboo houses were scattered near our path, and Placido would often stop to gossip and exchange betel nut with their occupants. We were glad of any rest. In every hut someone lay shivering and feverish with malaria. It was the season of the *lagnet*—the Big Fever—which was at its height now before the heavy rains began.

At last we reached Placido's house on the bank of the river, and seeing again the swift-flowing water sun-gleaming in the fresh morning light, I felt once more that sense of freedom, as though Ron and I had only to follow the river again to leave these mountains forever.

Placido's house was palatial compared to the huts we had seen, and to our starved eyes and stomachs, it had an air of prosperity and plenty. Dried tapa and corn hung from the bamboo rafter and mounds of *camotes* were stacked near the fireplace and a huge rice pot was hanging over a crackling, cheerful fire. There was the usual huge bamboo bed in the corner. As we entered, a scrawny woman with a gleaming gold tooth rose and greeted us with a fawning smile, and motioned for us to sit down on a bamboo seat near the fireplace.

"*Nagugutum na?*" (Are you hungry?), she asked, and handed each a cup of steaming soup from the rice pot. It was pig meat soup and as I drank, I felt the strength oozing back into me.

"*Salamat,*" we murmured politely to the woman who watched us avidly while we drank. I was conscious also of a pair of dark eyes staring at me intently from the bed. I turned to see a girl with long coarse hair who looked like a little Indian. Placido followed my glance and said, shaking his head: "Rosa—*sakit malaria!*" (Rosa sick with malaria). Rosa was the daughter of the woman who gave us the soup—Aling Ate—at present the wife of Placido, who was not, however, the father of the little girl. Nor was Aling the mother of the little boy who came running in presently with a fish—but Placido was his father. It was all rather complicated and it took us some time to get all the relationships—we never really got them altogether straight, since incest and polygamy were common and accepted practices there. Placido presented us with the fish, saying "*Dalag—mabute pagkain*" (Fish—good to eat).

Placido rose and motioned for us to follow. He smiled and said: "*Ding-ding bahay.*" We said goodbye to Aling and Rosa and followed Placido down a path in back of his house that ran parallel to a tiny stream cutting through the woods. My heart sank at the sight of these woods—were we to be hidden once again in woods that I hated so much? I still remembered with fear our months near Labug, but perhaps now it would be different—we were near these friendly mountain people who would take care of us, we would not be so utterly isolated nor so far from human beings as we were then. I realized with something like terror how dependent we were upon those people— they held our life or death in their hands, quite literally. What could prevent them from informing on us, if they wished? Or why could they not even hand us over to the Japanese and claim the reward they had on the heads of all Americans caught hiding out? The answer was that as long as we were regarded as their friends, they would never betray us to the enemy. They might run away and let us starve, but they would never betray us.

The three-peso *ding-ding* house that Placido had built for us, a snug little shack with a roof of grass and leaves and walls of bark, was only a few feet away from the stream. I tried to hide my disappointment at the flimsy roof which I was sure would not keep out the rain—I had had so much experience sleeping under such roofs that leaked like a sieve. Placido was obviously very proud of his handicraft because he kept pointing to the bark walls and repeating: "*ding-ding bahay.*" I was relieved when he left us at last after he had chopped some wood for the fire, assuring us that he would return tomorrow.

Again tomorrow. . . . Ron and I stared at each other: How many more tomorrows of this would there be, hiding in the woods, being hunted, hiding in the woods where at night a thousand eyes might be staring at you from the darkness of the jungle, where every sound was the footstep of the enemy ready to pounce on you . . .

The afternoon turned sunny and our little stream sparkled with light. Suddenly I felt cheerful and happy again as though we were starting on a new adventure. We had food enough for today and who knew what tomorrow might bring? Tonight we would have a wonderful supper of rice and fried fish and coffee. I even decided to take a bath to feel fresh and new—ready for anything. The next few days were the most peaceful we had known since we came to the mountains. Placido and Aling came every day to bring us either some fish or a bit of meat or some corn, and we began to feel stronger and more human and I knew that things were better when I found Ron ensconced at a spot by the stream writing again.

On June 14, I wrote: "I think I shall be a confirmed believer in miracles after what happened today. Fabian San Juan, that fine-looking

Filipino with the good face who took that note to Manila for me came today with his brother Epifanio, a former University of Philippines student. They had walked about fifty kilometers with packs, and brought us supplies of food and clothes and a letter from my friend, Mrs. Jaramillo. I was so overwhelmed that for the first time in months, I wept for joy. It was our first contact with Manila for more than eight months, and it brought back to me that incredible world before the war: teaching at the University, broadcasting and living freely. . . . Was it possible that I had ever lived such a life? That I had not been hunted? When I had eaten Bread? Now this primitive life in the jungle seems my only reality . . ."

I stared at the incredibly dainty underclothes Mrs. Jaramillo had sent me—silk panties and slips that I had always taken for granted, but now seemed to belong to another world—the world of sheltered, well-clad women. I wanted first just to sit and stare at them or stroke their soft silkiness. The food delicacies she sent were equally incredible—crackers and peanut butter, a can of real butter, some jams, a few cans of meat. Most precious of all was a bottle of 100 tablets of quinine and some aspirin for me. It should last us until the Americans came back.

I read Mrs. Jaramillo's letter again and again—how happy she was to hear that I was alive and to get word from me at last, but she said that it would be dangerous for me to come to Manila now because the roads were being carefully watched and even if I did manage to get there, it would be too difficult to hide, because the Japs were making periodic house-to-house searches and the house of an American woman was watched with great suspicion. She implored me to hold out and she would try to send me food, clothing, and medicine from time to time. . . . Fabian also brought me a message and parcel of food from another friend, Mrs. Ruth Lava, an unusually intelligent woman who, with her two children, had attended my classes at the University. Ruth, an American woman and the sister of Mrs. Claude Rains, was married to the brilliant Filipino scientist and inventor, Dr. Vicente Lava, then fighting with the guerrillas in the hills. She also warned me against going to Manila, as the Japanese had sources of information at that time through which they might learn of my anti-Jap activities . . .

I wrote in my diary: "Meanwhile I must have courage and try to stick it out . . . courage. . . . I thought of our soldiers at Bataan and of soldiers everywhere and suddenly what we were going through did not seem so awful. . . . After all, we were still free and alive and all around us was a world of incredible beauty and we were living among people who still lived by customs that had been prevalent when the earth was young . . ."

Fabian and Epifanio had also brought some fresh pork, lard, and bananas, so once again we had a feast. We sent some foodstuffs up to the Spaldings whom we had not seen since we had moved down here. Then while Fabian cooked the dinner, Epifanio talked to us, giving us the latest news. He seemed exceptionally intelligent and well-informed, and spoke a good English. He told us that most of the Filipinos believed that the American forces would be back by Christmas, if not sooner, and that we must not lose hope. The Americans were reported to be fighting in New Guinea and it was only a matter of time when they would be here. Even the Sakdals were beginning to be afraid, and were losing their nerve—they had found it not too pleasant working for the Japs.

I was interested in the differences between the two brothers, both physically and mentally. They represented two distinct types—one was the student and teacher, the other the simple *tao* or farmer. Epifanio was taller and had a lighter skin and was more delicate than Fabian, who was more stocky and stalwart. Fabian was obviously very proud of his older brother, who had been educated under the Americans at a great sacrifice by their poor parents. There were three other children—José, a carpenter; Ponciano, a high school student; and Carmen, the only daughter. While Epifanio talked, Fabian kept a respectful admiring silence, and would not allow his brother to do any manual work at all, but he himself chopped wood, made the fire, cooked the rice, and washed the dishes in the little stream.

The San Juan brothers slept on a nearby kaingin that night, since there was no room in our hut, but they came down early the next morning to cook breakfast for us—rice and fried meat. Then they started on their long trek home, with a promise to return soon. We felt marvelously cheered by their visit—the future suddenly seemed much more promising, more certain, now that we knew we had someone we could trust. From what Spalding had told us of these people, we knew that as long as our money held out, we could keep from actually starving, but after that, who knew? Meanwhile Placido's solicitude concerning our welfare increased even more after Fabian's visit.

The *tao bundok* had both a fear and respect and awe for the townspeople, and I think Placido sensed a possible rival in these brothers, who might eventually take us away from him, and thus spoil all chances of his reward after the war. And so every day he sent Aling or Rosa, who had completely recovered from her fever, to visit us and chop wood or cook for me. I began to pass the time by teaching Rosa a little English, incidentally also improving my Tagalog. I made a little book for her, with which she was delighted. But I was amazed at her stony look when she saw I had written in it that Placido was her father. I thought she would tear the book up, so angry did she become. It was very strange—apparently, she had learned somewhere that something was wrong, since she did not know her real father.

About that time I wrote: "Sometimes it is quite idyllic here and I think I am living through a pleasant dream—then I remember the reality. . . . Luckily I have my 'housework' and that keeps me from thinking too much, until the night falls. We have an invariable routine—in the morning I usually wake first, crawl out and make a fire, and cook some coffee. Then we have our breakfast—rice with a sprinkling of brown sugar, if we have it, and more coffee. . . . Then Ron either chops wood or goes down to his 'writing den' by the stream to work. I clean up our little house—straighten up the clothes we sleep on, roll up our mosquito net, and sweep the floor with a grass broom. After that I bring the dishes and dirty clothes down to the stream and wash, using as little soap as possible. Then I'm free to write or read or dream until lunch, then on goes the rice pot again. If we have any lard, I fry up the rice, or better still if there's any meat we fry that and really eat. Or it may be just rice and salt. In the afternoon if there are no visitors we either write or read until supper. After that nothing to do but crawl into bed after dark."

One day not long after Fabian's visit, Placido brought us a strange visitor—a tall, well-built heavy-set woman who obviously did not look like a *tao bundok*. She was much too well-dressed and even seemed to have an air of sophistication that none of these people possessed. With her shrewd eyes in a hard cold face she looked more like a merchant or shopkeeper. We learned later from Spalding that she was a trader from Montalban who exploited these mountain people shamefully. In exchange for rattan which they cut for her, she gave them rice or sugar or tobacco and by this barter system she had bound the natives to her in an involved debt structure and held the whip over them constantly by threatening to get the police after them. Later we were to find that they had to do almost anything she wanted because they were so much in debt to her. Delang typified the feudal overseer in this primitive economic setup, ruthlessly exploiting these people for her own ends. She rationalized her position by telling you she was a poor widow with eight children to support: "Life is so hard for a woman all alone . . ."

Placido deposited a pack of supplies in our hut, while Delang stood aloof, watching us with hard, cruel eyes in her pockmarked, handsome face. I distrusted her at once. *"Marami pagkain"* (Very much to eat). Placido beamed, looking from Delang to us. I think Delang was trying to size us up—to find out whether we were poor or rich

Americans. Placido had probably told her that we were not poor, at any rate not like the Spaldings. She looked sinister. I decided I had better make friends with her.

"Magkaano?" I asked her, and was surprised to see that hard mask crack into a smile. She must have been amused at my speaking Tagalog. She gave me the price in English, and after we had paid, she said stiffly:

"I have much pity for you—a woman in these mountains. Life is very hard here, is it not? I have been coming here many times. I would help you if I can." She smiled hypocritically as she pocketed the money and left with Placido.

Living in the woods began to oppress me again, especially at night when the darkness fell so quickly and we were completely walled in by blackness. Our life then radiated around the fire and since, for lack of wood, we could not keep it going all night, we would crawl into bed as soon as possible. Sometimes the night seemed endless and sometimes I would awake suddenly from a horrible dream in which the Japs were surrounding us and I would lie awake trembling until the dawn. We decided to ask Placido to build another house on the hill, so that we could at least get a view. . . . This time, Placido charged us five pesos, and we paid another five for Spalding's house, which he built a few yards from ours, on a high windswept hill overlooking the river and with a magnificent view of the mountains beyond.

THE RAINS

I CANNOT THINK OF THAT NEW HOUSE WHERE WE LIVED for the next three months without remembering how the Rains burst over the mountains with a sudden fury of a typhoon, and even now as I lie in the jail, I can hear that rain lashing and the wind howling and the river roaring, swollen and foaming with the yellow churned waters. Sometimes it would rain for nine days ceaselessly, and this the mountain people called a "*sham*"; if it continued to eighteen days, it was a "*sham-sham.*" No longer then were we walled in by woods but by rain, and it seemed to me that the whole world was dissolving in water around us, and our little house was like a boat riding the crest of a wave, as the wind rocked it back and forth.

Placido had built two houses of cogon grass on top of a hill that could be reached only by climbing a steep trail winding through his cornfields for about half a kilometer. Our view embraced the mountains and the surrounding country, and—most important of all—we could always see anyone approaching us. Directly behind our house was a wide field of cogon grass, lush and tall, where we could hide in a hurry, while beyond to our right stretched a huge forest of unbroken jungle vegetation. No Japs could possibly attack us from this direction, simply because it was virgin country—even the mountain people had not yet hacked their trails through the dense brush. Spalding's house, separated from ours only by fifty yards or so, looked directly into the valley sloping to the river, and in the months to come, it was our lookout; no person could come up the trail from Placido's house, unless he crawled through the grass, without being seen by the sharp eyes of the Spalding family.

Our new little house was very beautiful and sweet smelling, with its freshly cut cogon grass roof that hung over the sides like the hair over the eyes of a shaggy dog. But alas, despite all Placido's assurances, it did not keep out the rains, and I became resigned at last to the fact that we would probably never have such a house in these mountains; for these *tao bundok* are so much a part of the elements, so close to the earth and the wind and the sun and the rain, that they just do not mind getting wet. As for us, when the rains came, we would huddle on one part of the bamboo bed where the rain did not drip, and when Placido would find us like that he would wag his head incredulously, stare at the cogon and mutter: *"Oolan-oolan masama"* (bad rains)— *bukas mabute* (tomorrow good)—by which we were to infer that tomorrow he would fix the roof. But that tomorrow never came, and our roof leaked until the very day we had to flee for our lives some months later.

The first *sham* started on Friday, July 10, and three days later I wrote: "If only it would stop raining—sometimes I think we'll go mad if it doesn't. We can't do anything but sit and stare hopelessly at the rains and we haven't been able to take our clothes off for three days, it has been so damned cold and wet and muddy here. Everything is wet—the wood, the fireplace, our bed, our clothes. It's been hell trying to get a fire started, and today we didn't get any rice cooked until about noon, and we were weak with hunger by then. Poor Ron has chopped up all his fingers trying to hack the slippery wood with his bolo. The Placido tribe hasn't visited us for thee days now—will we live through this Rainy Season?"

Our new little hut was soon turned into a muddy foxhole and our nerves began to go to pieces—we would jump at each other at the slightest provocation. I knew Ron was suffering because he could not write; he spent most of the time chopping wood or getting fires started, and for relaxation would go over to talk to Spalding. Spalding was having his malaria attacks almost every day now, but was usually better by the evening, and then he would sit upright, wrapped in a blanket like a mummy, with only his pale feet dangling above the fire. I could not bear to go over to the Spalding's shack anymore, it depressed me so to see the children huddled together for warmth like puppies on the bed, skinny and dirty and unkempt. But most of all I could not bear to see Mrs. Spalding trying to stifle the baby's wailing by letting it suck at her dry breasts, while the fat, slatternly Corinne brandished a stick over the Ugly Duckling to keep her from whimpering.

And as the rains continued, I sensed a strange thing happening to me: I found myself growing curiously superstitious, and attaching extraordinary importance to the most casual occurrences. I remember one afternoon during that first *sham* while I was squatting by the fire staring out at the rain, a blood-red heart pigeon suddenly fell into our house, as if it had dropped from the sky. The lashing rains must have bruised its wings, for it lay trembling for a moment in the mud where it had fallen, unable to move. Ron picked it up gently and put it on our blanket on the bed, and let it lie there for about ten minutes or so. Suddenly we saw the exquisite wings fluttering spasmodically and then in a convulsive movement, it had flown quite freely out of our hut into the rain, and up towards the sky. And watching, once again, I felt a sudden sense of freedom, as though I were that bird flying away from the rain and the mud and the mountains and the Japanese, once more free. And it seemed to me also a good omen, as if the gods had sent this bird to us in our despair, telling us that all was not yet lost.

Living so close to the earth, I think unconsciously I was beginning to feel like these native peoples in their strange mystic worship of the elements. For these mountain people were the non-Christian tribes and worshipped not one God but many, like the pagan Greeks of old. In the *Philosophy of Solitude* Powys speaks of Heraclitus, the Greek philosopher, believing that "all things are composed of fire, and into fire they are again resolved." And this I remembered as day after day, hour after hour, I would watch the golden flames miraculously spring-ing into light, bringing us warmth into the wetness, life where there would be death, and unconsciously I began almost to worship this fire as though it were a god. I could understand then how these primitive peoples looked upon the Sun and the Moon, the Fire and the Rain as gods. And I could almost understand, too, their belief in the Magic Spell, for it was about this time the Placido, in the absence of the witch doctor of the tribe, first gave me the Magic Spell.

I think it was the morning of the fifth day of that first *sham* that it happened. Looking out of our foxhole, we suddenly saw a rift in the gray sky and thought it was clearing. We had been living on rice and mungo beans and some dried corn for the past few days, so we decid-ed to try to make it down to Placido's shack to beg, borrow, or steal something fresh to eat and also to get away from our soggy hut. The trail through Placido's cornfields was precipitous and slippery from the heavy rains, and we had to take off our shoes and crawl most of the way to keep from falling. Sharp twigs and cogon grass scratched at our bare legs and ankles, but we felt nothing, so eager were we to reach the bank of the river before the rains started again. Placido's shack was bedlam, crowded with women and children and Negritos stopping there in their journeys up and down the river. There was also the usual pack of wild-looking skinny dogs barking furiously at nothing, dash-ing aimlessly about. I had always been somewhat afraid of these dogs—they had such vicious snarling faces, more like wolves, looking as though they were always ready to spring. I was sure, that like the carabao, they always smelled and hated the white man. I was feeling this subconsciously, as we were crossing the room to where Aling Ate, Placido's wife, squatted by the fire, stirring something in the rice-pot when suddenly I felt something nip at my leg and swiftly glancing down, I saw a tiny trickle of blood over my ankle and at the same instant, saw the pointed, wolf-like head of a dog, his fanged white teeth bared in a snarl as he barked at me.

"Ron, I've been bitten—that dog . . ." I cried out hysterically.

At that moment, Placido came into the hut with a group of Negritos carrying a dead deer on their shoulders. I looked into the beautiful glazed eyes of the young fawn, its head drooping earthwards, and blood still dripping from the wounded carcass. I stared at them fascinated—they looked like figures in an ancient frieze depicting a savage hunting scene. My head was whirling.

Placido caught sight of us and beckoned in a friendly gesture for us to sit down. Ron shook his head and pointed to my leg and said: "*Asawa sakit* (wife sick)—*asu masama* (bad dog)" and began to pantomime a dog biting me. Placido grinned. *"Hindi masama asu"* (dog not bad), he said, and bent down to examine my leg. Suddenly he rose and began to talk very excitedly to the Negritos holding the deer. I saw their faces light up with a strange gleam as they moved towards me, completely surrounding me. Placido started to talk again in excited gibberish. We could not make out a word. One of the Negritos stooped down and began to blow several times on my wound, following this with some weird mutterings sounding like an incantation, and then he spit three times on my leg. It all happened in a fraction of that moment, so quickly I seemed only to have drawn a breath. I felt as though I had been bewitched—the blood of the deer, the wild, strange faces of these little people, and the weird mutterings: It was the Magic Spell. . . . I came out of my trance and saw Placido grinning broadly as he turned to Ron triumphantly and cried: "*Asawa hindi sakit.* (Wife not sick). Placido doctor." Ron grabbed my arm impatiently. "Come on, let's get out of here before he gives you any more magic—better get some iodine or something on it quick—" He dragged me out of the shack to the utter bewilderment of the natives and half-carried me up the trail to our house and deposited me on our bamboo bed.

We still had some iodine left from the medicine Mrs. Jaramillo had sent and Ron poured it into the cut. Then he called Spalding to come over to look at the bite. It was one of those rare times when Spalding was not having one of his malaria attacks, and was able to hobble to our house. He looked carefully at my ankle.

"Doesn't look like a dog bite to me at all—" he said, after a while.

Ron looked at me curiously. "Are you sure you were bitten by that dog?"

For a moment I was speechless. At last I said to Spalding:

"What does it look like then?"

"Looks like a cogon grass scratch to me—that's all."

I stared at the tiny wound. Unmistakably I thought I saw the tiny marks of a dog's teeth. "Can't you see the teeth marks?" I asked Ron.

"Might be anything—" he said impatiently. "Look here—if you think you've been bitten, then we'd better not take any chances. I'll have to cut it out with a razor—think you can stand it?"

"Wouldn't do any good—couldn't cut deep enough if she really was bitten," Spalding said before I could answer.

"Then we'd better get Placido to get her to town right away to a doctor. She'll have to get shots," said Ron starting for the door. "Hell, here's the old witch doctor coming now—damn it all, if he gives her any more spells, I'll—"

Placido came into our hut with two of the Negritos who had been holding the wounded deer. In his barbaric way, he must have been worried about the abrupt manner with which Ron had carried me off. He came to the bed where I was lying, while the Negritos stood in the doorway staring at me. Ron glared at him and turned to Spalding.

"Ask him if he can take my wife near town to some doctor. Tell him she is very sick."

Placido shook his head incredulously and then unleashed another volley of gibberish of which we could only make out the words "*Asawa hindi sakit*" and "*Haponese* doctor."

Spalding shrugged his shoulders.

"He says your wife cannot possibly be sick anymore after that magic spell he gave her. It is a very powerful spell here in these mountains and all the witch doctors use it. It never fails. Besides he says its impossible to go to town for a doctor because all the doctors in town now are Japanese. No Filipino doctors. He's afraid . . ."

Afraid . . . hearing that dread word we knew there was nothing more to be said. If Placido said he was afraid, no other native would make that trip—even for a thousand pesos. And we could never make the trip alone.

Ron looked at me helplessly. "Try to remember whether you were bitten or not. Think back . . . it's important."

I could only see the blood trickling down my leg and the wild dog barking at me and the blood of the wounded deer. Somehow it was all mixed up in my mind. Must have been the rains and the lack of food . . . pull yourself together, I told myself.

"Maybe I wasn't bitten," I said slowly, looking at Ron's face, the tension draining from it as I spoke.

"Well, you'll know in nine days," Spalding said cheerfully. "Personally, I still think you weren't." He glanced at the wound again. "Nope, looks like a cogon scratch to me."

Placido bent over my leg again. Then he beckoned to the two Negritos.

"Christ, they're giving you the Spell again!" Ron turned away in disgust. "Anyway you've got the iodine in it now."

The Negritos were muttering the strange words and blowing, and spitting three times. Placido started to jabber again.

"What the hell's he saying now?" Ron asked Spalding.

"Says the spell is so powerful it can make us all invisible if the Japs attack us. Says he'll give it to us again when the Japs come up here—"

The next day, July 14, I wrote: "I feel better today and ashamed of that hysterical incident, but the terrible part of the whole thing is that deep down I still don't know whether I have been bitten or not. I'll just have to forget this whole thing—it's just silly. But it worries me that my nerves could play me that silly trick. It's these damn rains . . ."

The Rains. . . . After that brief interlude, the rains lashed at us with a redoubled fury, and then the river began to rise. We could see it from Spalding's house—we could see the swollen waters heaving, churning, roaring, and I had the eerie feeling as I watched that it would rise and rise until it covered the earth like the biblical flood and that our little house was like Noah's Ark. I was glad that we were so high up on that hill. We had the bitter satisfaction of knowing too that the Japs could never cross this river now—we were safe from them, for a while at least.

But if it was not the Japs, it was food. We were running low on supplies again, and we could not count on Fabian coming up in the heavy rains. Our supply of mungo beans was running out—I used it only for the big meal of the day; for breakfast and supper we were eating rice and salt again. Aling and Rosa came up occasionally with a few ears of tender corn or a bit of shrimp—real delicacies for which I would trade a dress or a slip or anything else I still had. We knew that it was important above all else to keep the friendship of these people, on whom we now depended more than ever.

The rains began to taper off towards the end of the *sham,* until finally on the ninth day exactly the mists over the mountains parted and the sun shone hot and clear. I could have danced and shouted for joy, I felt as though I had never seen the sun before, never needed it so badly to warm our mildewed, damp bones. I threw everything out into the sun—clothes, blanket, and mosquito net. My nine-day "hydrophobia" period was almost over and I had become convinced that the incident was simply hysteria brought on by overwrought nerves. We decided then to go down to the river to take a bath, and this time I watched carefully to see that I was not cut by the cogon grass. We picked out a secluded spot on the river about a quarter kilometer from Placido's house and we took turns keeping lookout while we stripped and bathed and then soaked in some sun in the tall grasses along the banks. I felt as though I could easily become an idolatrous sun worshipper after all those days of rain.

And for a few days before the next *sham* started, we had an interlude of incredibly radiant weather, almost like the Indian summer of the States. Once again we could see the mountains towering in the distance, a shimmering green against the deep blue of the sky. On one of those days, Fabian came up with his younger brother, Ponciano, the high school student, for whom this trip to the mountains to see the Americans was the greatest adventure of his life. He was a sturdy, well-built boy, tall for his sixteen years, with a clean-cut, Boy Scoutish look, who would probably grow into another Epifanio. You could see he was both startled and awed by Ron's great beard, but they soon became friends, talking and swapping stories. I could not help thinking what an excellent guide or companion Ponciano would make for us in those mountains, for not only did he speak English well, but he cooked marvelously, as he proved that night when he made some chicken *adobo*. Fabian had also brought up two ancient and dog-eared "pulp" magazines, which we devoured for the next few days.

Fabian had told us that Placido was building a new house across the river, saying that his old house was now too small for his tribe. Actually we suspected that he was afraid to be so close to us when the rains stopped and the Japanese should try to come up the river. About a week after Fabian left, having eaten all the food he had brought, we decided to visit Placido in his new house, hoping to get a bit of meat even if it was only a meal. We knew Placido always had some fresh wild pig or deer meat, which he appropriated from the Negritos as they stopped in his house in their nomadic journeyings up and down the river. In deference to Placido's position as chief of the tribe, these simple people gave their hunting trophies willingly, in exchange for some betel nut or a little tobacco, which they would chew while they gossiped over the latest *balita* of the bamboo wireless.

The river was still high in some places, but after walking about a quarter of a kilometer along the bank we found a spot where we could safely cross. Little Doris had come with us to see if she could beg some rice or *camotes* from Placido and her sharp little eyes spotted Placido's new house at once. We were really awed by its size— it was about three times as big as his other hut, and looked almost like an inn with its motley assembly of people there, and we wondered if it was some special occasion. The whole scene was like a mural or a fresco painting—the half-naked Negritos squatting around the fire, the dark coarse-haired children running about, the native women pounding rice with the primitive pestle and mortar, and the wild-looking dogs. Placido was nowhere to be seen, but we caught sight of Delang, wearing a huge coolie hat that made her face look almost Japanese, sitting like a queen on the huge bamboo bed, flanked on either side by two pretty Filipino girls. Aling Ate was also squatting on the bed chewing betel nut and talking to Delang, while beside her lay a young half-naked native girl, the most savage-looking creature we had yet seen in these parts. She was obviously pregnant, and her huge dark swollen breasts lay exposed on her big belly around which was wrapped a cloth skirt. She wore gold loop earrings and her black coarse hair hung straight down her back. Her eyes were wild and fierce as she stared at us and then lethargically turned to spit a red stream of betel-nut juice into the fire. Delang looked laughingly from this savage to us, and then prodded her playfully, saying in Tagalog:

"Filomena, go now and see if the rice is cooked. The Americans will also eat with us." She turned to me. "That is the daughter-in-law of Aling Ate. She has come to stay here until her child is born. *Oi,* but she has a bad temper, that one, and she will do anything." She smiled at me cunningly. "You must watch your husband, Missus. Mena is a very bad woman and will take any man she can get."

I smiled at Delang. I was thinking about the meal to come.

"Even if he has a big beard?" I said jokingly. I knew how afraid these mountain people were of Ron's beard—some of them had never seen a man with a beard before and these people have very little hair on their faces.

Delang was in a playful mood and her mask-like hard face looked almost pleasant and human as she joked: "*Oi,* but he has such nice blue eyes. You must watch over him most carefully so he will not be stolen from you. What a pity that would be." She rolled her eyes mockingly at Ron.

"The old bitch—" Ron muttered under his breath. "It'd better be a good meal—"

We knew that Delang always brought up plenty of supplies for her own stay in the mountains—sugar, lard, and prepared dishes like *lechon* and *adobo.* This time she also had some delectable guava concoction. We sat around the fire afterwards, smoking and chatting with Delang. She said she was waiting for Placido to come from town with more supplies of rice and sugar and tobacco, which she would dole out to the mountain people in exchange for the rattan they cut for her. Already she had sold the rattan in town at a huge profit. Now they would also harvest her rice from the mountain kaingin they had planted for her. She turned to Ron.

"Sir, it is a great pity in the town now for the people. The Japanese are taking the rice from out of their mouths, sir. Soon I will not have rice to feed my eight children, sir, were it not for the rice I will get soon from my kaingin here in the mountains." She rolled her eyes

skyward. "*Oi,* yes, this war makes a great hardship for the Filipino people, sir." We bought some lard, sugar, and tobacco from Delang for
about five pesos. We knew we could get it for about half the price she
charged us if Fabian bought it for us in town, but we knew we had to
take what we could get and when we could get it, not knowing when
the next *sham* would start and keep the San Juans from coming. We
also bought a few things for the Spaldings, which Doris stuffed in her
sack together with some corn and *camotes* Aling gave her very grudg-
ingly. It was becoming increasingly difficult for the Spaldings to get
anything from Placido's gang in the rainy season, when food was
scarcer than ever.

It was already late in the afternoon, and we were getting ready to
go back, when Placido arrived. He was carrying a big load yoked to
his head and was followed by three more natives with packs. I immediately knew something was wrong when he put down his sack of rice
and without stopping to catch his breath started jabbering excitedly to
Delang. We saw Delang turn very pale and then all the natives gathered
around and started to talk all at once. We caught the words "*Haponese*"
and "*natatakut*" (afraid). At last Delang turned to us and said:

"Sir, the news in town is very bad, sir. The Rodriguez family has
been put in jail by the Japanese for helping the Americans and guerrillas." Spalding had told us about the Rodriguez clan in Montalban—
Rodriguez had formerly been governor of the province under the
Americas and refused to work for the Japanese. He had been suspected for a long time now due to his pro-American sympathies.

Delang looked at us with hostility. "Placido is very frightened. He
is worried that the Japanese will soon come up the river and shoot him
too if they find you here."

I glanced at the frightened faces of the natives. They looked like
badly scared children. I was glad we had already bought the supplies
from Delang, and that we still had about half a sack of rice left. It
seemed as if they would not pay us another visit for a long time. Ron

swung the sack with our supplies over his shoulder, as he said gruffly to Delang:

"Tell Placido not to be afraid. The Japs cannot come up the river now in these rains. And even if they should come, Spalding and I will shoot them with our guns."

I knew Ron was saying this for effect—he knew just as I did that if the Japanese ever did come, we would not have a chance, except to run and hide as we had done at Labug. But it was important to show these people that the Americans were not scared of the Japs, or they would start running away like rabbits.

Nobody came to visit us the next day, and when the rains started again, I was almost glad, for I knew it would calm Placido and his fear of the Japs coming up the river. It was the second *sham* and we could tell by the way the wind lashed at our little house, driving the rain in furious gusts around us, that this one was going to be worse than the last. The river began to rise again and even had they wished, the mountain people could not come up to see us. We knew too that it would be some time before Fabian could come and we prepared to dig in for the next nine days at least—we had enough rice and sugar and tobacco to last us that long. The Spaldings were not so fortunate—they still had seven to feed, but only had rice enough for about two people. And isolated as we were during those terrible days on that hill as though we had been shipwrecked, it was torture to hear the ceaseless wailing of the baby, its crying borne by the wind when the sound of the rain ceased for a moment. . . . Spalding was getting desperate—he knew that they could never live through another *sham*, there on that hill, and he began to think of some way to get out. He knew that his only hope lay in the chance that his friend, Kiko, the Negrito, who had been his guide on a long trip he once made in these mountains, might come to visit him again, as he had come once before, on the other hill. It was the barest chance, and he prayed for it. His plan was to have Kiko contact a Filipino friend of his wife, a rich man called Marcello, who lived not far from Montalban. Then Kiko could help them move on the first dry day to this man's house where they would be well taken care of. Meanwhile they must wait for Kiko, and while they waited, they had to eat and there was now only one thing left for them to eat—the young corn from Placido's cornfields.

Spalding knew of course that he was taking a terrible chance, but what could he do? And so under cover of the heavy rains, he sent the children stealthily into the fields, to pluck the corn, and from my house I could see little Doris and Robert, their figures bent under their loads and staggering like an old couple, drenched to the skin from the rains. Doris would often come in to visit me after one of these expeditions and squat by the fire and talk. She would reminisce nostalgically about her life in Manila before the war, when she was going to school, and when she could buy candy and sweets.

On one such day she came into our hut and offered to help me cook rice. She sat by the fire, blowing at it occasionally, looking a pathetic little waif in her thin dress and bare feet. I was always amazed at her sturdy resilience—I had seen her carry a load on her head that a white man could not bear without tiring. She started to talk, puckering up her pretty little face like an old woman.

"I would like to stay here with you, Missus," she said in her curious mestiza English with its singsong intonation. I was surprised that she spoke such bad English despite the fact that she had an American father. When I asked her about it she told me she saw her father rarely in Manila.

"Why don't you stay, Doris dear? I would love to have you," I said. And it was the truth—she would be a real help to me with her knowledge of Tagalog and Filipino customs.

"But my father would not allow me," she murmured and suddenly she burst into tears. "I don't want to go home—I don't want to go home!" she sobbed. "Please let me stay here with you!"

I carried her over to our bamboo bed and tried to comfort her.

"I'll ask your father if you can stay," I said.

"I know he will not let me," she cried again. "He will beat me with a big stick. He beats me when I do not obey," she said, seeing the surprised look on my face. "In Manila when I do not obey he says he will sell me." Suddenly she stopped crying. We heard her mother calling from the hut. "I will go now. I must help my mother. I will come back," she added and ran out into the rain . . .

One day the thing that Spalding had feared happened—one of Placido's gang caught the children stealing the corn, and in savage retaliation began throwing stones at them. Then Spalding knew he was lost. He knew now that on this flimsy pretext, these mountain people would let him starve to death rather than lift a finger to help him. And he knew then that he must leave this place, and he prayed and waited for Kiko to come.

And as the rains continued, surrounding us with their wall of wetness and wind, shutting us off from the rest of the world, we all waited: Spalding was waiting for Kiko, and we were waiting for the rains to stop so that Fabian could come up. We knew now that we were lost without Fabian. We could not trust the mountain people.

I think it was only once during that second *sham* that Placido came to visit us, deliberately ignoring the Spaldings. I think he was still afraid at that time to turn on us, because he still felt that we had some money and power through our link with Fabian and the San Juans of Montalban. I called little Doris in to tell Placido to get word to Kiko the Negrito that Mr. Spalding wanted to see him. Placido looked relieved at this news and promised to do this, and two days later we saw the handsome, curly-haired Kiko carrying the leg of a deer up the hill.

These people have a strong sense of loyalty and friendship and he would not accept any money for the deer, which he had brought as a gift. He promised Spalding to contact his friend Marcello and come up to move them on the first rainless day. Spalding celebrated that night with a wonderful feast of venison, to which we were invited, and for the first time since the rains started, he looked almost human again, like the night we first came up to the mountains.

True to his word, Kiko came to move the Spaldings on the first rainless day, the tenth day after the second *sham* had started. I had begun to measure the days by the *sham* periods and I found that these primitive peoples were uncannily—almost eerily—accurate in their measurement of the cycles of rain. It was a melancholy sight, and I felt the tears rising as I watched the Spaldings painfully crawling down the slippery trail to the river. Kiko bore their few miserable possessions and Spalding's gun, leaving them free to carry themselves, which they barely seemed able to do. I wondered how they could ever make it— Spalding said they would take it in slow easy stages and that they planned to spend the night on the next hill in Dugas' empty house, then in Barrio Puray. Somehow that seemed to me a bad thing—an omen of ill luck—for them to sleep in the house of a man who had been caught by the Japs, but Ron told me I was getting too superstitious. Still, it turned out later that I was right.

Our hilltop seemed strangely desolate and empty and quiet without the Spaldings. It had been torture to watch them slowly dying, but now I missed them—I missed the baby's crying and the Filipino women jabbering, but most of all I missed the sight of the children. As long as one could see children about, there was still a feeling that the world was all right. Now I felt lost, cut off, isolated from human beings. The Spaldings were not much, but they were human and they were Americans like ourselves hiding from the Japanese. Of course there were the mountain people, but we could not speak their language and we did not even know whether they had fled or still remained on the river.

The loneliness on the hill was unbearable, so we decided to trek down to Placido's house that afternoon. It was a dull, cloudy day, and everything seemed quiet, now that there was no rain, and suddenly I found myself listening for the sound of the rain and the howling wind. Placido's shack was completely deserted. . . . Where could they all be? Could they have gone for good? Again I felt that chill of fear creeping over me. Despondently we crossed the river again and climbed the kaingin to our house, and I was just starting a fire to cook the rice for supper, when we heard it: *"Hallooo . . . oo! Hallooo . . . oo!"* reverberating over the hill.

I could not mistake that call—I remembered it from the little woods where we had lived before we moved up here. It was Fabian, dear trustworthy Fabian, once again coming to us when we needed him most. His younger brother, Ponciano, accompanied him and both of them carried supplies on their backs for us. Fabian said he had met Placido and his tribe down the river on his way up—they had gone fishing for eels and would be back at nightfall. The situation in town was about the same: The Rodriguez family had not been released from jail yet and this had upset some of the townspeople.

"But we are not afraid, sir. The Japanese cannot come up this far, sir," Fabian concluded, adding to me: "Missus, don't worry, please."

The next two days were among those rare days that stand out in my mind like jewels against the gray background of the rainy season. Radiantly sunny, gold, and blue-white days: We loafed, we ate; we talked with our Filipino friends. After Fabian left, Ponciano went down to the river and caught a fish, which we fried for supper. The next day he washed all my things and bleached them in the sun, while we took baths and felt reborn after those terrible days of the *sham-sham.*

But with the suddenness of a tropical storm, everything changed the following afternoon. It must have been about three o'clock when Fabian appeared over the hill, panting, disheveled, distraught.

"Fabian," I cried, "what has happened?"

"Sir, the Japs are in Puray," he gasped. "The mountain people say they are coming here, sir."

Puray was the barrio about twenty-five kilometers away from the river. It was the barrio to which these mountain people had fled before they had come here. It was also the barrio where the Spaldings were to spend the night on their way down towards the town after their first night in Dugas' house.

"Is it *balita* that the Japs are in Puray, Fabian?" asked Ron.

"No sir, I saw them with my own eyes, sir. They forced me to talk to them, sir."

"What, the Japs got you, Fabian?" I asked. "How did you get away?"

"Better let him tell the story from the beginning," Ron said. "Let's get it straight. Fabian, begin at the beginning. Here, sit down."

Fabian sat down reluctantly and took a deep breath.

"Sir, the Chief of Police in Montalban who is my best friend, sir, ran to me early this morning and told me that fifty Japs are getting ready to cross the dam with one Sakdal as guide, sir. I followed them, sir, up to the trail until they reached Puray at noon, sir. Then I was unlucky, sir. A Jap saw me and pointed his gun at me, sir.

"I raised my hands and shouted to the Sakdal that I was a good man. The Sakdal told this to the Jap who came over to me to see if I was hiding a pistol. I was carrying only my bolo, sir. Then he asked me what I was doing in the mountains. I said I was going to help chop fire-wood to sell in the town. I said I was a poor man. Then he let me go and I ran all the way here, sir."

"You ran all the way from Puray?" asked Ron, incredulous.

"Yes, sir."

"What about the Spaldings? Did you see them?"

"Yes, sir, I saw them as they were leaving Dugas' house to go to Puray. I warned them that they must not go, sir. So Kiko is finding them a place in the woods to sleep this night, sir."

"What makes you think the Japs are coming here, Fabian?"

"It is only *balita,* sir. But it would be safer to leave this place, sir. All the mountain people have run away already, sir."

"Fabian——" I cried. "You mean Placido and his family have gone—— without telling us?"

"Yes, Missus. All the houses on the river are empty, Missus."

I was still trembling as I stuffed all our things into the sack, preparing to leave. So the mountain people had fled without warning us, just as we had feared. What if Fabian had not come up or had been caught by the Japanese?

"Do you think the Japs will come here, Fabian?" asked Ron.

"Sir, I don't know, sir," Fabian looked worried. "Perhaps they will not, sir, but it is not safe here, sir."

"Don't you think they would be here now, Fabian, if they were coming? And where would they sleep? Hell——I think they're just out exploring these mountains and they're not taking too many chances, going too far in one day. Bet they're almost back in Montalban by now——"

"Perhaps, sir, but it is not safe in this place, sir. Too many people in town know there are Americans here, sir."

Fabian was right; we could not take any chances. Too many people knew where we lived—the exact spot, the very house. Fabian's plan now was to find some deserted hut where we could sleep that night and keep a lookout for any Sakdals or Japs.

Placido's house looked desolate in the eerie silence that enveloped the countryside of that late afternoon as we followed Fabian and Ponciano down the trail along the river. We passed other empty little shacks—there was not a sign of a living soul anywhere. We turned up a path to the right and climbed steadily for a while, as we followed a worn trail made by the mountain people, until we came to a cluster of little huts. It was twilight and everything was bathed in a strangely mysterious light. We were passing the first house, when suddenly I stopped, startled. I thought I saw a motionless figure sitting on the bamboo bed, looking like an idol carved of wood . . . was it an apparition? I nudged Fabian and he stopped for a moment, and glanced back.

Then he said softly: "That is the blind man—the mountain people have left him here."

And suddenly I remembered China again: The people were running away from the Japs, but the old and the sick and the blind and the little children were left behind. It was the same old, old story. . . . We continued on our way until we came at last to a small clearing on a hill from which we could get a good view of the country and the river without being seen. Fabian and Ponciano threw the sack and other supplies on the bamboo bed of the empty hut and we all sank down exhausted. We knew that sleep would be impossible that night, so we decided to make some coffee to keep us going. Fabian made a smudge fire—lots of smoke to keep away the mosquitoes and also to smoke-screen the glow—and we squatted around and smoked while waiting for the coffee to boil.

"Do you think the mountain people will come back, Fabian?" I asked.

"Yes, Missus. I am sure of that. They have run away now only because they are afraid of the Japs. But they will come back."

It was a strange night. There we were, somewhere in the remote Philippines, an American couple and some Filipinos waiting for the Japanese to come at dawn. We were tense and excited and I remembered that we talked of many things, especially of what we could do after the war. That always made everybody happy.

When the Americans came back to Manila, we would have a grand celebration in the little town of Montalban and invite all the people of the town, and we would have roast pig and ice cream and candy for the children and lots of wine. Fabian also wanted us to have a week-end house in Montalban to which we could drive from Manila. After the war, Fabian wanted to have a business of his own—operating a fleet of trucks or something like that. But I could never imagine Fabian as a businessman—I can never see him, to this day, without seeing him always as the *tao,* against the background of the earth or the mountains. As for Ponciano, he wanted to go on to study at the University of the Philippines, and we would send him, of course—in fact, he might even be in my English class. . . . We all grew happy and excited dreaming about what we would do after the war.

I think that the strange bond between Fabian and us really was sealed that night, when we sat around the fire and looked up at the sky and wondered at the destiny that had brought us together. It seemed to me symbolic of the bond between the Americans and the people of the Philippines, who even at that moment all over the island were risking their lives, standing by us against the Japs. Fabian was deeply religious. "God has sent me to you," he said. "I am sure of that. And I will stay with you until the end."

And that is how it was. Fabian was with us until the very end—the bitter end when we were captured by the Japs. . . . But that night I could only marvel at the faith of this simple Filipino, and in these lonely mountains, waiting for the Japs to come, I felt a sense of hope once more that all was not utterly lost.

But the Japs never did come that morning. At dawn, Fabian hid us in a little bamboo grove behind the house and brought us rice and tappa he had cooked for breakfast, while Ponciano kept a lookout. The sun was already high when he told us that Aling Ate and a group of natives were coming up the path toward us. I still do not know how they ever knew we were there. When we saw Aling Ate smiling broadly, we knew that everything was all right. Bamboo wireless had reported that the Japanese had left Puray for Montalban and there were now no Japs around there. The danger was over—for the time being at least. Fabian said Aling Ate wanted to take us to their "secret place" about twenty kilometers or so down the river, where Placido and the rest of the mountain people were hiding. There we would surely be safe.

Suddenly I felt that I wanted nothing better than to crawl off somewhere in the jungle and just sleep forever. I was utterly utterly tired. I did not want to go on any more journeys. I was tired of being hunted, of hiding, of running away from the Japs. I wanted more than anything in the world to go home. I wanted America.

But the mountain people were waiting. We had no choice, and so we began another safari. It was a steaming hot day and I could feel the blazing sun beating down upon me, driving me on. I plodded breathlessly after Ron and the Filipinos through jungle woods and deep forest pools and down steep paths until at last we came again to the river. It was like a journey in a nightmare: Every bone in my body ached and I was like a wound-up robot, mechanically walking, walking. . . . On the banks of the river we stopped to rest and eat, and I felt better. For the rest of the afternoon, our trail was literally the river, which was there quite shallow, and we just walked through it, after rolling up our trousers. Fabian held my hand to steady me over the parts where the current ran swift.

The sun was already sinking, a fiery ball against the pale horizon, when we turned a bend in the river and waded up to a narrow strip of beach against a background of bamboo woods. Aling Ate stopped suddenly and uttered a piercing cry. We heard an answering *halloo*. Aling Ate smiled and beckoned to us to follow her up a path through bamboo woods a short distance to a flimsy lean-to hidden among the trees. We could hear riotous laughing and singing and the sound of a guitar, and then we saw them: Placido and Rosa and Filomena and the others. They laughed delightedly when they saw us appear, as if it were all a huge joke we were playing on the Japanese, as if they were children playing a wonderful game of hide and seek, and we had discovered their secret hideout.

On August 21, I wrote: "I like this place—this strip of beach gives me the illusion that we are at the seashore, and it is all very gay and festive after the grimness of those last days in the mountains. The natives have improvised tiny little bamboo shacks at various spots along the river. It seems that this is the place where they live while floating the logs down the river for Delang—she owns the lumbering business also. . . . Fabian made a tent for us right on the beach out of the canvas Spalding had given us when he left and we all slept there. It was wonderfully warm and there was a full moon, and after supper, the natives began to play the guitar and dance the *pandango*. It was an enchanted night . . ."

The next morning we watched sadly as Fabian and Ponciano disappeared around the bend of the river on their journey back to town. Before he left, Fabian had arranged with Placido to build us a temporary house behind his until they could return, and he had also pretended to scold him like a child for deserting us that day when the Japs were coming. Though king of his own tribe Placido was secretly afraid of the townspeople and he looked very shamefaced and chastened after Fabian's lecture. Besides, the cunning Delang was not there to counteract Fabian's good influence.

Our new house was in a bamboo grove about fifty yards behind Placido's lean-to. We could not see the river, but we did get a glimpse of the open fields around us so that we were not completely walled-in. I remember the first night in that house because it was the beginning of a terrible toothache that lasted for months and in a way was responsible for our attempting later on to get closer to town and so led to our capture by the Japanese. . . . All night long I tossed and tossed in the agony of the pain until I thought I would go mad, and decided that I had better have one of the natives pull the tooth out. But in the morning, when the pain stopped for a while, I thought better of it: I was sure they would pull the wrong one—anyway we had been told that these people never pulled any teeth but just let them rot away.

The next day we received a letter from Fabian, saying they would not be able to come up for a while because "Ponciano was muchly suspected." In that small town, people had begun to notice his long absences from home, and he was suspected of having joined the guerrillas who were just then being organized and were growing stronger every day. The Japanese were trying to nip these guerrilla bands in the bud and were exploring the hills as they did that day in Barrio Puray to look for both Americans and guerrillas. . . . Fabian sent us five gantas of rice and some tobacco to last us until he would return.

The following week was gloomy and miserable—the weather had become threatening as though another *sham-sham* were in the making, and we could tell by the way the natives acted that the rumors via the bamboo wireless continued to be alarming. The few times we came down to visit them, we encountered a stony silence, or mutterings about the Japanese being *hindi malayu* (not far). Then the rain started again, and as usual in our "temporary" house, the roof leaked, so that we were continually wet, and to make matters worse, my tooth again began to pain unbearably.

Maybe Fabian was right when he said that God had sent him to us, but whether Fabian or God, it seems to me now nothing short of miraculous the way he would suddenly come to our rescue, invariably when we were at our lowest point, when we thought we could no longer endure our misery. Once more, he burst upon us one morning as we were desperately trying to get a fire started to cook some rice and hard corn. He had two companions this time—an older man, José, and his son, Andoy—and they all immediately took over. One started a fire, the other chopped wood to keep it going, and the third prepared the rice and fresh meat they had brought. Then they started to build another house opposite ours, one that would be really rainproof.

Fabian told us that he had arranged to stay with us for a few weeks, since Ponciano could not come. To allay suspicions in the town, he had told his neighbors that he and José were going up to the mountains to chop logs and float them down the river like the mountain people. We had enough supplies now to last a while, and we could also negotiate with the Negritos for wild pig or deer.

And that is how we came to live through the final *sham-sham*—it lasted eighteen days—of the rainy season in the mountains. On

August 29, I wrote: "The *sham-sham* continues, but with Fabian and his friends here, we could say to that howling rain, like Lear to the wind, 'Blow, blow and crack your cheeks.' For now that they are with us, we just don't care. . . . Of all the houses we have seen or had since we have been in the mountains, this new little one that they made for us is by far the most perfect and beautiful. It is a little gem and it looks like a house in a picture postcard. It is exquisitely made, down to the very last detail, with a fenced-in fireplace and shelves and a little bamboo bench. It also has two bamboo beds, instead of the customary one— and miracle of miracles, it has a roof that does not leak!"

After the house was built, Fabian began to cut down huge trees and carry them on his powerful shoulders to our place, where he would chop them up with his bolo and stack the wood neatly near our fire- place. In those rains, he felt that we should always have an ample sup- ply of firewood—and in this as well as many other respects, Fabian showed himself to be one of those rare Filipinos who think beyond the present. José, the friend of Fabian, was a jocular, friendly little man with a wonderful sense of humor and he and Fabian were always laugh- ing uproariously at some joke or other. He also seemed to know a lot about herb medicines, and immediately mixed me some kind of queer concoction for my aching tooth, which temporarily stopped the pain.

Following the curious pattern of our life during those months, the next few days belonged to one of those strange peaceful interludes we had occasionally in our hunted, hectic existence. I felt safe and secure and snug there with the friendly Filipinos who cooked and chopped wood for us and brought us food. In the afternoon, Fabian and I swapped lessons in English and Tagalog, and I found him unusually alert. He had a certain native intelligence that amazed me. And at night we would all sit around the fire and tell jokes or sing. Fabian at heart, like all Filipinos, was an incurable sentimentalist—his favorite song was "Springtime in the Rockies" and we had a wonderful time singing it together.

After a few days, Fabian sent Andoy to town to contact Ponciano and tell him to come up with more supplies for us. On September 6, I wrote: "Ponciano and a boy called Bino came up from town today with supplies and terrible news: Spalding's family has been picked up by the Japs but Spalding himself is still in hiding."

Nobody seemed to know much of the details of the story, but the intimations of what was known were frightening. There was no doubt that the Japanese would force the Spaldings into talking, especially that imbecile Corinne—and then what? Ponciano said that he had also seen Delang in town and she was so petrified by the fear that the Spaldings would inform on her, as a friend of the Americans (though we were not quite sure she could be called that) that she had been afraid to come up here even though her lumber business was now at stake . . .

We knew that this news could mean only one thing for us—we would have to move again . . . but where? I was beginning to feel like Io, pursued by the gadfly, doomed to wander eternally. . . . At any rate, we could not move while the heavy rains were on. Fabian thought the best thing would be to wait for the time being until we got more news, and he sent Ponciano and Bino back to town the next day for that purpose. A few days later, Bino came back alone with word that the Spalding family was being kept in the schoolhouse by the soldiers who were grilling them. No doubt they were after Spalding, and it was only a question of time.

Delang appeared a few days later, so we surmised the news could not be too bad—she would never risk her neck if she could help it. Fabian said she was stirring up Placido and the mountain people with all sorts of stories and telling them that if the Japs came there after us, they would also be killed. She had put the very devil of a fear into Placido, who came one day to tell us that he was moving his whole tribe away as soon as the logs had been floated down the river. It was very exciting to watch the people riding the huge logs, looking like Lilliputians as they maneuvered them so dexterously. But Placido meant what he said, for soon after the logrolling was finished, he moved out with all his tribe—and Delang with him. We were glad to see the last of her. Her parting bit of news to us was the rumor that the Japanese were shooting any American they caught on sight—no questions asked.

Once again we would have been utterly alone on that desolate riverbank if it had not been for Fabian and his brothers. One day Ponciano brought up the only brother we had not yet seen—also called José—who was a carpenter by profession, but a barber by avocation. He gave Ron a haircut and trimmed his beard, and tried to persuade him to shave it off. But Ron swore he would keep it until the Americans came back.

The rains continued drearily, but we felt comfortable and snug with our friends. At night we would roast corn and *binosa* and discuss plans for the future. Ron brought up the coast idea again, but now the only guide we could possibly have was Fabian, and he could not leave his family. The only alternative was to get some mountain family who would take care of us—but in a more certain way than Placido. José thought it would only be a matter of months until the war ended—all the people in town expected the Americans back by Christmas. Soon after, Ponciano and his brother José left to go home.

Before the last *sham,* the last and most terrible, we had another spell of fine weather—brilliantly clear sunny days and nights of full moon. Sometimes Fabian and José went off to explore the neighboring country and remained away overnight. Before they left, Fabian would ask jokingly: *"Hindi ka kao natatakut sa aswang?"* (Are you not afraid of ghosts?). He himself, like most Filipinos, was very superstitious, and believed very strongly in spirits and ghosts. Strong and fearless as he was in all other ways, he would never sleep alone in the woods. On September 24 I wrote: "Another radiant day—are the rains stopping at last? These nights the full moon has turned the woods into a *Midsummer Night's Dream* and like Meg in Keats's 'Meg

Merrilles' when he says: 'and for supper many a night she would feast full hard upon the moon'; so I sit and stare at the full moon, thinking, and wishing and dreaming . . ."

But three days later, we awoke to a torrential downpour and for the next two weeks the rain streamed down until I thought we would surely be inundated this time. It was really typhoon weather, and as the river began to rise I became quite afraid, because there we were not on a hill but on the same level with the river. On September 30 I wrote: "The river has risen over Placido's house. We are marooned, and we have only a little rice and hard corn left . . ." October 1: "The wind is dying, but the rain seems to be abating somewhat. We may still be saved. . . . My tooth has started paining me again, and I have discovered that only by putting red-hot chili peppers in the hole can I stop the pain for a little while. It burns up my whole throat and tongue but it's worth it . . ." October 2: "Still raining but not so hard. . . . The river has gone down somewhat but is still swollen. . . . Fabian and José decided to risk it and swam across the river with a tin can to get rice from one of the natives living on a kaingin over there. They swam back with the rice in the tightly shut can floating on the water . . ." October 3: "Rain stopped at last this morning and Fabian and José decided to leave for town to get supplies. We are completely alone . . ."

The next week was hell—literally hell. It was a week of waiting, waiting, waiting . . . living on rice and hard corn . . . listening for footsteps. There was not a soul around for miles and we knew that there would be nobody to warn us if any Sakdals or Japs did come. Sometimes at dusk, we would go down to the river and there on its banks would be the wreckage of Placido's little shack . . . utter silence, only the sound of the flowing river. It was as though there had been a flood and we were the only two human beings left on the earth. And standing on the banks of the river, I could not but recall the first night on that beach, the soft air, and the warmth, the natives playing the guitar and the girls dancing.

I think the last day of that horrible week was the worst: We were gaunt and weak from lack of food, but it was mostly the fear that I was afraid would drive us *"lo-loco,"* as the Filipinos say, fear and anxiety about Fabian. We imagined all kinds of scenes in which he was captured by the Japs and tortured to tell our whereabouts. At any moment we expected them to surround our little house and in the dead of night I would awaken listening for footsteps until I lay trembling in a cold sweat. . . . At last we could stand it no longer: we decided to hide all our things in the bamboo woods behind our house and try to make our way towards town. Perhaps we would meet Fabian en route—it was either that or die of starvation . . .

Then once again the miracle happened—Fabian and José suddenly appeared as we were already hiding in the woods. They had been delayed by the rains and the swollen river. They brought good news: They had found a mountain man who would take care of us for the next few months. His name was Mariano, also a *tao bundok,* but he had broken away from Placido's clan to live with his five brothers and their wives and children on the kaingins beyond the next mountain. . . . And that very night Mariano came with his son Gregorio to move us to our new home.

THE HARVEST

I T WAS THE SEASON OF THE HARVEST IN THE MOUNTAINS when the people gathered in the *palay* and pounded it into that sweet young rice which is called *taclooban,* and at night as we lay in our hut in the valley below the house of Mariano, we could hear the rhythmic strumming of the guitar and the steady beat of the pounding of the rice. And they also gathered the *calabasa* (pumpkin) and the *camote cahoy* (cassava) and the pink or red *camotes* (sweet potatoes) and the *pepino* (cucumber) that they had planted months before on their kaingins. But strangest of all was their digging into the very bowels of the earth for an occult root called *ubug* which they roasted and ate when they did not have rice, and it was said that the wild Negritos, who do not plant rice kaingins, often lived only on this root.

Mariano had taken us to his lonely kaingin, which he and his three brothers had claimed as their own and where they had planted their rice. Long ago, Mariano had quarreled with Placido and his tribe, and had left them to go their own way. And when the time came for him to marry, Mariano chose his bride, not from the tribe of mountain people who followed Placido, but from the natives who roamed the coast near Infanta and had settled at last in a barrio inland, Santa Inez. Mariano had traveled many kilometers to get his bride, Victoria, and bring her back here to his kaingin, but he considered her well worth the trip. He was very proud of his choice, for not only was Victoria handsome, but she could even speak a little English, having gone to the school built by the Americans in Santa Inez, and she was also familiar with the art of the witch doctors of the coast.

We first saw Victoria as we climbed the hill to Mariano's house and, from that distance, her bent figure under its wide coolie hat might have been that of a Chinese peasant woman in the rice fields. A little girl was working beside her, cutting the *palay*. When Victoria came to greet us with her daughter Carmen, we saw that they were both covered from head to foot with a fine gray dust—the powder of the *palay*—that gave them a strangely camouflaged appearance, as though they had just come from some ancient mystic rite of the fields and the earth. Victoria had a wide peasant face with lovely expressive eyes, unusually intelligent for a mountain woman. She seemed different from any of the other women we had met in these parts, more understanding and sympathetic, perhaps, because she belonged to that younger generation of mountain people who had grown up under the Americans. Her English was very literal and naive, with its childish singsong intonation, curiously like that of her own daughter. The bright, sturdy little Carmen (if her mother's hopes were realized after the war) was to become a teacher and live in the town, a most amazing ambition for these primitive people and a further indication of Victoria's difference from her clan.

Victoria was fascinated by Ron's beard—apparently she had never seen a man with a beard before, nor an American either for that matter; the combination must have pleased her, for she stared at him, she smiled broadly, saying to me:

"Very big *bulbous* (beard) you husband. You like?"

I smiled at her and nodded my head, amused at her reaction of pleasure rather than fear, the usual one among these mountain people. Victoria took out a tiny bag from her bosom and extracted a curiously shaped substance. She broke off a piece, put it in her mouth, and offered the other half to Ron.

"You husband like betel nut?" She smiled delightedly when Ron accepted.

For the next three months we lived with Mariano and his family on that lonely kaingin, isolated from the other mountain tribes, and nobody but Fabian and Mariano and his brother knew where we were, so well did Mariano keep the secret until the flight of the mountain people half a year later. Our house was built in a bamboo wood near a stream deep in the valley below Mariano's kaingin. Once again we were in the woods but Mariano had told Fabian this was only a "temporary" house and as soon as he had harvested his palay he would build us a *maganda bahay* (beautiful house) with a view of the mountains.

The bamboo woods . . . the little stream . . . the temporary house . . . it reminded us of the house Placido had first made for us when he said he wanted to take care of us, and we remembered the black pearl ring—and wondered if Mariano would turn out to be another Placido. But Fabian assured us that Mariano was much more dependable, and had promised him never to leave us alone and had also agreed to bring us supplies when he could not for some reason come up from town.

The rainy season was over and it was the time for the harvest. We had now lived in these mountains for almost a year—it would be a full year at Christmas—and there was still no sign of the Americans coming back. But we dared not think of that, for we could not go on. We lived merely within the circumference of each day, and always at night that trapped feeling and that blind questioning would seize me: How would all this end? How much longer could we possibly survive here in these mountains, here in these woods? I was afraid. Yet, somehow, as I stared wearily at our new home—perhaps the twelfth house that had been built for us—and thought helplessly of the months to come, I felt prepared for anything after what we had already survived—the burning heat and the lashing rains, being hunted and machine-gunned by the Japs: We had lived through it all and we were still alive.

Alive? We must have looked like ghosts then, if you can imagine a ghost with a beard and a woman with long, wild hair. It was as though we had been shipwrecked; Ron, a tall cadaverous man with a bushy beard, ragged trousers, and a dirty white jacket hanging loosely over his gaunt body, and me, a wild-looking woman with long black hair, my worn, patched slack suit covering my thinness. I was glad when the days grew warmer and I could change into a dress that the natives had given me—a kind of sarong-like affair—and take off my shoes and walk around like a native woman. I felt curiously at home in these woods dressed that way. In fact, without being completely aware of it then, I see now that a strange thing was beginning to happen to me psychically: Living with the native people for so long, I was unconsciously beginning to go native myself, imitating their habits, their gestures, their movements. I found myself squatting the way they did when they talked or cooked the rice over the three stones, watching the flames embracing the rice pot until they died down to the gray ash. I felt as though I were living in some aeon of the earth's primitive history, thousands of years past, a primitive woman in a jungle cooking rice over three stones.

The Ritual of the Rice—for me it has remained the everlasting symbol of the life of the year I spent in the mountains of the Philippines, where all life revolved around Rice as the life in the West revolves around Bread: the planting of the seed, the gestation during the rains, the harvesting of the *palay,* and its pounding into rice. All this I saw as I squatted watching the warm golden fire licking the black earthen pot, the visible symbol of this rice ritual.

I learned the art of cooking rice from the mountain people: Measuring the rice carefully out of the *tuba* (tiny tin holding about a cup of rice) washing it three times at the stream in the rice pot, measuring the exact amount of water necessary for its cooking, preparing the raging fire, and feeding it constantly until the rice foamed and boiled. As in the crescendo of a symphony, so these preparations were important to the climax in the cooking of the rice, and everything had to be perfectly synchronized. As the fire died down slowly, the moist rice stood on the ashes of the fire, until at last it was dry and each kernel stood out distinct from the other. This was the perfect Rice.

Our world was very simple—fire, water, wind, rain, sun, moon, stars, and the jungle vegetation. Living so close to these elements, and depending upon them for our very life, I could understand that primitive awe of them and the pagan worship like the Aztecs in Mexico, and that same mystic feeling I had experienced about the fire during the rains, I now began to feel about the sun and the very earth itself. It sprang from the sheer joy and relief at merely being alive, and at dawn, when I awoke and went down to my little stream to wash, I would wait breathlessly for the early morning sun, and when its first rays burst upon me, I would recite aloud that Egyptian poem of Amenophis addressed to the sun: "Homage to thee, O Ra, thou risest, thou shinest . . ."

I became strangely aware of the mystic significance of every living thing, as if life had been reduced to old allegories and fables; if one saved a life, whether it was a bird, a beast, or an insect, perhaps ours also would be spared. And I remembered this when once again a wild blood-red heart pigeon was brought us, this time by a little mountain boy. He had caught it in a trap in the woods and cruelly broken its tiny leg. Once again we nursed the bird gently and let it fly away.

The mountain boy Mariano had sent us to chop our wood and cook for us was Roberto, a skinny runt of a kid with spindly legs and funny-shaped head and buckteeth. Roberto was the nearest link to the Placido tribe we had seen among these people, with his extraordinary laziness, his *mañana,* his listlessness, his prevarications. But Roberto outdid even them in laziness—it seemed an effort for him even to lift one foot after the other, and I always wondered how he ever managed to get about. Roberto seemed to be an orphan—at least we never saw any visible father or mother of his unless they belonged to Placido's tribe—and he took turns staying with each of Mariano's brothers, most often with Lucindo, the eldest brother who was the bachelor of the clan.

One by one we met Mariano's brothers and their families: Lucindo, well-built, exceptionally tall for the mountain people, and also very shy and timid; the second brother Donsalo, squarely built and squat, who came to visit us with his wife, Beatrice, and their little boy. Beatrice was half-Negrito—the offspring of a *tao bundok* and a full-blooded Negrito—and had a star tattooed on her forehead—the mark of her clan. Like the other Negritos I had seen, Beatrice had the wild, savage beauty of a creature of the jungle woods, with her tiny perfect face and lethargic movements. I never tired of watching her: There was something remote, dreamy and detached about her as though she came from a different world—the world of *Green Mansions.* Finally we met the third brother of Mariano, a small wiry man called Albino, who also brought his wife, Maxima, a sleek, fat, and handsome woman with gold earrings, who looked quite chic and almost sophisticated.

Though I hated being in the woods again, we did not feel too isolated because someone of Mariano's family came to visit us every day, bringing fresh vegetables and occasionally even a bit of meat. Mariano was much more provident than Placido: On his kaingin not far from our house he had planted squash, corn, string beans, and cucumber (*pepino* they called it). This *pepino* I enjoyed voraciously because of its green freshness, and for weeks afterwards I had nothing but rice and cucumber and salt for breakfast. Later on when the *camote cahoy* was in season I even tried making a stew. What we lacked completely all this time was citrus fruit and it was partly because of this that my teeth began to decay. One morning I awoke to find that part of one of my front teeth had chipped off, reminding me only too vividly of what would happen if I did not see a dentist soon. But of course for that we would have to go to town and risk running into the Japanese. Naturally, a dentist was unheard of among the natives—they did not pay any attention to things like toothaches and let their teeth rot merrily away. That was exactly what was happening to the tooth that had pained me so a few months before: It still hurt occasionally and I kept a supply of chili peppers on hand for "treatment"; but it was slowly rotting and crumbling away, and I was sure I would lose all my teeth if we had to stay there another year.

On October 24 I wrote: "I remember that this is my sister Stella's birthday and silently send her felicitations. How far away America and that world seem now! We seem to be living in some prehistoric age, or somewhere on the moon or another planet. . . . Talk about the primitive life—maybe it was all right for the cave-woman but God it is dull here now . . . sometimes a terrible futility and melancholy grips me so hard that I want to run out of these hateful woods and get to town no matter what. . . . If only we could contact some guerrillas or other Americans, but it seems impossible. . . . there are no guerrillas operating in these parts and the mountain people won't take us where they are. . . . We are stuck here and must wait, wait, wait . . ."

Only a few sporadic rains during the next months reminded us of those terrible days of the *sham-sham* and by the end of October, dry clear days of sun and wind had set in. If it had not been for the unchanging green of the jungle vegetation and the tropical heat of the sun, I would have thought I was in the autumn of the States. On these days our little wood had a special beauty of its own: In the afternoons the sun turned it into a green paradise as it lit up the velvety mossy rocks and the overhanging foliage, through which flashed the scarlet and yellow wings of the great big-billed kalow and the white cockatoo and the bojong bird. And as the afternoon wore into dusk, through the porous stillness would come the regular plaintive hoot of the tropical owl, low and sad, like a child crying.

Sometimes I would follow our stream for about a quarter of a kilometer, walking on the stones where the water was shallow, until I came to a huge rock from which I could get a clear view of the mountains beyond Mariano's house, stretching out into the blue immensity of sky . . . and I would sit and stare at them until dusk. At first the glare of the sudden light hurt my eyes, but gradually I became accustomed to it—I had a feeling of hope and joy just to see something beyond these woods. I felt as if I had only to start walking, to go beyond these woods and I would be free and I remembered Yeats: "I will arise now and go to Innisfree." And I also remembered the cities I had seen: I remembered New York and Paris, Shanghai and Moscow, and there in the jungle, they seemed infinitely fascinating, infinitely glorious, and I had only to say their names and they conjured up all the beauty, all the warmth, all the richness of living of the ages.

"How tired I am of this imprisonment," I wrote then, "of this diet of rice and vegetables we have been having this last week—rice and cucumber for breakfast, rice and mungo for lunch, rice and squash for supper. . . . Will this waiting never end?" And it was about this time that Ron came down with a high fever, and Victoria "cured" him with the Magic Spell. She took one look at Ron, his flushed face and feverish eyes and went to the nearby woods, returning with some strange-looking herb that she boiled in the rice pot. She made him drink it and solemnly administered the "Spell": Three times she blew on the back of his neck and muttered those strange words we had heard the Negritos chant over me. That night Mariano and Victoria and the two children slept in our house on their *banig* (mat) before our fireplace—a grandiloquent gesture to show their friendship and sympathy to us in our time of need, a gesture that deeply moved me. In the morning, Ron's fever was gone.

Things got still better that very day, for late in the afternoon Fabian came at last with food—*lechon,* lard, sugar, bananas, and a real surprise: some stuffed sausages his wife had made for us. This was not only a rare delicacy, but most practical, since we could hang them up from our bamboo rafters and keep them for a week at least, that is, unless the rats got them.

The rats. . . . I can never think of those woods without the rats and I often wished some jungle Pied Piper would magically appear and conjure them away. As soon as darkness fell, the rats would attack us, swarming over our heads, scampering across our shelf and climbing up and down our bamboo rafters. I was deathly afraid of them, and their singing—a steady droning song, like the hum of crickets—filled me with dread and loathing. I was especially afraid that they would climb onto our bed, and I always kept our mosquito net tucked in tightly; but one night Ron must have pushed his foot through the net during his sleep, for when he awoke the next morning he had a bite on his big toe—a rat bite.

Since the harvesting would be soon over, Fabian said that Mariano had promised to make us a new, beautiful house—*maganda bahay*—with a wonderful view of the mountains and then we would pick a spot, and we would move when he would finish the gathering of the *palay* in his kaingin at Tuay (about twenty kilometers away, where Mariano formerly had his home). Alas, I knew it would be a month at least before we would leave these woods.

In December the winds began to increase in fury and intensity, and listening to the music of their rushing turbulence I felt as though I were hearing some great symphony, and listening I would sometimes read aloud Shelley's "Ode to the West Wind":

Wild Spirit, which art moving everywhere,
Destroyer and preserver, hear O hear . . .

The windy days continued and the wind carried down to me the song of the natives as they strummed their guitars and pounded the *palay* into rice. Meanwhile, I slept badly and had terrible dreams. I was beginning to forget what I looked like—a clouded pocket mirror showed me angles of my face, pale and gaunt and shadowy. I felt like a wood nymph—somebody not quite real, without substance. Only the presence of Ron seemed to give me any semblance of reality.

On December 8 I wrote: "This is the day when our world collapsed around us last year. . . . Since then I have known all war has to offer to civilians but the finality—death: Will that come too—here? Bombings, the invasion, flight, being hunted, raided by the enemy, and now their weird primitive existence from day to day.

"If we ever come through alive, I know I shall never be the same again . . ."

Not long afterwards Mariano and his brothers left for their kaingin at Tuay to finish their harvesting, and we were alone. We decided to keep a lookout on the trail just in case our whereabouts had leaked out via the bamboo wireless, so we picked a spot in the tall cogon grass on Mariano's kaingin where we could see without being seen. We usually went up after lunch and lay there in the sun until dusk, when we would go down to Mariano's deserted house and sit there watching the sun sink beyond the mountains. At last we would go down into the woods again, this time following a little brook back, so that we could stop at Mariano's *calabasa* patch and pick some squash. I remember the nights that followed not only because we were alone again, but also because they were the "white nights," I called them, remembering Peter in *Marius the Epicurean*. Again we had moved into the white light of the full moon, those enchanted nights when the jungle woods around us became eerily alive with the barking of the wild deer and the cry of the night birds and the rushing sound of the flying insects and once we heard the unmistakable crashing of the wild pig thundering past our little hut.

I should not say we were completely alone at this time—or I would be forgetting the two creatures with us: an incredibly beautiful wild bird that little Gregorio had left with us and a pullet hen that Mariano had given us. Gregorio had trapped this wild bird in the woods and was trying to tame it so that he could eventually take it to town and get a good price for it, and now whenever he went on a journey with his father he left the bird with us. Sometimes I would be tempted to untie it and let it fly away as I watched it in its agony of struggle, its iridescent wings flapping helplessly in wild desperate plunges to get free. Our own brown hen was docile enough, and I fed her well knowing she would eventually lay and an egg in these parts was worth a thousand pesos.

Later on I wrote: "My own dear hen continued to lay an egg a day for me and I must confess that I spoil her, giving her every delicacy that I can. . . . I do not know what I would do without her, especially on the days when we have only rice—if it were not for her, I think I would not have the strength to walk. . . . I know she wants to hatch and she keeps peering around for that egg that I steal away from her nest every morning . . . poor thing, I fear she is doomed to frustration. . . ."

When we moved from place to place I always carried the hen with me and it was well worth it. And of all miracles, once when we stopped on the trail, I put her down in a bit of cogon grass and she laid an egg for me right then and there. I ate it with the rice we cooked in the open. . . . By the time we had to leave the mountains, the little hen that had been so faithful had laid fifty-five eggs in all. I let her fly into the woods to become wild and free at last. . . .

I wrote on December 10: "Still waiting for Mariano's return. . . . No rice or wood—life centers on rice and wood and my daily existence revolves around the fire and the rice pot. . . . No wood, no fire, no fire, no rice, no rice, no fire, and so on. All the simple things of living like food and cooking that I never gave a second thought have now taken on more than ever a symbolic significance . . ."

On the fifth morning of our solitary vigil we were startled by the sound of five shots fired in staccato from the direction of Mariano's house. Suddenly I remembered the Japanese raiding our house in Labug—the same rifle shots sharply cutting the stillness—and the same icy fear crept through me, and subconsciously I waited for the rat-a-tat of the machine guns that peppered our woods that morning. . . . But Ron was already pulling me away from our house towards the jungle woods across the stream, and we scrambled panting through the choked underbrush for about a quarter of a kilometer until we came to a small clearing where we could get a view of the trail to our house without being seen. The hot tense hours wore on as we watched, until we knew it was noon by the blazing sun beating direct-ly upon us. It was then that we saw him—a small skinny figure carry-ing a shotgun sauntering lazily towards our house. We could never mistake that walk. It was Roberto, and I could have wept out of sheer relief when I saw him. He was nonchalantly poking up a fire in our hut when we came down.

"What was all that damn shooting about, Roberto?" asked Ron, as he rolled a cigarette.

"Sir, that was the brothers of Mariano many *pung-pungs* now." The impish Roberto grinned.

"What do you mean—'many *pung-pungs* now'?" I asked.

"Sir, you come to Mariano's house. We see many *pung-pung*," was the laconic reply.

We followed Roberto up the steep precipitous trail behind our house and had to practically climb on our hands and knees clutching the earth as we went and when we emerged suddenly into the open field under the hot sun and crystal-blue sky, we were dazzled momen-tarily by the blinding glare and had to shield our eyes. I felt as if I were a mole living under the earth and had suddenly come up into the sun-light. Mariano's house was crowded with all the brothers and their families, and in the center of the floor, Victoria and Maxima were pounding the rice to the rhythmic beat of Donsalo's guitar. Mariano pointed to Lucindo and Albino outside the hut putting up a bull's-eye target on a tree at a distance of about 100 yards, and grinned happily as he took up his home-made shotgun which the family used for hunting. "Pung-pung-pung!" he cried as he took aim for the bull's-eye and missed. Then each brother took turns trying out his luck and each missed. Lucindo then handed the shotgun to Ron. I held my breath— I knew that he would lose face if he, as an American, missed, and I did not see how he could help missing, he was so out of practice. Ron fired and hit the bull's-eye. The brothers surrounded him, laughing and jabbering excitedly. Mariano had a proud glint in his eye, as if he had suddenly discovered that his prize hen was laying golden eggs. He began to talk to Victoria.

"Mariano says you husband shoot deer tomorrow," Victoria explained to Ron. "We will have very good to eat then."

Ron looked at me in comic consternation—what could he do now? He was doomed and he knew it. They would give him no peace until he went hunting with them. "Hell, I don't want to shoot a deer even if I see it," Ron said to me later. "But the odds are we'll never even get the smell of one. I might as well get it over with."

At dawn the next morning Mariano came to get Ron. I made them some coffee and they started out. I was worried about the whole business—either way it would not be good. If Ron missed a deer, all his prestige would be gone, and if he shot one, he would be miserable. I waited anxiously.

At noon they returned and I could tell by Mariano's dejected face that the expedition had not been a success. Ron was in good humor. "Just as I told you," he said happily. "Neither sight nor smell of it. They had their dogs out trying to track one down, but no luck . . . guess they'll just have to leave it to the Negritos to bring in the deer."

But if these mountain people could not track down a deer, they made up for it by their undisputed prowess in shooting monkeys. They were always hitting one of these poor creatures, caught unawares as they huddled together in the trees. Usually when we heard a series of shots one right after the other followed by a silence, we knew they had killed a monkey, and one afternoon not long after the deer episode, Albino brought one to our house. It seemed so terribly human, like a little man, as it hung limply from Albino's arm and I took one look at it and ran in terror into the woods behind our house and thought I could never stop crying. Later they sent down the frizzled monkey meat to us and I was sick right on the spot. Ron fed it to the dog that had been hanging around our place.

To celebrate the completion of the harvest, on Christmas Eve, Mariano was having a great *pandango* to which we were invited, and that night he came to guide us by bamboo torchlight up the steep trail to his house. It was the last night of the full moon and the sweet-smelling cogon fields lay green-white as though touched with frost under the wide sparkling sky and white-blue clouds. I felt as though I had never seen the night before and I wanted to kneel down and worship its beauty. . . . Already we could hear the soft strains of the guitar chant fluting through the grooves of dark stillness.

Mariano's house was very gay and festive: The red-orange flames of the roaring fire lit up the faces of the mountain people as they squatted on the floor or lay on their bamboo bed. The women were clapping their hands rhythmically to the beat of the guitar, while the impish Roberto danced in the light of the fire. Lucindo began to pass around *alak* in bamboo cups.

The *pandango* was a "danse solo" and now each one took his turn, called on by the others who shouted their names. After Roberto, came little Carmen, graceful, measured, almost as if she were about to step into a minuet; then sturdy little Gregorio, waving his arms grotesquely and making fierce faces so that everybody shouted with laughter; now Victoria, heavy and clumsy, shuffling her feet to a slower tempo; then Mariano, whirling dervish-like, brandishing his arms wildly. . . . They were shouting now for Beatrice, and as she rose to dance, it happened that at that very moment I drank the *alak* that Lucindo had given me in the tiny bamboo cup; instantly I felt a burning sensation as though I were on fire and then the room began to spin around me and all I could see then was the star on Beatrice's forehead, whirling round and round, as she danced, lithe and graceful, with subtle provocative movements, her hands weaving through space with Balinese art, and as the music mounted and the clapping increased, the star whirled faster and faster, and suddenly I felt I was watching some wild bacchante of the woods dancing before the fire with abandoned grace and joy in a circle of savage men of a primitive tribe. Then the clapping of the hands ceased, and the star was no longer there and I heard them shouting at me, pantomiming for me to dance. Mesmerized by the steady insistent beat of the music and the hands clapping, I began swaying in the center of the floor, my feet dancing to the beat, my body bending to the rhythm of the music. . . . The music stopped—and the *pandango* was over.

The next day was Christmas and it was a Christmas I never forgot . . . our first Christmas in the mountains—just a year since we had left Manila, just a year that the Japs had been in the Philippines. But to us it was a wonderful Christmas because it was a symbol that the Filipinos were with us, that we were not alone. For on that day, as a wonderful surprise, the four San Juan brothers came to visit us and they brought everything—supplies, newspapers, magazines, medicines, marvelous food, and a package of delicacies for me from Mrs. Jaramillo—canned butter, jellies, fruits, candies. We were all much too excited to sleep, so we just sat around and talked and talked until dawn.

The news was good and even though the Americans had not arrived yet, as the Filipinos had expected, they were more hopeful than ever as word came in of the island-to-island strategy, and they knew that it was only a matter of time. But the really significant news was the fact that the guerrillas were growing stronger every day and the fact that there were very few Sakdals left. From small isolated bands, the guerrillas were becoming well-disciplined units and making life most uncomfortable for the Japs.

The week before New Year's Day was one of those peaceful, almost idyllic interludes, which to me always presaged a sudden storm or catastrophe. After the San Juan brothers had left, Ponciano remained with us to help us move, and as usual relieved me of my monotonous chores of cooking and washing. We gorged ourselves on the food—chocolates, cakes, milk, and oranges, and I wrote: "I am reveling in all the different tastes which seem exotic to me after so long a time. . . . I am also a lady of leisure, with Ponciano here to do the work. Lazy, luxurious days. . . . I spend my time lying in the sun and dreaming of the war's end. We are full of hope for the future and feel that it is only a matter of months now. On New Year's Eve, we stayed up to see the old year out and the New Year in over a roaring fire, and I felt as I stared into the flames, a prophetic intuition of the American victory . . ."

The next morning we moved to the *maganda bahay*. We lived there for exactly one week . . . One week—and then began that fantastic period that I have called our Flight: For the next three months we were in constant flight with the mountain people and from the first of the year to April, when we moved near the town of Montalban, where we were finally captured by the Japanese, we had traversed at least a hundred kilometers over mountains and hills, through forests and streams, in fields and valleys, and we had lived in about a dozen more houses made for us by Mariano and the other mountain people.

It was the beginning of the terror unleashed upon the mountain people by the Japanese to wipe out the guerrillas whom they suspected were hiding in these hills. With the beginning of the New Year, the Japs began to reach out tentacles here by sending out exploratory squads (like the Japs who had come to Puray the day Fabian had warned us) to root out guerrillas or Americans. And the rumors of their coming, whether true or false, spread over the bamboo wireless with the speed of the wind, and scattered the mountain people like birds in flight. And when the mountain people fled from the Japs, they took us with them.

Our new house was perched on the edge of a precipice, looking out on a range of knife-ridged mountains, their green backs arched against the sky. For days, a typhoonish wind lashed the flimsy bamboo trees around us, "howling at all hours." Staring at the gray sky I almost anticipated a real blizzard with ice and snow, and somehow it brought me back to that strange afternoon we waited in the station at Manchuli, to me the edge of the world, when great drops of ice-snow fell from the leaden sky. But then it was August with a blizzard raging and this was January, in the tropics, so a real blizzard was impossible, and soon the scorching sun would blaze out. So at that moment, knowing it would not last, I was almost glad of that windy interlude, for it seemed to blow away the fog of my memory and I remembered once more happy moments of the past and felt alive again and on "the threshold of things." I began to lose that terrible feeling of futility that had overwhelmed me at times in those woods. At dusk, with the gray veils of mist enveloping the mountains, with the wind howling about us, the place looked like a lost world, a Lost Horizon.

I do not think I was ever so sorry to leave a house as I was to leave that beautiful one where we stayed just one week. After that, Mariano took us to his "secret place," where the rest of the clan was hiding, a tiny barrio in a deep valley where we found Mariano's three brothers and their wives and children. Ruling over this little world was the *Matanda* (the old woman), Mariano's ninety-year-old mother, who had walked a distance of about twenty-five kilometers from Tuay to that spot. It seemed unbelievable, she was so old and shriveled, with her wrinkled parchment-like skin and her wasted body. Yet she reigned over her brood like some ancient queen and her least word was law to these childlike people.

Poor Mariano built us still another house on a hill above their barrio and from this height on a clear day we could see almost to Manila
Bay. It gave me a strange feeling, as though soon we would be going
closer to town. We lived there for about two weeks in another one of
those rare placid interludes; then, once again, we started on our flight.
. . . I was always more cheerful and happy living on a hill, away from
the lugubrious woods, and it was there that I started a "school" for the
children. I made books for them, taught them to write, and read stories to them, and in return they would gather wood for me or carry
up water from the stream in huge bamboos. At night we would go
down to the little barrio and dance the *pandango*.

But the reports and rumors via the bamboo wireless continued
alarming: The Japs were on the rampage and there were even stories
of Americans in the hills being captured. We also had news again of
Spalding and his family: Spalding himself was still supposed to be hiding, but his family was working for the Japanese. We knew it was only
a question of time before Spalding himself would be taken. No doubt
the Japs also knew we were in the mountains but did not know the
exact spot. With news like that, Mariano began to talk again of moving us, and if the *Matanda* had not fallen very ill with the *"lagnat"* at
that time we would not have stayed there as long as we did.

We moved soon afterwards to our new house in "Death Valley" as
I called it, where I felt we were living in the very bowels of the earth.
The climb down was so precipitous that I thought we would have to
use ropes to keep from falling, and I never would have been able to
make it if Mariano had not held my hand all the way. It was a sheer
drop of about a kilometer on a trail through bamboo woods and jungle underbrush, and when we finally made it, Mariano said with a
grin: *"Mabute lugar—wala Haponese dito"* (good place—Japanese not
here). We were surprised to see that there were three little huts in that
spot. Mariano said they were the houses of Donsalo and Albino, who
came there to cut *yantok* (rattan), which they later sold on the river to

the townspeople. Gregorio again left his wild bird with us tied to one of the bamboo poles in another hut. Then again we were alone.

The next morning we heard a ghastly wailing reverberating into our valley that made us strangely uneasy. The *Matanda* had died at last. . . . After the funeral there was to be a nine-day wake. They sent to town for alak for the celebration and went hunting for wild pig or deer. . . . I can never think of the death of the *Matanda* without remembering also the death of little Gregorio's wild bird—for it happened that very same night. We were suddenly awakened by an unearthly shriek that sounded so human that we sat up in horror. I remembered the woods in Labug—it was the same terrible cry. Ron grabbed his bolo. Around us the darkness was so black and thick you could have cut it with a knife and then as Ron fumbled in the direction of the sound it stopped. In the morning we saw that only the beautiful iridescent feathers and a few bones remained of the wild bird. It had been attacked and eaten by the wild cat. How I wished then that I had set it free.

After this our Death Valley seemed more lugubrious than ever—we seemed to be in some kind of Dante-esque world, deep beneath the earth. I became very moody and melancholy, and began to get strange premonitions of disaster.

Then it came—the news of the surrender. . . . Fabian brought it one day when he came after what seemed an eternity of waiting. Fabian gave us a typewritten carbon of a letter written by Colonel Thorpe, American leader of the guerrilla forces in the area. The essence of the letter was this: After his surrender to the Japanese, Colonel Thorpe called upon all guerrillas and Americans hiding in the territory to lay down their arms and surrender peacefully to the Japanese, who promised them full clemency in accordance with the recent edicts of the Emperor. It was only later we learned that actually Colonel Thorpe had been captured, and after terrible torture, forced to sign the letter.

We were stunned. . . . I think we were more shocked by the news that we could surrender than if Fabian had brought word that the Japs were coming—we were used to that by now. I was confused, bewildered—I simply could not quite grasp the idea that it was possible to surrender to the Japanese, so long had I been living subconsciously with the fixed determination to stick it out there in the mountains until the end, until the Americans returned. . . . And for one moment this surrender seemed almost a way out of our terrible impasse there in these mountains where we might slowly die of starvation or illness. But Ron pooh-poohed the idea at once.

"Sounds like a phony trick of the Japs to get the Americans in and then shoot them, don't you think, Fabian?" he asked.

"Sir, that is how I think also, sir," Fabian said. "The Filipinos do not trust the Japs only, sir." And then he added casually, dropping a bombshell, "But, sir, Mr. Spalding has surrendered to the Japs, sir."

"What—Spalding has surrendered?" I cried. "What happened to him?"

"Missus, we don't know, only. But, sir," he said to Ron, "the Japs did not shoot him, sir. He is only working for them, sir. The people in the town think it is very bad, sir, to see Mr. Spalding with the Japs."

Spalding surrendered—working for the Japs . . . it all seemed incredible, impossible.

"The dirty rats—Japs and their surrender," Ron said bitterly. "They either shoot you or force you to work for them. No surrender for us, Fabian—we'll stick it out."

"Oh sir, I am very happy, sir. It will be easy, sir, and if you like, sir, I will take care of you on my own kaingin near the town, if only you will come down, sir. It will be easy, sir, and I will bring very much food for the Missus."

"No, Fabian—too dangerous near the town. We'd better stick it out here for awhile yet, then if it gets too bad we'll go down."

"But sir, there are only seven Japs in Montalban, sir. The news is very good, sir; only last night there was a blackout in Manila, sir. They say the Americans bombed Cavite, sir."

Blackout in Manila, Americans bombing Cavite . . . the first good news after more than a year of waiting. Was the tide beginning to turn at last? Maybe we ought to go nearer town—I could get to a dentist, perhaps, even a doctor if I needed one, better food. . . But what was Fabian saying now?

"Sir, also the Japs are promising the Filipinos independence if they will fight the Americans, sir. But the people in the town believe it is a trick only, sir."

Independence to the Philippines—that could mean only one thing—that the Japanese would try to conscript an army to fight the Americans when they returned.

"Do you think the Japs could get the Filipinos to fight the Americans when they come back?" asked Ron.

Fabian looked aghast.

"Oh no, sir—the Japs will force them, sir, but they will run away, sir. The Filipino people will never fight the Americans, sir."

But with this independence business Ron thought more than ever it would be dangerous to go nearer town.

"We'll stick it out for a while and see what happens," he told Fabian, who promised faithfully he would come to get us when we needed him.

All that night we lay awake discussing the implications of the startling news Fabian had brought. Ron was still dead-set against the idea of surrender, but he admitted he was worried about my being able to stick it out much longer.

"It's up to you," he said finally. "If you want to take a chance on surrendering, we'll do it."

Suddenly it came to me in a flash . . . even if I had been tempted to surrender, I could not . . . I could never surrender. The Japanese military police must surely know all about me: how I had been black-listed by them in China, how I had even been broadcasting against them before the war. I would never have a chance. They would torture me—kill me. . . . I could never surrender.

The next month was the same old story—of constant flight, of fear, of hiding, of endless waiting, and of starvation, until we began to feel trapped like animals at bay. Wherever Mariano and his family went, they took us with them, and hid us in the woods until the next scare. But it was not until the *balita* came that five hundred Japs were coming up the river—news that struck such panic into these little people that they left us alone for days and weeks at a stretch—that we decided at last that we could no longer stay with them. Now we had only one hope left and that was to contact Fabian and ask him to bring us to his rice kaingin near the town, where he himself would take care of us. Here, in these barren mountains, we knew that we would slow-ly starve to death, or be caught unawares by some prowling Japs.

On March 13, I wrote: "The tension we are living under is becom-ing utterly unbearable—I can't sleep nights or when I do I have terri-ble nightmares and wake up screaming. . . . We have been slowly starving—sometimes we even run out of rice, and are lucky to get *camotes*. . . . Our only hope now is Fabian . . ."

The Harvest was finished and we were leaving at last. The Seed had been planted, had gestated during the Rains, the *palay* had been cut, and pounded into Rice. . . . We had lived through the cycle of the planting, the rains, and the harvest . . . except for the rains, it had been a perpetual summer and for the past two long strange years I had entirely forgotten what the coming of spring was like. Now the fields lay dry and barren, and everywhere we passed was desolation as Fabi-an one day led us stealthily down the river, past the Mariquina Dam, and to his rice kaingin near the town.

The Guerrillas

Lying in the jail, I felt once more that same strange sense of loss I had that afternoon we followed Fabian down the river away from the mountains forever, and I remembered the story these people tell that if a mountain child is taken to town, he will try for the rest of his life to return. All afternoon we followed the river and then continued through the woods at night with bamboo torches. Occasionally we passed an isolated barrio and heard the mountain people singing and laughing and shouting, the guitar playing and the hands clapping to the beat of the *pandango,* and again that feeling of sadness at leaving this free wild life overwhelmed me and I wanted to go back and be one of them. For no longer did I remember the pain and suffering and starvation of that year in the mountains, but only its free primitive life and savage beauty, and with a prophetic intuition of the terrible months to come, suddenly I could not bear to leave. But we never saw those people again.

On and on we went, stopping only at dusk to cook rice by the river-bank and as quickly as our bamboo torches went out, Fabian replaced them with others, until at last we came to the broad river leading directly to the Mariquina Dam of the town of Montalban—the very same river I had crossed with Gabriel more than a year ago. A pale white moon, brooding over the countryside like a human face, lit our way until we came to the ladder of the Dam, and holding Fabian's hand I climbed with shaking knees, as though momentarily I expected some Japs in ambush to leap out from the blackness. And then only the open highway stretched before us and Fabian's house, where we were to spend the night.

The highway gleamed ominously white between the blurred blackness of the fields on either side; it might have been a battlefield beyond which lay the enemy awaiting us, so dangerous was it then because of the possibility of sudden Jap forays in search of guerrillas. But it was very late already, and if we took the roundabout route through the fields we could not reach our destination before dawn. Fabian decided to take the chance. He walked swiftly ahead, ready to give us the signal momentarily to drop flat into the fields. My body was tense with fear and fatigue, and my legs seemed to be moving entirely of their own volition, as though they had an independent life over which I had no control. Only a sharp cramp near my left thigh was threatening to stop me with the sheer agony of its pain, and I fought and fought it until I saw Fabian veering quickly to the right, and with a terrible relief, I followed Ron's white, gaunt, shadowy figure in the direction.

I do not remember much of the rest of that night—another little house, a candle being lit, and a young woman with long braids and the face of a Madonna bending over me as I sank upon the floor . . . then somebody shaking me and I pushing them away, and Ron bending over me, whispering: "We must go now." Painfully I opened my eyes to see Fabian silhouetted against a blue dawn and then mechanically once again, I began to move. Would we ever rest? Must we be forever wandering? . . . Where were we going now?

"I will hide you in a little woods until night, sir," said Fabian. "It is too dangerous to walk through the fields in the daytime, sir. At night we will go to my rice kaingin, sir."

More woods—I looked at Ron in despair. Would we ever be done with woods? All that day we hid in the dry, hot, little bamboo woods where Fabian and his wife, the lovely young girl with the braids and the Madonna face, brought us deliciously prepared dishes and fruits, and even ice cream, until at last in the coolness of the dusk we felt revived, and ready to continue our journey. When we emerged from our woods, the light was just fading, and I was startled to find that we could see the houses and the church steeple of Montalban, and I was suddenly filled with an uneasy feeling at being so close to town. Like the mountain people, I was now afraid of the town, and especially afraid of this town where there were still Japs.

There was a slight delay in our plans to go to Fabian's rice fields that night—there was no house for us to live in yet. But that was a small matter to a Filipino—had we not had at least twenty-five houses in the mountains?

"Sir, my father is now building a house for you on the hill near our rice kaingin and it will be ready surely very soon, sir," Fabian assured us.

Meanwhile, that night we were going to the house of an old American who had been hiding out with his Filipino wife. Fabian said the Filipinos all held him in great esteem, considering him quite venerable with his snow-white beard and hair. His name was Magna and he had lived in these parts before the war. He was the direct antithesis of Spalding in every way—a large, stout, florid man with a loose jaw and a protruding chin. With his ruddy complexion he looked very fit, as though he had been away on a vacation instead of hiding out for a year and a half, and I could not help recalling the poor, sickly, thin, half-starved malaria-ridden Spalding. Magna's white beard and hair did give him that kind of dignity the Filipinos respect so much, indeed, even associate with the color white, but his venerability ceased as soon as he opened his mouth and spoke with a Texan drawl out of the corner of his mouth. He sounded too smooth. In fact, I did not like him at all—but I could see that he had a way with Filipinos all right—he could twist them around his little finger. He was one of those Americans—bamboo Americans they call them—who had come over in 1898 with the Army and just stayed on, worked as a bartender in a dive, had many native women, and spawned more children than he could keep track of. But his latest wife had certainly stuck by him and managed to hide him all these months—he had never been raided either by Sakdals or Japs.

I liked his wife better than I liked him. She was a fairly tall, thin Filipino woman, handsome rather than pretty, and really smart. She could outwit any Sakdal any time, and she was liked and respected by the townspeople who went out of their way to warn her of danger. With genuine solicitude, she began to mother me at once and insisted, somewhat to Magna's embarrassment, that we stay there until our house was built, offering me the luxury of a "private bedroom." Magna's house was very large and comfortable, divided into three rooms—a lean-to kitchen and two bedrooms, which were reached by climbing a small foot ladder, and screened with bamboo walls. The flooring of the shack was made of bamboo strips, instead of the usual bare earth. That night for the first time in a year, I slept on clean sheets and a clean pillow, under a huge, pavilion-like mosquito net and I felt I was in heaven.

For the next day or two we just ate and loafed and talked with Magna who told us of the guerrilla situation around Montalban.

"There are two rival bands here—Lieutenant Navarro and Ocampo. They useta fight like cats and dogs but now they settled down to fightin' Japs. . . . You'll meet 'em—I think they're just kids, playin' with guns—"

"What about Hukbalahaps? Any around here?" asked Ron.

"Nope not here," drawled Magna. "Pampanga's their hangout. The nearest to 'em here are Marking's gang in the hills with that dame Yay . . ." He turned to me. "Maybe you hearda her before the war in Manila—she was a writer . . . Yay Panilio—wrote for the *Herald*—a Communist, I guess . . ."

"Yay Panilio!" I shouted in my excitement so that Ron shushed me, looking around. "Yay—is she here in these hills?" I had known her when I was broadcasting over Station KZRM and admired her brilliant writing and wit and humor. Being the mother of four children was no obstacle to her career as a newspaperwoman. She was the first woman to penetrate into the dangerous territory of the Moro headhunters. An Irish-mestiza by birth, she was well known in Manila as a tough fighter for the underdog. I had often thought about her in the hills and feared that the Japs might have killed her.

"Sure, she's right up in the hills near Yuhan—where you were—or not far from there," said Magna, looking at me curiously. "Just livin' with Marking they say and fightin' just like a man—"

I turned to Ron. "Maybe I could contact her—maybe we could join them—"

"Maybe we could—we'll see what the situation is down here," Ron said. Then he grinned at me. "Maybe the war'll be over by the time we get back up to those mountains again—"

The few days we were at Magna's, Fabian put us on exhibition. We were his show. He had been waiting a long time for this—almost a year—and he could not resist the opportunity of letting his "best friends" and his own family and his cousins' cousins take a look at us. We were Fabian's "Americanos," and they came to see if we were really alive, or merely a figment of his imagination. And we were a good show—many of these simple Filipinos had seen American soldiers before the war, but scarcely one of them had yet seen an American woman who had lived in those wild mountains for well over a year and was still alive. They came with food and presents and remained to stare at me, laughing and whispering among themselves, examining me carefully from head to foot. "Nakawaawa" (such a pity), they would say, "Ano ang pagkain sa bundok?" (What did you eat in the mountains?). Invariably I replied: "Asin at kanin" (salt and rice) and "Ubug" (the root the Negritos ate instead of rice), a word that filled them with horrified awe, and they would look at me with great pity and shake their heads, for most of these townspeople have never tasted this root, which has for them all the mysterious connotations of the strange customs and habits of the Negritos themselves.

We also met Fabian's father, a tall old man with an unusually intelligent face, who told us of his memories of the Americans in the Spanish-American War; his sister Carmen, very shy and pretty and subdued and who immediately took all my clothes to wash; his mother, an old, old woman, dried and wrinkled . . . and his children—two boys and a girl.

Lieutenant Navarro came to see us the night before we left Magna's place. A .48 swung from his belt and the five guerrillas accompanying him carried rifles. I was surprised at the extraordinary youth and beauty of this guerrilla leader, whose daring exploits and ruthlessness towards Sakdals had made him an almost legendary figure around Montalban. He was one of those extreme guerrillas who gave no quarter and he was greatly feared by the people. From his reputation I had expected to see a big, husky desperado; instead, in the dim candlelight that gleamed on the cross he wore around his neck, he had an almost feminine beauty, with delicate features and wavy black hair. Only his eyes—hard, cruel, impenetrable—revealed the real man he was. He had come to tell us that as Americans, we could count on his help at any time and that he would send us food and medicines.

"Perhaps, sir," he said to Ron earnestly, "you would also like one of my men as guards for your wife, sir?"

Ron said he did not think it was necessary—yet—but thanked him for the offer. "I might take you up on that, Lieutenant Navarro," added Ron, "if the situation should grow more dangerous. There are not many Japs around now, are there?"

Navarro smiled grimly. "Only seven, sir, but you never know when they will bring more, only, sir, maybe after the next few weeks. We must have revenge for what they did to Colonel Thorpe, sir." His eyes flashed vindictively.

"You worked under Thorpe?" asked Ron.

"Yes, sir. We took orders from Colonel Thorpe, sir. Now I make my own orders, sir."

"What about Marking's guerrillas? Ever think of joining up with them?"

"No, sir. Marking is directed by a woman only, sir. She is smart, all right, but my men never take orders from a woman, sir." Navarro smiled softly, as he glanced at me for a moment. Then he said, changing his tone: "Sir, we came also tonight to find out from you about a certain Gabriel, sir, who claims to know you and your wife."

"Gabriel?" I cried. "What about him?"

The guerrilla's face was a hard cruel mask. "He is in most serious trouble now, sir," he said to Ron. "We are trying him for his life in a few days, sir."

"What is the charge, Lieutenant?"

"He is suspected of working with the Japs, sir."

"That damn fool Gabriel—playing both sides again," Ron said to me, then to Navarro: "Gabriel saved our lives in Labug."

Navarro shrugged his shoulders. "Sir, we will consider that in the trial." Then he smiled. "Sometimes my men are hotheads, sir. . . . They kill first and ask questions afterwards. Gabriel is not liked by the people, sir,"

"Gabriel saved our lives—I am sure he isn't really bad, Lieutenant Navarro," I said impulsively.

He glanced at me in surprise. A Filipino is always moved by a woman—and his face softened.

"Perhaps we will give him another chance, Missus," he said with a smile. Then he signaled to his men, saluted smartly, and was gone.

"That damn fool Gabriel—" Ron repeated.

The next morning we moved to our house on a little hill overlooking Fabian's rice fields and Fabian left a young boy, Domingo, who worked in the fields, to take care of us when he could not be with us. When I think of Domingo, I immediately think of carabao milk, for it was he who introduced me to that delicacy; each morning he appeared at daybreak with a jug of carabao milk which we boiled for our coffee, making a kind of café au lait. It was the first fresh milk I had had in a year and a half and I lapped it up. We had other fresh food at that time also—melons and guavas and papaya and mangoes and fresh eggs and meat brought by Fabian's family and friends.

Beyond the next hill, about a quarter of a kilometer from our house, was the camp of Lieutenant Ocampo, the other guerrilla leader, and one morning, without warning, he visited us with ten of his men. Some of the guerrillas wore caps and even Japanese uniforms and as I saw them coming up the trail, my heart stopped for a moment: I thought they were Japs or Sakdals. Luckily Fabian was with us and he hurried down the trail to meet them. Filipinos are very far-sighted and he had recognized Ocampo at once.

"Don't worry, Missus," he said. "They are the guerrillas."

Again I was struck by the youthful appearance of these guerrillas as they filed into our house—they looked like high school boys carrying guns. Ocampo himself seemed a more rugged type than Navarro, but the thing that I remember most about him was his unusually intelligent eyes, in which there was not the slightest trace of the hardness or cruelty I had seen in the other's. And I liked his open, frank manner of speaking and the earnest way he tried to impress upon us that his guerrilla band was not just a gang of hoodlums but also a well-disciplined unit of men. He told us that most of their guns as well as uniforms had been captured from the Japs.

"We drill like a regular army, sir," he said to Ron. "We would like to know about army pay for guerrillas."

Ron said he thought it would be necessary for him to join some guerrilla band that would be recognized by the Americans.

"What about Marking's guerrillas? They're supposed to be a good outfit—why don't you join them?" Ron asked the same question he had put to Navarro and received the same answer.

"My men would never take orders from a woman, sir," said Ocampo with a rare grin. "As long as Yay Panilio gives the orders, sir. Besides she thinks we are just kids—she is always telling us to grow up, sir," he added indignantly, then as an afterthought: "But, sir, she's also a good woman and very smart, sir. She gave me two books when I was at Marking's headquarters, sir. Perhaps you have read them, sir."

"What are they?"

"One book is *Red Star Over China* and the other is *Revolt in the Desert* by Lawrence of Arabia. I have been studying them very hard, sir, to learn more about guerrilla tactics. I can learn from Lawrence like the Arabs learned too, sir," Ocampo said gravely.

"Very good books, Lieutenant," said Ron, then he asked abruptly: "What do you know about the Hukbalahaps?"

"They are the guerrillas in Pampanga, sir, They fight very good against the Japs, sir, but they are communists, sir," he added. "But they have very good organization, sir. They have their own money, just as we also will have soon to pay the people for what we take, sir. But now the people are always glad to give us everything, sir. . . . We will soon send food and anything you need, sir," he said proudly. "We will also keep a guard on this hill to watch night and day, sir. You will be warned immediately in case of danger, sir."

Ocampo kept his word. During the month we stayed there on that hill, a guard kept a twenty-four hour vigil, and I certainly slept easier because of it. He also sent fresh meat and eggs and chicken. After a while we were amused at the way Ocampo and Navarro competed with each other as to who could take better care of us. We could not become accustomed to all this rivalry and Ron repeatedly urged them to unify.

"First unify," he told each guerrilla leader, "then you'll get recognition from MacArthur. MacArthur won't recognize small roving bands. After you're recognized and big enough, you'll be able to form a government and print money and organize a real army."

In the May of 1943—a year and a half since the Japs had landed in the Philippines—the guerrilla movement was gathering momentum, preparing for the day of MacArthur's return by keeping the spirit of resistance alive among the people. And here, as in China, the guerrillas had their roots among the people, who gave to them freely—their rice, their cows, and their carabaos, even their women. For it was enough in the beginning for these desperadoes merely to adopt as their slogan "Kill Japs" to become heroes, so deep and instinctive was the Filipino hatred of the enemy, so great the desire for freedom. And even later, when their popularity waned because of the ruthless tactics of some lawless bands who fought among themselves for confiscated spoils and the Japs stepped in to bring "law and order," the Filipino people never ceased their support of the guerrillas.

There in the Mariquina Valley—where the American soldiers were to fight some of their major battles against the retreating Japs in 1945—the guerrillas, as in other parts of the islands, had started out as small bands of former Filipino soldiers or jobless civilians wandering aimlessly around. With their open defiance of the Japanese, particularly among the young students, some of whom had never held a gun before and who reveled in the romantic life of the outlaw, living in the hills on the spoils of a Jap raid or what they had confiscated from the people. One of the first good things the guerrilla bands did in Montalban was to kill off systematically all the Sakdals or fifth columnists, so that at the time we reached the town there was hardly a single one left, or if there was, he must have been in hiding.

The Japanese began a subtle campaign to try to win the Filipino people away from the guerrillas. First they posed as the great harbingers of peace and prosperity, bringing order out of chaos, with their "Greater East Asia Co-Prosperity Sphere." The Filipinos promptly reacted with passive non-cooperation; their guerrillas could loot and fight among themselves, but as long as they continued to kill Japs, the people would support them. Then the Japs started the "Neighborhood

Associations"—to promote friendship between the Filipinos and the Japanese. It was the duty of "good neighbors" to report to the Japs whether his own neighbor was being a good friend of the Japs or whether he was hiding some American or supporting the guerrillas. The guerrillas answered that one for the people: Whereas they had confined themselves heretofore only to killing off known Sakdals, they now began to kill one "good neighbor" for every slain guerrilla or guerrilla sympathizer. They shot first and asked questions later. Nor did they merely kill—they would sometimes brand the bodies of these "good neighbors" and leave the faces so that they could be recognized when they floated the mutilated bodies down the river into the town. The guerrillas always went the Japs one better and the number of "good neighbors" decreased with amazing rapidity.

During the period we lived in the hills near Montalban the two guerrilla bands we knew were in complete control of the Mariquina Valley. Not a Sakdal dared show his face. The guerrillas wandered freely in and out of Montalban, mingling with the people, bringing news via secret radio sets of the American victories, and persistently harassing Japanese communications lines and blowing up trucks. Yet the two guerrilla bands were not completely on their own, for they were receiving orders for surprise moves on the Japs from the Americans.

Ocampo also told us about the remarkable bravery of the women guerrillas in other parts of the province, particularly a certain Dr. Avelina Alcantara. Later when I met this amazing young Filipino woman, who looked little more than eighteen and was only four feet seven, I marveled that so much energy could be contained in such a tiny, delicate person. Having graduated from Santo Tomas Medical College just before the outbreak of war, she began her guerrilla activities in May 1942 in the New Bilibid Prison Hospital. At that time, the Japanese were putting their war prisoners of all nationalities there and the little woman doctor was the connecting link between the captured guerrillas and their units and families. In spite of the stringent rules imposed by the Japanese, she managed to smuggle guerrilla leaders and relatives into the prison hospital disguised as patients. Twice a week she was visiting physician at the Correctional Institute for Women at Mandaluyong, thus giving her an excuse to go to Manila and contact guerrillas and women prisoners. Dr. Alcantara founded the R.O.T.C. guerrillas' women's auxiliary corps with ten members at the start. When the Jap campaign against the guerrillas was at its height she arranged her transfer to the Philippine General Hospital, where many wounded guerrillas were being sent—Remedios Lucero, head nurse in the emergency ward, hid the guerrillas' guns. Although Dr. Alcantara became seriously ill in May 1944 and had to be confined in the Bilibid hospital herself, she did not lessen her guerrilla activities; on the contrary, she was more energetic than ever in working against the enemy. In June of that year, her brother, who was a guerrilla officer and a prison guard, masqueraded as a Japanese officer and engineered the escape from the prison of sixteen guerrilla leaders. The Japs, of course, were enraged, and Dr. Alcantara's brother, father, uncle, and sister were captured and tortured. The doctor mobilized the women guerrillas to serve as spies. One, who worked in a Japanese barracks, stole maps and important records; another was a courier and carried messages and arms; the rest, posing as buyers and sellers of food, made sketches of enemy strongholds.

One night, Ocampo brought us a letter from Tomas Confesor, leader of the big guerrilla movement on Panay, giving the guerrilla line to be followed that year: First, there was to be no surrender to the Japs in their recent pacification drives, no matter what they promised; second, the guerrillas were to be prepared for a long rough campaign in which the Japs would do everything to exterminate them before the Americans returned; third, President Quezon urged patience and courage for at least another year: MacArthur would probably not reach the Philippines until late 1944 or 1945 at the earliest.

To us, who had been waiting so agonizingly this last year and a half, it seemed impossible that we could hold out for another year—perhaps even longer. We had been living from day to day, and now we were being asked to think in terms of another year. I couldn't, couldn't . . . I would die. . . . To make matters worse, my teeth began to pain me all over again and even the chili peppers lost their effect. Navarro visited us one day as I was trying to treat myself with the peppers, and he laughingly asked about it. When I told him what was the matter he said he would take me to a dentist in town, who was the brother-in-law of an American woman married to a Filipino, Mr. Bautista.

Navarro came for me the next evening with one of his men. He said he had made arrangements for the dentist to meet us the following day at Mr. Bautista's house, where we would sleep. He brought me a wide-brimmed Filipino peasant woman's hat to shield my face as we walked across the fields, and for Ron he had brought khaki soldier trousers and shirt—he would have been too conspicuous in his white suit. I was uneasy about this outfit, however—I could not help thinking that he could so easily be taken for a soldier in case we were caught.

It was a still cloudy night as the three of us—Fabian, Ron, and myself—followed Navarro and one of his guerrillas through the rice fields and across the river to the town. It was my first trip into Montalban since the year before when we had driven through it so hurriedly, and I was excited and nervous. Even in the darkness, it was strange to be walking up a narrow lane instead of a trail or a path, among so many houses—real houses . . . with real doors. That was what struck me that night about Mrs. Bautista's house: It was a real house, the kind you see in little towns in America—a beautiful white house with a garden and chicken coop and a fence, and inside there was real furniture, a table and chairs. I remember most of all the rocking chair. I had not seen a rocking chair all the time I had been in the Philippines—only an American woman would have had one.

Mrs. Bautista was an American of German extraction who had lived there for the past twenty years or so. She was a handsome woman, a trifle too smooth, I thought—I had heard it said that she got on well with the Japs, but she also knew which way the tide was turning and was anxious to have it known that she helped the guerrillas and Americans. Naturally she had to be careful, because the Japanese were very suspicious of American women married to Filipinos—since she had not been interned, she was carefully watched. The Bautista White Leghorn chickens had been well known even before the war, but the Japs now were her best customers and often came to the house to buy eggs.

I felt almost uncouth, like a wild creature of the woods, as I stared at Mrs. Bautista, elegantly attired in a housecoat, her sleekly brushed brown hair drawn back into a neat knot. She seemed nervous and apprehensive, I thought, as she spoke quickly with her slight German accent. She told us that Lieutenant Navarro practically lived at their house now, so that he was beginning to be almost a son to her.

"I have only daughters—four daughters," she said laughing. "And they all like him too much, he's so handsome. But he is such a hothead— I am afraid he will get into real trouble with the Japs one of these days, won't you, you bad boy?" She playfully shook her finger at him.

Navarro looked flattered by all this attention and flashed a shy smile at her, showing dazzling white teeth.

I sat as in a dream. . . . I still could not believe that I was in a real house talking to another American woman—I had not seen one for a year—and I felt as though all this would vanish and I would be squatting over three stones cooking rice in the woods. I was dazzled by the electric lights and awed by Mr. Bautista, a tall, handsome Filipino, meticulously dressed in a light tan coat. He was smoking a big expensive cigar and offered one to Ron. At the wonderful supper of fried pork, scrambled eggs, apple pie, and coffee, Fabian sat with us at the real table, eating with real knives and spoons, and he looked as uncomfortable as I felt. That night we were much too excited to sleep. The

noises echoing through the town seemed very loud to us after the stillness of the nights in the woods, and when we finally dozed off, we
slept fitfully and were aroused constantly by the barking of the dogs,
and our one thought was that the Japs were coming.

After a miraculous breakfast of hotcakes and eggs and coffee, we
went to the living room to wait for the dentist. I sat in the rocking chair
and I asked nothing more from life at that moment than to be allowed
to sit and rock until the war was over. Mr. Bautista, now in immaculate
white, and again puffing at a cigar, sat and talked with Ron, who, with
his rough beard and long hair, looked almost savage and barbarous by
contrast. Presently the dentist arrived with his drill, an ancient foot-
pedal affair. He was very friendly and genial, though somewhat nervous. He examined my teeth and shook his head. He would have to
pull that bad one and fill all my front teeth—about five in all.

I shall never forget the next moment as long as I live: The dentist had the drill in my mouth when a Filipino boy rushed in shouting: *"Haponese dito!"* (The Japs are here!) The dentist let go of the
drill so quickly that it almost cut me. I heard Mr. Bautista say to Ron:
"Take your wife in there—quick!" He pointed to a door. Ron
grabbed my arm and pulled me into the room—it was the bathroom. We stared at each other incredulously. Suddenly, in spite of
everything, I wanted to laugh and laugh. It was the funniest thing
that had happened to us in a year and a half—in fact it was the only
funny thing: After all the hiding we had been doing in the underbrush, it seemed so incredibly stupid to be hiding in a bathroom with
Japs downstairs. I had a mad impulse to turn on the shower and get
under it. Ron looked at me helplessly—there was not a single thing
we could do.

At last the door opened and Mr. Bautista beckoned, smiling broadly.
"It's OK now," he said. "They have gone."

The dentist was nervously smoking a cigarette. I wondered if he
would be able to pull my tooth.

"Close shave," he remarked.

Mrs. Bautista appeared and threw herself down on a chair, almost prostrate with relief. "Thank God that's over!" she exclaimed.

"What happened?" I asked.

"Two Japs came to buy some eggs. I was scared they'd want to go upstairs to talk—they do that sometimes to get a chance to look around the house. But today they just bought the eggs and left—"

Mr. Bautista gave us a drink of wine and we all felt a little better. The dentist finished his cigarette and brought his drill from the other room.

"We better get to work now," he said.

He began to drill gently and filled my five front teeth. Then he let me rest. It was almost noon and Mrs. Bautista decided I had better eat before my tooth was pulled. It was the last civilized meal I was to have for a long time.

After lunch the dentist pulled my tooth. I have always trusted a Filipino dentist after that—he did it so beautifully I scarcely felt it. He gave me novocaine and the tooth came out easily because there was not much of it left—it had been crumbling away bit by bit in the mountains. When it was over, Mr. Bautista gave me another drink and I went into the bedroom to lie down to wait for the novocaine to wear off. Then I must have fallen asleep . . .

Ron was shaking me. "Time to go. Fabian is waiting . . ." I sat up bewildered . . . where was I? . . . where were we going? My face hurt where the numbness of the novocaine had worn off—and I remembered. I stood up and felt my knees cave in and would have fallen if Ron had not caught me. "Are you all right? Think you can walk back?"

"I don't know—can't we get a drink first?"

I felt better after the drink but still had to lean on Ron as we left and I could only make it a short way after that. I was glad we did not have to go far. My face throbbed and I began to sway. Fabian looked at me anxiously.

"Sir, I must carry your wife or she will fall, sir. Will you allow me, sir?"

Ron nodded and Fabian picked me up in his powerful arms and carried me until we reached Magna's house. We rested there a while and then continued on to our house on the hill. Fabian said he would sleep with us that night. I was glad he was there the next day to cook for us since I was too weak to do much more than merely lie on the bamboo bed and dream of the rocking chair in Mrs. Bautista's house.

Ocampo's guerrillas were still keeping a day and night lookout on our hill. One night one of his men came with the news that the Japs had attacked the Marking guerrillas in the mountains and the *balita* from the mountain people was that the Japs had even used planes and bombs in an all-out effort to exterminate them. A few of Marking's men had been killed, and in retaliation, the guerrillas had ambushed a whole truckload of Japs, wiped them all out, and scattered over the hills. My first thought was of Yay Panilio, but nobody seemed to know anything about her. Meanwhile the Japanese garrison in Montalban had been increased to fifty now and they had organized "suicide squads" that were out hunting for guerrillas everywhere. They were picking up suspects indiscriminately and torturing them to talk.

"We are breaking up camp tonight," Ocampo told us. "This place is no longer safe, sir. We will move you with us, if you like, sir."

We glanced at Fabian. His honest face was taut with anxiety.

"Shall we go, Fabian?" I asked. "You'll come with us?"

"Of course, Missus. I go where you go." It was as simple as that to him. He turned to Ocampo. *"Malayu ba?"* (Is it far?)

"No, we will not go far tonight, Fabian," replied Ocampo. "Near Barrio Isidro, only six kilometers from here. Then we will wait and see."

So that night we moved with Ocampo's *borobo* (guerrilla force). It was a strange journey . . . a journey to the end of night, I thought, as we followed the long line of Filipino men with rifles and packs on their backs, shadowy silhouettes in the pale darkness. But I also felt a kind of exultation that night, born of that same feeling that we were not alone or lost any longer in those islands, and that these people were one with us, and the Japs could never win out against them. And there was that feeling of continuity of struggle against a common enemy: I had seen the Chinese people fighting the Japanese in China, and now I saw the Filipino people fighting the Japanese in the Philippines. We were moving with the guerrillas . . .

From Barrio Isidro secret trails led to the mountains by which the guerrillas could escape in case of a sudden Jap attack. Ocampo suggested to Fabian that we stay for this night in one of the little houses in the barrio, near a wood and tomorrow he could make us a house in the woods nearby. Meanwhile the *borobo* would pitch camp on a nearby hill.

"It is best to keep the Americanos hidden," Ocampo said.

Fabian slept with us that night and at dawn the next morning took us into the little woods nearby, where he made a fire and cooked rice. I shall always remember that little bamboo woods because it was so much like that first woods at Labug. A year had passed and once again it was May and the dry season: The thin bamboo leaves hung withered from their flimsy branches and fallen bamboo crackled under our feet as we walked. Everything had a desiccated look, as though the very trees longed desperately for water—but there was no stream in the little wood. Fabian had to carry water for us in a huge bamboo from the barrio. He built a lean-to with a grass roof, and once again, we settled down to wait.

The actual situation was far more dangerous than we knew then. The Japs had ringed Montalban with a steel cordon in the effort to keep anyone from contacting Marking's guerrillas hiding somewhere in the mountains. They had terrified the mountain people by killing two of them who attempted to flee as they approached, and the Japs threatened to exterminate them all if they were caught protecting the guerrillas. Each day the news grew worse, and each day it became more impossible to move forwards or backwards—the Japs were using everything they had to spot guerrillas in the hills and they had stationed a permanent squad in the hills and they had stationed a permanent squad at the dam night and day to search and question anybody coming or going.

On our third day in those macabre woods, Fabian came at dusk, breathless from running. "The news is very bad, sir," he told us. "The Japs are watching all the roads from Montalban, sir. I could not leave this morning, sir. They are also searching the houses in Montalban for guerrillas, sir, and the *balita* is that they will also search this barrio, sir. The people are very frightened, sir."

"What about Ocampo?" asked Ron. We had not seen the guerrilla leader that day and it worried us.

"I think they are planning to leave tomorrow, sir, for the mountains by the secret trails, sir. But it will be very hard for the Missus to go that way, sir. Perhaps it will be better just to hide here, sir."

"Did Ocampo say he would come to see us today?"

"Yes, sir. He has told me he will ask you about coming with them, sir. He will come surely tonight, sir."

The woods were stifling in the noonday heat. Not a breath of wind stirred and every leaf hung motionless, as though suspended for eternity against the white blazing sunlight, waiting, waiting . . . Suddenly I had the feeling we were trapped there, trapped in that horrible, macabre little wood.

"Fabian, I am very thirsty," I said suddenly. "We have no water . . ."

"Oh, how sorry I am, Missus. I will get some—" he slung our two empty bamboos over his shoulders and disappeared on the path leading to the barrio.

I heard Ron's voice as in a dream: "Do you think you'll be able to make it with Ocampo tomorrow? It's our only chance—"

I was thinking: Better to die fighting with the guerrillas than trapped in this little wood. . . . If Fabian was picked up by the Japs in

town we would die here anyway of lack of food and water . . . Better
to die fighting . . .

"Of course—" I was glad then when I saw Ron's anxious look
change to one of relief.

It was at that moment we heard the shots and everything afterwards happened as in a speeded-up motion picture: Fabian was running towards us and waving his hand as if we were trying to tell us
something without shouting and then we caught on and saw that he
meant us to make for the heart of the woods and Ron grabbed my
arm and began to pull me with him as he ran with Fabian following
us. Then somehow we were following Fabian, darting tortuously
deeper and deeper into the woods, on and on, higher and higher, until
it seemed to us we had penetrated their very depths and at last we
came to a wide ravine in the heart of the woods. Fabian stopped and
pointed down into it. "Hide there," he panted and sank exhausted on
the ground.

"For God's sake, what happened, Fabian?" I asked as soon as I could
catch my breath.

"Japs—" Involuntarily he glanced around as though he expected to
see them popping out from behind the trees.

"Japs? How many Fabian?" cried Ron.

"About one hundred, sir. I saw them marching over the hill
towards the barrio, sir. Perhaps they will search the houses for guerrillas, sir . . ."

Then I remembered the fire I had left burning in the woods. I had
started it to cook rice before Fabian came.

"Fabian!" I cried in horror. "The fire . . . the smoke . . . you think
the Japs will see it and come here?"

Fabian's eyes dilated with sudden fear.

"I don't know, Missus," he said finally. "We must wait and see—"
Suddenly I saw him stiffen and lean forward as though he were listening.
Then we heard it too: a faint *rat-a-tat-tat, rat-a-tat-tat,* now louder,

more insistent. I could never mistake that sound anywhere—burned as it was in my memory from the raid on Labug—the peppery sound of machine-gunning. . . . Instinctively I crouched deeper in the ravine, pressing against the earth slope. Ron and I stared at each other and I knew we were both thinking the same horrible thought: The Japs had seen our smoke and were machine-gunning the woods.

I do not know how long we crouched there: The machine-gunning stopped after awhile and then we heard the planes zooming over us, the thud of bombs falling, and impulsively I fell flat on my belly in the ravine. Ron and Fabian sat tense, staring at the sky. It began to grow hotter and hotter and I felt the sweat oozing down my legs and the sun burning my head. I began to feel like a crocodile in a dried-up riverbed, dying of thirst. After awhile I heard Ron and Fabian talking, but I think I was only half-conscious by that time—I must have had some kind of sunstroke—and remember only as in a dream Fabian carrying me through the woods and then I was feeling beautifully cool with water on my face and on my lips. I opened my eyes, to see Ron bending over me, holding a bamboo cup of water to my mouth. It must have been late afternoon, for everything seemed cool and quiet.

"Japs—where are the Japs?" I murmured.

"Gone. Don't worry now," Ron said. He looked haggard and worried.

"Where's Fabian?"

"Cooking rice—"

Thank God for Fabian; he was still there, squatting over the fire, dear, dear Fabian—as long as he was with us, nothing could happen . . . Then I remembered.

"What happened this morning? The Japs—did Fabian find out?"

"They raided Ocampo's guerrillas on the hill—"

I sat up.

"My God—did they get any of them?"

"Seven—the rest escaped."

"Ocampo?"

"No—"

"Did they kill them or just capture them?"

"Got them alive—" Suddenly he put his head in his hands. "I don't know what we're going to do—looks like we're really trapped this time. Our chance to get out with Ocampo is gone." He stared at me hopelessly. "We have no supplies and Fabian's got to get back to his family tonight and see what's happening in town—we'll have to stick it out somehow until he gets back—"

Fabian left us and once again we were alone in the woods. It was a horrible, nightmarish night—I tossed feverishly, unable to sleep, and when I finally dozed off I was always running away from the Japs . . . Japs . . . Japs.

I think it was the next day, when Fabian did not show up—that I began to get that "feeling" . . . the feeling that the end had really come . . . this time. We had come up against a blank wall, and there just was no going any farther. Before this, somehow I had always felt that we would still escape to the mountains, but now deep down, I knew that there was no escape. I did not say anything to Ron—he was worried enough—and because he was always hypersensitive to my feminine intuitions, his sixth sense, he called it. I had the feeling all day long that we were trapped—and that the end was near. But I was afraid to think too much about that end—a dead end—that always led in my mind to the same picture: being surrounded by Japs with cruel eyes boring through me . . . As long as they don't catch us in the woods, I prayed . . .

All that day, we hid in the woods and crept back at dusk to cook rice and wait for Fabian. We knew he could not possibly make it during the day now to our place, with all the roads being watched.

Lying in the jail now, it seems to me that everything in those last days was leading irrevocably to that terrible dusk of May 20, when Fabian suddenly appeared. For a moment I did not recognize him, he looked so changed, and then I knew at once that something awful had happened. He seemed to have visibly shrunk in the last day, and his face had a gaunt, tormented look, his eyes were dull and listless and he did not look directly at us, but into the distance, and as I stared at him, I felt a sudden clutch of fear at my heart. . . . It was the end.

"Fabian!" I cried at last.

He did not look at me even then . . . just stared into the fire. Then he spoke at last to Ron, dully, quietly, as though he were talking about the weather, "Sir, the Japs are keeping my family in jail, sir."

"Jail—your family?" echoed Ron.

"Yes, sir—my father and my wife and my children—they are in the Jap jail, sir."

"And you—the Japs—"

"The Jap captain let me go to tell you, sir. He says if I do not surrender you and your wife, he will kill them all, sir."

As in a dream, I heard Ron's voice, questioning, questioning. I knew that the end had come at last.

"Who is this Jap?"

"Sir, he is Captain Tanaka," replied Fabian.

"Just what did he tell you?"

"Sir, he said to me only, sir: 'I know you are hiding Mrs. and Mrs. Johnston. Tell them if they surrender peacefully, I will take them to Santo Tomas, if not—'"

"If not—?"

"He will kill my family and force me to lead the Japs to you and they will kill you both, sir."

Ron's face was a white, swaying, shadowy blur . . . Nothing seemed real at that moment, not even Fabian.

"Santo Tomas?" I cried. "Fabian—did he say Santo Tomas?"

"Yes, Missus—"

"If only we could believe that damn Jap—" Ron muttered. He turned to me impatiently. "But what can we do now? We can't let Fabian's family be killed for us—come on, what are we waiting for?

Let's get ready . . ." He turned abruptly to Fabian. "When are you supposed to bring us in?"

"Tonight you will sleep in the house of my father, sir, and Captain
Tanaka said he will come tomorrow morning to get you, sir."

I do not think I ever knew pity until that moment when I saw it on
Fabian's face as he looked at me. It was as though he wanted to sacrifice anything then—himself, his family—to save us from the next
twenty-four hours. But he could not . . . and we could not live without him. It was the end.

Mechanically I stuffed the remains of our miserable things into the
sack. The leather portfolio containing my diary and Ron's writings I
gave to Fabian: We were afraid to take it with us and he said he would
bury it in his rice kaingin until the end of the war.

We set off on our last walk through the fields towards Fabian's
house. Behind us lay the mountains . . . I was afraid to look back—
afraid I might suddenly drop everything and run back to them . . . I
was afraid of everything then . . . afraid of what lay ahead . . . and afraid
of the Japs and of what they might do to me.

10

THE LOWER DEPTHS

L YING IN THE DUNGEON AT MALOLOS, TIME CEASED TO EXIST for me, and I noted the passing of the days only by the marks on the stone wall of my cell. We might have been there for months or years or centuries for all I knew, buried as I was in that abyss where only the past seemed real . . . the present was that square of blue sky I saw through the bars and the light in the prison courtyard and the few moments during the day when I could see Ron. After the first week, I lay in a kind of coma from which I would start up only at the sound of footsteps or the rattle of keys. But the curious thing was that as I felt myself growing weaker physically, my mind seemed to become extraordinarily clear, almost clairvoyant, and I found that no longer did that nightmare of the Jap eyes obsess me. . . . It was as if I had become free at last by reliving my past experiences in memory through the endless nights in the jail and integrating them step by step with the present. And I knew then that I must accept the fact that I was here in this dungeon in the Philippines as the inevitable link in the long chain of events of the last ten years of my life. It was inevitable from the very first moment years ago when I had decided to throw in my lot with the Chinese in their fight against the Japanese: first in America, then in China—and it was only by sheer luck that I escaped at that time, and again when I took up the fight in Manila by my broadcasts. And I knew also that it was this fate—being captured by the Japs—that I unconsciously feared from the instant I had decided to go to China and it was because of this that I had been haunted by that strange dream that had become such a reality for me. But curiously enough, it was through this very realization of my haunting dream that I lost my fear and now understanding the picture as a whole, I was able to face its implications with more equanimity: torture or rape or even death . . . as a prisoner in the hands of the Japs . . .

One morning when the marks on the wall showed that we had been there for thirteen days, two Japanese officers and some soldiers came into the jail. I saw them go to Ron's cell and Ron staggering out with his hands tied and then they came to my cell and told me to come out. They unlocked the door and I came out dragging the sack. The Japs stared with grim faces at me and the sack but said nothing. They motioned for us to follow them through the outer prison courtyard. I felt the eyes of the Filipino prisoners watching us as we disappeared through the same archway by which we had come that terrible first day. I was so weak, I do not know how I ever managed to drag out the sack, but I felt possessed of some superhuman energy. For the moment it did not matter where were going; the important thing was that we were leaving that jail at last. I felt the blinding sunshine around me and the sky stretching to infinity and I wanted to sing and to cry with the feeling of being free again.

We followed the officers to the street where two trucks packed with soldiers were waiting. All the time I was dragging the sack and when I reached the truck, I was panting for breath. One of the Japs yelled an order to the soldiers and untied Ron's hands and pushed him into the truck. Then I lifted up the sack to Ron and climbed aboard. The soldiers climbed on in front and we were off.

I do not remember much of that ride because I was in such a weak and dazed state. I felt like an animal, who has suddenly been released from a dark cage and I kept lifting up my head to the sun and the sky to drink in all the light and space above us. In the truck soldiers with fixed bayonets hemmed me in, and I tried to see past them out to the green fields and the hills I had dreamed about in my cell, but it was all a moving blur as we roared along the dusty roads.

I wondered whether by some miracle we might be going to Santo Tomas, and it was with a terrible sense of foreboding that I saw the trucks veer off the main highway into a small town—and I knew then we were not going to Manila. The trucks drove at breakneck speed through narrow unpaved streets and stopped before a large spacious house that looked as though it might have belonged to some wealthy Filipino before the war. I remembered Captain Tanaka's house and felt glad that at least it was still daylight and not the dead of night, and anyway it could not be as bad as that dungeon—and perhaps we might even have a bed to sleep in. The soldiers were jumping out of the truck and we climbed down after them and followed them into the house.

We entered a large vestibule and went into a small room where a Japanese man was sitting at a desk writing in a large book with another in shorts and white shirt watching him. They glanced up for a moment when we came in and both stared at me as though they had seen some strange apparition. Then they looked at each other and started to giggle, but I was feeling too horribly tired and dazed to pay much attention to them. I felt unbearably weary—weary of everything—as though there was little sense in going on much longer. . . . Then everything began to swim around me: I steadied myself against the wall and looked vaguely about this strange house. As in a dream I was conscious of soldiers going up and down the stairs outside and a door opening across the room and Japs sitting at some desks.

I felt something queer about this house, something I could not quite define: It had a curious mixture of formal officialdom and the informal atmosphere of a high-ranking officer's living quarters.

I glanced back to the desk where Ron was standing and saw the little Jap begin to frisk him and put his things on the desk—passport, pencil, cigarettes, and matches. He examined each article and then wrote something in his book. . . . Suddenly I was afraid—where were we and what kind of house was this? At that moment I had the weirdest feeling of eyes watching me from behind. I was leaning against the wooden wall or what I thought was a wall of that horrible room. Impulsively I whirled around and then a sickening wave of fear swept over me. Unmistakably I was looking down into a pair of eyes peering at me through the wooden bars of what I thought was a wall; actually it was a cage below the floor level . . . some prisoner inside was staring out. . . . For an instant I thought I would faint, then I saw Ron beckoning me to the desk.

I stared into the cold eyes of the little clerk. He pointed to the shabby handbag I was clutching under my arm and motioned for me to empty the contents on the desk. I took out everything—a small cracked mirror, a broken compact, sliver of lipstick, a few bobby pins, a comb, a pencil, my green-covered passport, and a dirty handkerchief. He separated the passport from the other things and wrote something in his book. The other Jap picked up the lipstick and compact and examined them curiously. He nudged his friend and they burst out laughing and pantomimed the act of putting on lipstick. They gave back my bag intact except for the passport.

They turned the sack upside down and shook it and everything was scattered on the floor—my mosquito net, our dirty clothes, and those khaki trousers that always caused trouble. But I was especially worried about my books—if only they did not take them away, I thought desperately. But I need not have worried. The Japs had eyes only for the khaki trousers. They glared from them to Ron and asked the same old questions.

"You soldier, yes?" Why had I not sense enough to leave those trousers in the other jail? But we had left so suddenly I had not had time to think at all.

The other Jap picked up the books and leafed through them disdainfully, then threw them down contemptuously on the pile of dirty clothes. I imagine they were looking for guns or bolos or pistols— some torn books did not matter at all. The Japs motioned for Ron to put the stuff back in the sack.

As we stood there uncertainly, one of the Japs took a bundle of keys from his pocket . . . there was something sinister about that gesture. At that moment I wanted more than anything in the world to leave that house. I felt a terrible sense of foreboding and fear.

"Ron!" I whispered, but he was already following the Jap and my legs moved automatically after them. The Jap had started off in the direction of the doorway, then turned sharply to the left into a small, dark hall and stopped so quickly that I was thrown against Ron and clutched him to keep from falling. I heard the turning of a key in the lock and a door opening . . . The Jap stepped back and gave us a violent push so that we fell into the semi-darkness below at the precise moment we heard the door slammed shut behind us.

For a while we were blinded by the blackness . . . then we gradually distinguished some figures sitting upright and staring at us. I sank down on the sack and looked at Ron in horror, but I could only see the white blur of his head. I buried my face against his shoulder and I felt I wanted to remain there forever and never again look up to see where we were. . . . I was startled out of my trance by a sudden whisper in Tagalog:

"*Huwag matakot—Filipino kasama* . . ." (Don't be afraid—we are Filipino friends.)

I looked up and now clearly saw four Filipino men squatting upright along the wall on our right and staring at us, and then one of them smiled. I glanced around the narrow oblong cell that was about ten feet long and five feet wide. There was a tiny window high above at the lower end of the cell that was barred by the same wooden planks that walled in the rest of the cell on two sides. Again I had that uneasy feeling about this house. Here we were in the sunken Cage and yet outwardly the house looked like a well-to-do Filipino home. . . . Suddenly I wanted to be back in the dungeon at Malolos with José and my jailbird friends.

It could not have been more than three or four in the afternoon but it was like dusk or even night in this dark cell. Staring through the gloom, I noticed something in the far corner on the left near the window—some square object: It was a large tin can—they must use it as a toilet. I was overcome by nausea . . . no wonder this place had such a fetid, filthy smell. I buried my head in my hands again. What was the use of seeing or feeling or thinking any more?

I was aroused by the sound of Ron's voice and then a strange one in English. "What's this place called?" I heard Ron ask.

"This is the San Fernando, Pampanga, Military Police Headquarters," someone replied in a low voice.

I looked up and saw a shadowy face peering in through the bars and staring more intently I thought I detected Filipino features.

"When do you think we'll leave here?" Ron asked.

"Three days—" There was a sound of clicking boots somewhere near and suddenly the face and voice vanished.

"Who was that?" I whispered to Ron.

"Don't know—he just started to talk to me through the bars— must be some Filipino the Japs forced to work for them." He buried his face in his hands. "Three days in this hole—God!"

"Three days." I remembered the "tomorrow" of that Jap in Malolos that had stretched into thirteen tomorrows. Would it be the same here? But it was impossible—they could not keep me here with all these men—it was like a cage for wild animals.

I was beginning to get sick again from the ghastly smell and I felt I would choke from the bad air. I turned around to put my face between the wooden bars we had been leaning against and was startled to see that I was looking across the length of the room to the desk where the two Japs had signed us in. . . . Then this had been the "wall" I had been leaning against and one of these Filipino prisoners had been staring up at me, watching me all the time. That explained that uncanny sensation I had had of the eyes behind me. . . . Now I, too, could stare out at the desk for any new prisoners . . . and I watched with loathing the two little Japs jabbering. I saw them suddenly stiffen to attention as a swaggering Japanese officer, dressed up in a uniform replete with sword and boots, strutted up to the desk.

I saw them start in my direction. I waited for the door to open. Maybe then I could get a little air and not faint. Then I looked up and saw the officer standing outside the Cage staring in with a cruel mocking smile that bored through the semi-darkness and I felt that if I looked long enough into those fanatically cruel eyes, I would go mad. It was as though at last he had captured the animals he had been hunting for so long and now had them locked behind bars where he could examine them triumphantly, at his leisure. And there was no hurry—he had been waiting twenty years for this—even longer. . . . When I looked up again he was gone.

I heard one of the Filipinos whisper: "*Masama-ito*" (This is a bad one). Then I relapsed into my torpor and vague inchoate images began to float through my mind. And for some fantastic reason everything seemed to revolve around that ghastly object in the corner—it was as if it symbolized all the horror of this place. I wondered how I would get out of the cell to go to a toilet—surely there must be one in the house—all these Filipino houses had them . . . would the Japs let me out? In the dungeon I had learned the Japanese word for toilet—*benjo*—I would try it on them when they opened the door again.

It was very quiet in the cell. We might all have been figures carved out of stone as we sat fixed in our immobile positions. The Filipinos were still staring at us, but did not talk, even among themselves, which is strange indeed, for Filipinos are usually very gregarious and talkative. They must have been afraid—maybe the Japs beat them for talking. I felt a terrible apathy and despair envelop me and I think I was falling asleep when I jerked up to the familiar sound of footsteps and keys rattling outside the Cage.

Someone pushed open the door and I saw one of the Japs standing beside a thin figure in civilian clothes holding two plates of rice. The civilian bent down to hand the plates to Ron and me and I looked at him in surprise—he was unmistakably Chinese, a pathetic-looking creature in tattered shabby clothes. What was he doing here? He vanished as suddenly as he appeared.

Mechanically I began to eat my rice and I was halfway through when I felt something in the rice. I looked down: It was a piece of fish. The Chinaman had apparently hidden it there for me. And after that, whenever he brought the rice, there was always a bit of fish in it.

I finished eating and was awaiting my chance to get out of the Cage when they came for the plates. As the door opened and I saw the guard, I cried out: "Benjo—benjo!" and held my breath at the startled look that came over his mask-like face. Then the mask cracked into a smile.

"OK—you go." He motioned for me to follow him and after he had locked the door, he led me through the big room past the desk to a door at the other end.

It was a filthy hole, probably used by the Japs, but at least I could close the door and be by myself. The first thing I saw was the iron-barred window and I rushed to put my head between the bars and breathe in the fresh, free air. That funny little song we used to sing as children: *If I had the wings of an angel* . . . I could not get enough air to replace the foul stench of the Cage. A blue light bathed the garden gleaming with sprays of purple and orange bougainvillea.

There was a dirty washbowl in the corner and hastily I splashed my face and hands with cold water and longed to throw it over my whole body. With water dripping from my face and hands, I opened the door and followed the guard back to the Cage. As we passed the doorway, we almost ran into some soldiers who had just come in and started stamping noisily up the stairs.

It was very dark in the Cage now, with only a dim reflected light from the big room, and the others were just vague shadows; only Ron's dull white jacket made him stand out. I felt cool now and able to breathe again. Ron whispered that we ought to get ready for bed before it got completely dark. Bed? I looked around at the four Filipinos—how could the six of us sleep in this narrow hole? It seemed impossible, but the Filipinos were already standing and motioning us to move to their end of the cell near the window and indicating that they would take the small space near the door. And so once again I took the ragged, dirty mosquito net out of the sack and tied the ends to the bars, thanking heaven that it was the kind of net one could look out from but not into. I spread my blanket on the floor and rolled our old clothes into a pillow. We crawled in and stretched out—that is, I stretched out, for Ron had to tuck his long legs almost up to his knees. I was grateful for the darkness that blotted out the horror of the place.

Suddenly a powerful light flooded the room, almost blinding me. What now? I sat up wearily and wondered if this was to be another inspection. I felt no fear—I was simply too tired to have any emotion. I could see the Filipinos lying crisscross like corpses along the width of the cell, blinking at the dazzling light. The guard stared in at us as if he were counting us to make sure no one had escaped, though how we could ever get out of there was beyond comprehension. They kept the light on all that night.

I do not know how or when I fell off, but I must have eventually slept despite the glaring light, for the next thing I remember was opening my eyes to the sight of the Filipinos squatting outside our net in a pale sickly dawn. I lay still for a few minutes, resisting the thought of the Cage and what lay ahead and stared through the bars of the high window at a glimpse of sky, watching the blueness brightening into white. I saw again the morning light of the many dawns in the woods and hills. At last I turned to Ron, who was still asleep, and as in the old days in the mountains I shook him. We smoothed our mussed-up clothes and crawled out of the net. Desperately I longed for the hot tea and cakes we had had in the dungeon at Malolos. Here in this filthy Cage everything was cold and dismal. Ron was tense and jittery without a first morning cigarette. We sat straight up against the wall, waiting. Then I began to concentrate on getting out again to wash. Peering through the bars I cried to the Jap at the desk: *"Benjo, benjo!"* I am convinced to this day that there was magic in that word—perhaps it was their hearing it spoken by a foreigner, particularly a woman. Anyway the effect was instantaneous: He looked up startled, then he grinned, reached for his keys, and shuffled over to the Cage. Once more I was out. Then, and in the days to come, the word *"benjo"* was for me the "Open Sesame" to a fragment of freedom. Cool water on my face and the freshness of the flowers glistening in the golden morning light.

When I returned, Ron was still sitting upright against the wall, pale and gaunt, staring fixedly at a placard on the opposite wall in Tagalog and English.

PRISONERS MUST NOT TALK TO EACH OTHER.

PRISONERS MUST NOT SMOKE.

PRISONERS MUST SIT UP AT ALL TIMES.

PRISONERS MUST NOT READ.

So that explained the strange silence of the Filipinos last night. I looked at them now, motionless and staring. Suddenly I thought I would go mad if I had to stand this much longer.

But the door was opening again. Someone was handing in plates of rice to the Filipinos who passed them on to us. I peered out to see if I could see the pathetic Chinese creature of last night but he was not there. We were given some squash with the rice and I was so hungry that I gagged the whole thing down with water. That was breakfast and now ahead of us stretched an interminable wasteland of the hours until the next meal—no smoking, no talking, no lying down.

I heard whispering and turned to see one of the Filipinos talking to Ron. After awhile Ron said: "Telling me why they're in here—this is their third day. They're not political prisoners anyway—not guerrillas—the Japs wouldn't put us in the same cell if they were. If their story's true, it's almost funny—seems they were picked up by the Jap Army for selling contraband stuff to the Jap Navy."

It was late afternoon of the third day in the Cage, and we were dazed with the heat and stench and foulness of the air. All day we had waited anxiously for a sign that we would be taken out at last, remembering that the Filipino had said "three days," and all the hours crawled agonizingly and nothing happened. At last we gave up hope and fell into a kind of stupor. The most torturous thing of all was trying to sit up when we longed so desperately to lie down and sleep, and during those terrible hours, as Ron and I leaned against each other, one of us would doze off and fall over suddenly, and awake with a start. At last I decided to vary the monotony by squatting near the bars and watching the Japs at the desk—at least that would keep me from falling asleep. Clerk bending laboriously over some papers, making precise little marks with a brush pen . . . soldier boots marching through the hall, and clattering upstairs . . . civilians in khaki shirts and shorts dashing about. . . . Suddenly I sat up startled, and peered more intently through the bars. I was looking at a pair of huge, dirty bare feet, stumbling behind the strutting Jap boots, now halting before the desk. Big feet and long legs emerging from torn, tattered trousers. I almost pushed my head through the bars in my frenzy to see more; up and up and up my eyes went, past torn khaki trousers to torn khaki shirt and black beard and dark unkempt hair—an American soldier. . . . There was no mistaking those big feet and long legs—he was even taller than Ron, must have been all of six feet two. "An American!" I almost shouted in my excitement, shaking Ron as he lay half-asleep against the wall.

I lowered my voice to a whisper then: "The Japs have brought an American soldier here! Look . . ." Both of us peered through the bars again and saw him, half-turned towards the Jap officer now, leaning against the desk as if for support, but we could not see his face distinctly. The little clerk began to frisk him, feeling through his shirt and trousers. I saw him take out a box of matches and hold them out to the officer, who turned swiftly and slapped him sharply on each side of his face—once, twice, three times, four times, and screamed something in Japanese. I turned away—I did not want to see any more. But I heard the sound of the boots as they approached the Cage and the Jap still shouting, and the key turning in our lock and the door scraping open and I looked up in time to see the guard kick the American violently so that he fell into the Cage.

I do not think I will ever forget Banks, that American soldier, as long as I live. It was not only that he had a rare sweetness and simplicity—it was also what he came to symbolize to us during those agonizing days and nights in the Cage. He was just a G.I. from Texas who had enlisted when the war broke out and was shipped to the Philippines. He had been in all the fighting and escaped on the Death March from Bataan by lying in a ditch and pretending he was dead. At night he managed to crawl into some woods and hide there for a few days, living on roots and berries until some friendly Filipinos found him and took him up into the mountains around Pampanga. He lived up there for more than a year the way we had in our hills until the Japanese started rounding up all the mountain people and he was forced nearer town to get food. He was caught in a little hut with his two Filipino friends in the middle of the night. The Japs shot the two Filipinos right away and then started to give Banks the "works"—they knew he was a soldier and thought he was connected with the Hukbalahaps, the communist-led guerrillas roaming through the hills of Pampanga.

They beat him up and when he was almost unconscious, gave him the "water-cure"—sticking his head under water and pulling him up and then sticking it under again. Then they threw him into solitary confinement at one of the local jails near here for another week, torturing him with all their infamous methods to force him to talk. Then they threw him into our Cage.

Banks was the first American soldier I had seen who had fought in Bataan and as I stared at him lying there in the dim light of the Cage, looking for all the world like a dead Abraham Lincoln, my emotions were curiously mixed: A terrible pity and despair and pride and hope and rage and futility were all jumbled together in my mind. Banks was a symbol of what the Japs had done to America at the start and he epitomized what they would do to all of us if the Americans did not come back.

He lay with his eyes closed, the sweat pouring down his face, and he was trembling violently. I took out an old handkerchief and wiped his brow. He opened his eyes for a moment looked started when he saw me, then he said, "Thank you, ma'am." He smiled weakly. "Malaria—"

Ron moved him so he could lie in the center of the Cage with his long legs stretched out, and covered him with our blanket. "Thank you, ma'am," he had said and those three words took me back to the America I had lost and seen only in my dreams for the past three years: the wide stretches of the prairie land, the shining train speeding across the country, its mournful whistle a lonely wail in the night. A great hope surged up in me and I had the feeling that all was not lost. America suddenly seemed very close.

I think if it were not for Banks and the fact that he suffered so much more intensely than any of us, I certainly could not have endured the deadly monotony of our existence. Except for the privilege of *benjo,* the Japs paid no more attention to me during the first five days than if I had been a stick of wood. The fact that I was the only woman in a filthy cell with six men did not seem to disturb them in the least, for which actually I was glad, fearing the possibility of a solitary confinement. Sleeping was a problem but we solved it by trial and error method: We three Americans stretched out lengthwise—Ron and I under our net—at one end of the Cage and the Filipinos crosswise at the other end.

The first two days and nights, Banks was very ill with malaria and we were really worried about him. I had two quinine pills left in my bag, which I gave him and that helped some. The attack finally left him on the third day and he just lay there limp, staring at us with the most extraordinary pair of sad eyes in his gaunt, black-bearded face. His leanness and great height made him look more than ever like Lincoln, and when he spoke in his backwoods drawl, it evoked a picture of log cabins and rail splitting in a pioneer America.

He told us his story in snatches. Born in Texas, raised on a farm, very little schooling, left by his father's death to support a mother and sister at an early age, he had done odd jobs all his life from farmhand to ranching, migrating from state to state and taking his mother and sister along with him. Somehow they had scraped together enough money to buy a small farm in California and, ironically enough, during the last few years before the war they had been growing rice for the Philippines. He could not bring himself to eat rice then, he told us, and he swore he would never touch it again if he ever got out of this alive.

I noticed the name Maria tattooed on his forearm.

"That's a girl I lived with in the mountains," he explained. "She was good to me—her family gave us lots of food. We had plenty to eat an' things were pretty good . . . *tuba* to drink—the mountain people make it up there—plenty o' deer an' wild pig . . ."

Again I began marking the days on the wall—this wall that was scrawled over with the names of former prisoners. On the fifth day, the Inquisition began and one by one we were called out for our grilling. I was scared when it started but I was also glad because it was a break in the monotony and my head had taken to paining me from the horrible heat and stench of the Cage, and I had a desperate longing for fresh air. The Filipinos were called first. I was the last to be questioned, right after Ron, and I did not even have a chance to find out what they had asked him. I was afraid that our stories might not coincide—the Japs were always waiting for a chance to trap you if possible.

I followed the guard into the hall and past the staircase to a large room with many desks at which Japs in civilian clothes were writing. A skinny officer with a close-cropped bullet-shaped head and cruel eyes looked up with a mocking smile as the guard brought me to his desk. I glanced at the papers in his hand and was startled to see a large bottle of perfume on his desk. Perfume—what in heaven's name was this Jap doing with perfume? In my primitive world, I had forgotten its very existence. . . . The Jap was speaking in halting English. I looked at him. There was something definitely queer about him, the odd-shaped head, the way he looked at me with that sly mocking expression.

He put the same questions to me that Tanaka had asked: When were we captured? Why did we hide out so long in the hills? Were there any other Americans in the mountains? At each reply he glanced down at his papers as though he were checking my answers against his information. At last he pushed a paper to me and told me to sign it. He leaned back in his chair, took a cigarette from a box on his desk, and offered me one. He regarded me through the cigarette smoke.

"You—one woman—many men here—very hard, yes?" he hissed.

"Yes," I murmured, evading his reptilian glance.

"Japanese punish you because you not surrender soon. Now woman stay with husband—where husband sleep, wife must sleep . . ."

What was he driving at? I put my hand for a moment to my aching head. The gesture did not escape him. He smiled sadistically.

"Head hurt?" he asked, pointing to his own ugly head.

I nodded.

"Too many men where you sleep—yes? You like sleep upstairs—alone?"

I shook my head. Suddenly I felt I had to get away from this sinister man—even the Cage was preferable.

"I must stay with my husband," I blurted out. Then to my surprise I heard myself say: "My head hurts—we get no exercise."

At the mention of exercise, he grinned. The Japanese are like the Germans in their fanatical obsession with calisthenics.

"Exercise?" he repeated. "OK—tomorrow exercise." He spoke to the guard, then turned to me and leered:

"You smoke and we talk again?"

I was frightened and could only nod as I rose. Now what have I let myself in for, I thought miserably. Asking for exercise—God knows what the Jap would ask in return. Back in the Cage, I told Ron about it and he was worried, too.

The next morning the guard told us all to line up to go out. The Filipinos looked scared, as though they were going to be shot. Luckily Banks could walk by himself, though slowly, and Ron walked directly behind him in case he should fall. I brought up the rear. We must have made a funny picture to the Japs who stopped their work to laugh when they saw us—four little Filipinos and two tall skinny Americans with beards and a woman in a black suit. They marched us past the kitchen and out into the backyard of the house where they lined us up against a wall. We all looked straight ahead, but out of the corner of my eye, I could see some Filipino girls washing at a trough—they stopped their work and were staring at us.

We were dazzled by the sudden sunlight and blinked our eyes and in that light, the prison pallor of the men was ghastly. We had only a moment to drink in the sunshine and the wonderful green of the banana tree leaves and then the voice of the soldier barked out: "One, two, three . . ." as he began to give us his exercises, which were like setting-up drills at school. All of us were terribly weak from the lack of food and frightful conditions of the last month and more than once I glanced in alarm at Banks and Ron to see how they were taking it. Banks looked as though he would keel over any moment but somehow kept doggedly on. The Jap only wanted an excuse, we knew, to vent his usual sadism on the Americans.

At last he stopped. The exercises were over and we stood there panting and breathless. As we followed the guard back to the house, I greedily gulped in all the fresh air I could.

At dusk the Japs would invariably play sentimental and patriotic songs on a screechy gramophone and the soldiers joined in the choruses at the top of their voices until we thought we would go mad with the din. But it was the occasional lilting, singsong, typically Japanese melody that I hated most—it seemed to epitomize the essence of Japan, our deadly enemy.

It was a strange house, this Japanese Military Police Headquarters of San Fernando, Pampanga, with its eerie, sinister atmosphere and odd combination of military and civilian personnel—soldiers strutting about in uniforms and clerks running around in kimonos and slippers. What went on upstairs was a mystery to us at first. Sometimes at night we would hear a fearful shrieking and when once we were awakened by the screams of a woman and a man shouting in Tagalog we knew: The upstairs was used as a torture chamber, just as the rooms downstairs had been converted into prison cells. It was the horrible house where the Jap Gestapo pried out information about guerrilla movements and Americans in hiding in Pampanga and then swooped down upon their victims in sudden night or dawn raids, the way they had captured Banks.

But why were we being kept there? We had been captured in an entirely different province, and they had not called us again after that first perfunctory questioning. As the days wore on, a ghastly futility began to gnaw at me—I had the feeling that we would never be free again, that the Japs would move us from one jail to another until we rotted of dysentery or malaria or some other awful disease.

That night after chow, we were leaning against the wall of the Cage in the usual half-dazed and stupefied condition, when suddenly we heard the grating sound of the key turning in the lock and the next moment the guard was peering in at us insolently. His gaze focused on me and he motioned for me to get up and come out. I stared at him incredulously . . . then startled and frightened, I glanced at Ron. Why was I being called out at this strange hour of the night? Ron looked at me helplessly with anxious eyes.

I followed the guard as he made his way across the hall to the big room where I had been interrogated the previous morning. The desks were empty now all except the one in the corner from which rose the familiar bullet-shaped head. It was that same officer who had questioned me. He looked up smiling when he saw me, and dismissed the guard with a few words in Japanese, and we were alone in the room. I stood there uncertainly.

"Sit down," he said, still smiling.

I stared at the bottle of perfume. What did he want, I wondered.

"Smoke?" I took the Japanese cigarette he offered and suddenly I wished I could save it and take it back to Ron.

The flame of his match lit up for an instant the cruel, mocking eyes, now dilated with a strange, excited look. The first puff at the cigarette seemed momentarily to ease my mounting sense of fear.

He was leaning back in his chair now, staring at me through the smoke . . . then I heard the clipped singsong words in rising intonation cutting the silence.

"You—American woman—no babies—no?"

So that was it. I was glad of the curtain of white smoke between us. "No."

"American women like babies, yes? Why you no have babies?" he leered, ogling me.

Carefully I avoided looking at him, as I took another puff at the cigarette, not answering, waiting. He must be sex mad, I thought. That cruel fanatical look . . .

His sudden shriek tore through the silent room, frightening me to a stark awareness.

"Japanese hate Americans . . . kill all Americans soon . . . good, very good!" he shouted. "No more American babies . . ." It was a crazy jumble—the psychopathic ravings of a lunatic. The voice continued: "Maybe you not know—Japanese bomb California—next Washington . . . soon all America!" He was shouting again. "Japanese kill all Americans!"

I sat rigid with fear, staring at the perfume, not daring to move. I half expected him to draw his sword and decapitate me on the spot—after all, I was an American, and I was completely at his mercy. Suddenly I was startled by the soft singsong intonation of his voice, gliding through the silence—the same voice I had heard when I entered the room. I glanced up in surprise.

"America very big, yes? You living where? California?"

"New York."

"*Sodeska* . . . New York . . . big city . . . good." He reached for a pencil and paper. "You write down your house . . . maybe I go soon. I see you mother—father—" He looked at me questioningly. "You have mother . . . father, yes?"

"Yes . . ."

"Good—maybe I see them."

I wanted to laugh then from sheer relief . . . laugh and laugh. It was all so fantastic, so mad. Here I was in a Cage, a prisoner of the Japs in the Philippines and a lunatic Jap officer was telling me he might see my mother and father soon. He was standing up now and shouting something in Japanese and the Jap guard was at the desk, waiting.

"OK now—go." He leered at me as I stumblingly followed the guard back to the Cage. Anyway, he had not asked me to go upstairs . . .

On our eleventh day in the Cage, in the late afternoon, we were leaning against each other, numb after the searing heat of the day. We had been taking turns lying down while the others watched to see that the guard was not looking. Suddenly we snapped upright at the sound of harsh Jap voices and heavy footsteps approaching the Cage . . .

another inspection? We had already had three during the past week. Then the door was opened and we saw a heavyset, dark youth handcuffed between two Japs. An officer peered into the Cage and counted us, then signaled to the guard to remove the boy's handcuffs. With the usual, vicious shove, the guard pushed him into our cell and locked the door.

The whole thing happened so quickly that Banks, whose long legs took all the remaining space between the Filipinos and Ron and myself and who had been staring fixedly at the boy, did not have time to move so that the boy just tumbled over among us, and then stood up against the wall. In that moment as the boy recovered his balance, I heard Banks whisper to Ron: "Spy—don't talk . . ." and then hastily drew his long legs under him to make room for the boy.

"Whew!" said the boy, as he squatted. "Not much room, is there?" He spoke in an unmistakably New York accent. He was looking around now, getting his bearings and his glance fell on me.

"Christ, they got a dame in here, too! How'd you get here?"

I pointed to Ron.

"My husband," I whispered.

"Why all the whisperin'? Don't they even let you talk in here anymore, for Pete's sake?" He spoke in such a loud voice that I looked involuntarily to see if the guard had heard him. Ron pointed to the rules notice on the wall and the boy turned to look at it.

"Don't pay any attention to 'em—make believe you can't read if the Japs squawk." His white teeth flashed in the gloom of the Cage.

I stared at him in wonder. His voice, his accent, his nonchalance— it was all music to my ears, just as Banks had been. Could he really be a spy?

The boy recognized Banks. "Hi."

"Hello, Tony," Banks answered.

"You been here all this time? Christ, they took me to Bilibid an' I sure hoped they'd let me stay there fer good. No kiddin', Bilibid ain't so bad—compared to this stink hole, it ain't." He looked around to see if a guard was in sight, then lowering his voice, he said: "The Japs here are the worsta the lot. They bumped off plentya our guys right here in backa the house. You havta know howta get around 'em. They kept me here two weeks before I got wise an' started playin' upta that pansy officer, Wada. After that it was a cinch. They let me play their records an' fool around the kitchen an' even go out to hick dances in town. Thought they'd get me ta give 'em the dope on the guys in the hills. Oh yea—I gave 'em the dope all right, but it was all the wrong dope, see? Then I beat 'em at their own game an' gave 'em the slip one night. Thought they'd kill me when they got me again but Wada still had use fer me. Then Bilibid an' now back here. Christ, do I haveta see that Jap fairy again?"

Pansy Wada . . . the Japanese officer with the perfume . . . so that was it. But why had he asked me about sleeping upstairs?

The boy talked as though it did not matter whether anyone answered or not but as if it were the most important thing in the world just to talk. . . . He was rather good-looking—and he certainly did not look as if he had been starved. He turned towards the door at the sound of footsteps. It was chow time . . . the usual mess of rice and greens.

"What slop!" Tony grimaced. "Not fit fer pigs!"

In the dim light I again had a fleeting glimpse of the pathetic Chinese man and as we ate, I asked Tony if he knew anything about him.

"Jeez, that poor guy! The Japs sure gave it ta him fer fair. He useta be a big shot before they came but he'd always been against 'em and they never forgot. It's a wonder he's still around at all."

It's a miracle how we all slept in the Cage. I was jammed up against the bars while Ron, Banks, and Tony filled the rest of the space at our end.

The next morning Tony was taken out by the Japs, presumably for grilling, and we had our first chance to ask Banks why he thought Tony was a spy. He said Tony had been in one of the local jails and that had been his reputation, though there was actually nothing definite to prove it.

"It all started," Banks said, "when Tony was seen around town hob-nobbin' with the Japs, especially Wada. The Filipinos got the idea that Japs liked him—they never figured Tony mighta been playin' 'em fer what he could get outa 'em, watching' for a chance to escape. The Japs are purty dumb sometimes. Anyway, one night Tony got outa this very jail—jest slipped over the wall. The Japs were maddern a nesta hornets when they found out—an' took it out on the resta the pris-oners. Tony didn't stay in the hills o' Pampanga long after he got out. He got tied up with too many Filipino women an' got the natives against him. He's just a crazy kid out fer adventure an' allus gittin' into some kinda trouble."

If Tony was indeed a spy, he certainly used naive tactics. He was forever talking about himself and there was not much that we did not get to know about him. He was only nineteen and had come over as a pilot on a bomber that was shot down near the coast. He was the sole survivor of the crew. Filipinos hid him and lent him a *banca* (native boat) in which he tried to escape. But he was picked up by a Japanese cruiser and brought ashore. He made his first getaway to the moun-tains, living with one guerrilla band after another and gradually drift-ing toward Pampanga. He told us his people were Italian and that he came from Brooklyn. He had married just before he left but had no intention of going back to his wife after the war.

"Just one o' those things," he said. "She roped me in."

"What are you going to do—after the war?" I asked.

"Hell, jest see the world—like my brother who wenta Spain—knockin' around, fightin', having' fun.

"What side was your brother on in Spain?"

Tony scratched his head. "Dam' if I know—but what the hell diff'rence does it make, anyway?"

That night the heat was so fierce none of us could even pretend to sleep. Besides, the Japs must have all been drunk, for they were making an awful racket, screaming and singing and shouting. The gramophone was on full blast, and with the dazzling glare of the light, sleep was utterly impossible. Our guard must have been drunk too, because he paid little attention to us and so we just sat and talked in whispers.

Our talk that night, drifted inevitably to food. Tony began telling about the wonderful spaghetti his mother made. I asked him whether she could make those marvelous all-whipped cream pies I used to have at a little Italian restaurant in New York. Banks said he did not care much for Italian cooking.

"Jest gimme good plain American home cookin', Texas style. Boy, that's eatin'! Chicken pie an' dumplings and a big hunka apple pie an' cheese." He sighed. "An' there ain't nothin' like American coffee . . ."

Even Tony agreed to that but he still liked Italian cooking best. That started a discussion on international cooking and we argued hotly on the relative merits of French, Russian, Swedish, Hungarian, Chinese, even Arabian, food. We had a wonderful time eating in our imaginations and when I finally fell asleep, I dreamed about endless strings of spaghetti dripping with rich meat sauce and mountains of whipped cream pies.

Were my dreams that night prophetic of the future—of the days when I would be free again, walk through the streets of a city, and once more eat bread? For, though I did not know it then as I slept, it was the last night we were to spend in the Cage. At dawn the next day—the thirteenth day—a terrific shouting awakened us. I felt Ron shaking me and heard him whispering: "The Japs . . . they're telling us to get ready to go. . . . Hurry up."

Nothing was real anymore: neither the coming here, nor the waiting, nor the sudden going. Now where were we going? To another jail—this time the dread Fort Santiago? . . . Now we were filing out of the Cage—Banks, shaky and deathly pale and gaunt, Tony still swaggering, dirty, and unkempt, Ron and myself. . . . But the Filipinos remained squatting there as we had first seen them and their smiles flashed bravely at us as they silently bid us farewell until I could no longer see them for the tears blinding me. I have often thought of them since, and wondered if they ever came out alive to see their forces victorious.

We were lined up before the desk now, and the clerk was calling our names and when we stepped forward, he handed Ron and me our passports. It was a good omen, I thought, as we followed the officer out of the house and the Cage forever into the shining morning light and sun.

11

AFTERMATH

A TRAIN WHISTLE CUTTING THE STILLNESS OF THE LONG NIGHTS in the jail, piercing the hard stone walls of the dungeon and the bars of the Cage, came to me out of the freedom of the night and journey through space. Slowly I lifted my head and listened, and as I listened, I felt once more the joy and the hope that all was not yet lost. I was speeding through the night away from the jail, away from the Japs, away, away. . . . I was a child again, feeling the magic of the train like a great chariot flying through space, stopping at strange places, filled with strange people and faces. . . . I was free again. . . . This was the miracle wrought by the sound of the train in the night, and even as I lay in the jail, I had felt that as long as I could hear this sound, there was still hope, and somehow I knew that it was on a train that we would leave this place forever.

And so it was: We were on a train at last, leaving San Fernando, Pampanga, heading for Manila—perhaps for Santo Tomas, perhaps for Fort Santiago, who knew? But this morning I did not care, as long as we were leaving the dreaded Cage and the Japanese military police behind us. There were six of us on the train—a Japanese lieutenant and his guard, Banks and Tony, and Ron and myself, on this Filipino train crowded with Filipinos staring at me with frightened, curious, and pitying eyes, seeing an American woman in a rumpled black suit, her long black hair framing a pale, haggard face with burning eyes; a tall, thin, fair-haired man with a bushy beard, ragged dirty-white trousers flapping over his dirty bare feet; and two handcuffed soldiers—one tall and gaunt with a black beard that made him look like Abraham Lincoln, the other short and stocky, dressed in khaki. The lieutenant, dressed smartly in well-tailored uniform and shining black boots, sat stiffly across the aisle from us with the soldier, watching us out of the corner of his eyes, as though he expected us to make a frantic dash through the moving train window and escape.

On the train speeding towards Manila—a Manila that I had not seen for eighteen long months, a Manila that I had dreamed about through those desolate afternoons as I stared at the barren mountains, and through those endless nights in the jails—green fields flashing by, a Filipino farmer plowing through his rice field with his carabao, and the sudden joy of release surging up in me as I stared out at this Filipino earth that has become forever a part of me, and the train speeding on, the wheels turning, and at last the slowing down.

We were at the station in the city of Manila and we were following the lieutenant through a maze of milling people, staring with pity and fear at the "Americano" prisoners of the Japs. Then we were walking through the crowded streets, on and on until at last we came to a massive stone building that looked like a prison.

The Jap stopped abruptly, and my heart almost stopped with him, as he spoke questioningly to the soldier: "Bilibid?" (Another prison, I thought with horror.) We were entering the gate . . . "Bilibid—" Banks whispered to me. . . . It was the same pattern and the courtyard. . . . but how could they bring civilians here?

Suddenly I saw a tall, fair, husky American in clean shirt and shorts and wearing a pith helmet coming toward us. He bowed slightly to the lieutenant and glanced significantly at us, and then he did a remarkable thing: We were standing on a kind of little porch in the courtyard where there were a few chairs and the American pulled over one of the chairs towards me, motioning for me to sit down. The whole pantomime took merely a few moments, and I may only have imagined that the Jap noticed it . . . but for me that simple gesture suddenly brought back a world that I had forgotten, where men looked upon women as more than mere appendages and cherished and took care of them. For months I had been a captive of the Japanese, and I had been made to feel like their women, to be held in contempt or ignored. I stared at the American in wonder, for in that gesture of offering me the chair, he had made me feel in that moment that I had come home to my own people at last.

"Two soldiers—" the Jap said curtly, pointing to Banks and Tony, "coming to Bilibid. This one—" he waved in Ron's direction, "coming to Santo Tomas. With wife—" he added.

The American must have known my joy that welled into tears at that moment—the first moment we had heard the spoken word that we were actually going to Santo Tomas—for he grinned at me happily as the lieutenant turned to go. And as we followed him, we bade a silent farewell and good luck to Banks and Tony. I never saw Banks again.

Out on the street the lieutenant turned to the guard and said something in Japanese. The soldier bowed and then started off down the street where we saw him strutting through the traffic and waving at a passing *carromata*. It stopped and he got in and came riding back to us. I stared at it unbelievingly—I had forgotten that there were still *carromatas* in the city; the little carriage seemed to belong so much to my pre-war world of Manila, when I used to ride in them as a lark after classes at the University, drive along Dewey Boulevard and stare out at the bay glittering in the tropical sun. Now we were sitting in a *carromata,* prisoners of two Japs, riding to the concentration camp at Santo Tomas, just as if we were going for an afternoon drive, and I thought sadly of the Saturday afternoons when we would explore the twisting narrow lanes with their Chinese shops and strange restaurants.

We rattled down a broad avenue and at every crossing we saw pill-boxes built of sandbags, but except for the yellow-painted Japanese trucks there was very little traffic and few people. The throbbing heart of the Manila I remembered seemed to have slowed down to a faint, sleepy beat. For a few blocks, we drove along a long low concrete wall, and then we stopped before a gate with a pillbox and a Japanese sentry with fixed bayonet. The lieutenant stuck his head out of the *carromata* and yelled in Japanese; the sentry bowed and motioned the *carromata* driver in through the gate. We drove down a wide roadway lined with trees, beyond which stretched green level lawns, until we came to a gray Spanish-style building with a cross on top of its domed tower. We were at Santo Tomas.

And because I had dreamed of it so long, I could not believe in the reality of that strange afternoon: It was too much for my mind, which only a few hours before had been steeped in the horrors of the Cage, to accept as reality this well-ordered place with its neat clean lawns and the people—*my* people—walking about freely, looking at us curiously. I stared at them in amazement—clean-shaven men in clean shorts and shoes, and the women, so elegant to me in their well-tailored blouses and slacks that they seemed to belong to another world. . . . I saw some of the women gather in a knot across the road and glance at us, talking among themselves. I felt like singing or shouting for joy but I only smiled at them radiantly as we followed the Japs down the road towards a smaller building. At the door hung a sign, "Office of the Commandant," and in smaller letters, "Only those on official business may enter." The lieutenant pushed open the door and we followed him in. A tall, well-built, black-haired man who looked British rose from a table as we entered and came to meet us.

The Japanese commandant looked up as we approached, staring at us as the British-looking man began to talk to him in Japanese; he did not say anything in reply, just nodded from time to time, then he waved his hand as though to dismiss us. We followed the interpreter to his desk near the door.

"It's all right now—you're formally registered at Santo Tomas. Now I'll turn you over to the Administration Committee and you'll be on your own."

As we approached the entrance of the gray building, a woman suddenly broke away from a group watching from the roadway, ran up to us and threw her arms around me, crying: "Thank God you're alive! Don't you remember me? Mrs. Jenks? I lived in the room next to yours at the Manila Hotel." She turned to the interpreter. "Let me take her to the showers and give her some clean clothes and some food before she goes through all the red tape. She looks as if she'll faint—"

I was in a happy daze; listening to well-modulated English voices instead of the singsong of the Japanese was like hearing music again, and walking through the corridor of the University among groups of white faces, I felt I had entered into a strange, wonderful world, clean, civilized, and well ordered. That first day in Santo Tomas, I did not see that already these "civilized" people were beginning to feel like zombies in their regimented; confined existences, slowly dying of starvation and their waiting, endless waiting, through the long weary days of the eighteen months they had been prisoners. But we had arrived at a most fortunate time in Santo Tomas. We escaped the chaos of the first weeks and months when thousands of people had been thrown into a dirty unsanitary building, without adequate bedding or medical facilities or food. Without the Philippine Red Cross, hundreds of people would have died outright, for the Japanese military did not begin to send in supplies until months afterwards. The internees, both men and women, had made a fairly livable place out of the old University: They had built several kitchens, a clinic and a hospital, a school and a library, and even fixed up the outdated plumbing with showers.

We had arrived during the period when Hirohito declared his policy of "clemency and forgiveness" towards prisoners of war—probably the only reason we were brought into Santo Tomas alive. And the Japanese military had said: "As long as we are victorious, we can afford to be magnanimous." They were still allowing the Filipinos to send in food to the Americans and granting passes for sick persons to get treatment at outside hospitals.

After the miracle of a shower and a clean towel, my body seemed reborn; I had felt I could never wash off the horror and filth of those months in the Japanese jails. Mrs. Jenks was waiting with a bathrobe and slippers, and led me through the long corridor to her room. Instead of doors, a curtain hung at the entrance of each room. Mrs. Jenks pulled a straw basket from under her bed and took out a dress.

"Here—I guess this will fit you—you've gotten so thin you're about my size," she said. "What do you want to do with the rags you're wearing?"

The dress was size 12 and while I had usually worn 16, I could easily slip it on.[1]

"Burn them if you can," I replied.

"Good idea. Guess I can get the men on the kitchen detail to do it—" She looked at me critically. "I suppose you could do with some lipstick and powder," she said and pointed to the mirror over the bed.

I stared at myself incredulously: It was the first real-sized mirror I had seen in a year and a half, and I felt at that moment as though I were meeting a stranger—this pale, thin woman with the dark rings under enormous eyes. I hoped Mrs. Jenks would not notice my trembling fingers as I applied the lipstick and powder.

"Relax," she said. "You look fine. Let's go and have something to eat, then we'll meet the men."

It was about three in the afternoon. "Can you get food here at this time?" I asked, surprised.

[1] Editor's note: The approximate equivalent of dropping from a size 8 to a size 4 today.

"Not officially," she replied. "The chow line starts at five. But there are places where we can still get something—"

We went through a hallway that skirted a little patio in the center of the building. I caught a glimpse of grass shacks with tables and chairs ringing the little garden in the middle of the patio. There were people everywhere, hurrying through the halls, washing dishes at the faucets, or sitting idly in their shacks. In back of the kitchen we came to a rather large shack of bamboo with several tables and chairs placed as in a restaurant. In the corner, a man was cooking over a charcoal stove.

"What would you like?"

"What can we get?"

"No steaks or french fries, but you can get hotcakes and eggs— How about it?" I must have looked slightly dazed, for she called out without waiting for my answer: "Jo, one order of hotcakes—the works—and two coffees." Mrs. Jenks took a Rosita cigarette from a straw cigarette case and offered me one. "Don't think the Japs give us this for chow. Hell, no . . ." She puffed vigorously at her cigarette. "These are only the extras for people who can afford it. Some men like Jo have opened up little restaurants like this to make some money."

"Where do they get the food?"

"Buy it from the Filipinos outside—contact them at the gate. It's possible to get a limited amount of stuff like flour and eggs, which, of course, the Japs would never supply for us."

"What do you get on the line?"

"Two meals a day—mush for breakfast, rice and mungo beans for supper. Sometimes they add a banana with the mush, and a little meat with the rice. And some watery coffee or tea—dishwater—ugh!" She made a face. "But the beginning was the worst. You should've seen this place when the Japs dumped us in here—filthy bathrooms with broken plumbing, no beds—we slept on the floor for days—no nets, no blankets. . . . It was awful! But I guess it wasn't as bad as what you went through." She looked at me with an avid, expectant expression. "They didn't—uh—rape you or anything, did they?"

"No—"

Here were the hotcakes and syrup and eggs. I had not eaten them since Labug and the eggs made me think of my chicken, and I was glad she at least was free somewhere in the mountains. Before I began to eat, I just wanted to stare at the plate, not touch it, but after I finished, I wanted to lick the plate clean. The coffee was marvelous. Mrs. Jenks offered me another cigarette, and I leaned back, satisfied at last. Mrs. Jenks rose. "We'd better get you to the Administration Office or you won't have a room to sleep in tonight—or a bed . . ."

She stopped to pay Jo one peso for the hotcakes, forty centavos for two coffees. "Luckily I brought some money in here with me. Filipino friends were very generous too."

I almost did not recognize Ron standing in the doorway of the main building. He was dressed in clean khaki shorts and a beautiful new blue shirt, and when I came closer I saw that he had had a bath and a shave and his beard was trimmed like a Van Dyke. He grinned when he saw me.

"Hello, Beautiful," he said. "Where did you get the dress?"

"And where did you get the blue shirt?" I countered.

The interpreter led us to a large room on the right where a thin woman with horn-rimmed glasses behind one of the many desks looked up.

"Your room will be No. 54 on the third floor," she said pleasantly, "but I'm afraid your husband will have to sleep for the time being in the gym because there's no room in this building now."

"You mean we're going to be separated?" I asked, startled.

"Why yes—all married couples are separated in Santo Tomas. It's a Japanese rule."

Suddenly I wanted to laugh—I remembered the Jap pervert asking: "Why you no have babies?"

Everything was wonderful that first day in Santo Tomas, the Santo Tomas I was to grow to hate with horror and fear, with the same hatred that these thousands of internees felt after a year and a half; for whereas to me that day it was a haven from the Japs, to them it was a grim and frightful prison surrounded by a yellow concrete wall.

Once in my room, I sank down on the straw mattress of the bed, and wanted to lie there forever—after the hard wooden floor of the Cage, it was heavenly. I opened my eyes for a moment and saw the curious glances from the women around me. Miss Kane, the Monitor of the room, sat down at the edge of my bed and said in a whisper: "Be careful what you say here—don't talk much. But there is one woman here to be trusted completely—a missionary, Ruth Harris."

She called to a white-haired woman with a sweet, youthful face and spectacles. "Ruth, won't you come here a moment?"

"Of course." The woman smiled, put down her book, and came over to my bed.

"Ruth," said Miss Kane. "Would you happen to have an extra sheet for Mrs. Johnston? And a pillow case?"

I was to find out in the months to come that whatever Ruth had she shared. She was known as the "angel." Ruth brought me not only a sheet and a pillowcase but a Bible as well; I had often wanted one in those months in the jail and I accepted it gladly. I felt a curious thing that I could not analyze—now that we finally had been brought to Santo Tomas and were comparatively safe, I felt a strange sense of gratitude to the gods or a God who had seen us through and I also noticed another strange thing—that here among all these people, the pagan feeling I had had in the mountains had disappeared. I began to wonder whether I, the agnostic, was becoming religious. But the real bond of friendship between Ruth and myself began when I learned that she also had spent some time in a Japanese jail down in Iloilo, when she and the rest of the Baptist group had been rounded up after living in the hills for a few months. After that, we could talk freely to each other about our experiences, and it was a relief to be able to talk to someone who understood.

I had been lying on the bed about ten minutes or so when a thin, bird-like face appeared through the curtain and a treble voice piped: "Is there a Mrs. Johnston here?"

As I stared at this thin gray little woman I had the strange uncanny sensation that Proust must have had when he wrote about the friends of his youth growing old in *Remembrance of Things Past*. The only recollection I had of Professor Benton's wife was that of a plump, comfortable housewife. Two years earlier she had come from Ann Arbor to join her husband for the year he was to teach engineering as an exchange professor. He had been a very good friend during the time I taught at the University of the Philippines.

"My dear, you had better come along and eat with us tonight—we'll give you plates and things. Where are you meeting your husband?"

"At the entrance to the main building at five."

"It's almost that now—the chow line must have started. Let's go."

As we walked down the corridors, Mrs. Benton chattered excitedly. "It's such a pity you were assigned to Room 54! It's the worst room in the building." She lowered her voice somewhat. "It has a simply terrible reputation—and the most awful characters in Santo Tomas—you'll have to be most careful—" She whispered: "There is that Shanghai prostitute—'Shanghai Lil' they call her, although her real name is Ruby Heller. She just got back from Mandaluyong, the Filipino insane asylum. Her behavior in camp was so frightful that nobody could control her—neither our Committee nor the Japs—she'd scream and rave at all of them. So the Japs just packed her off there. She was there about six months. They say she's much quieter now."

We descended the main staircase to the lobby. I caught sight of Ron in front of a large bulletin board. As we followed Mrs. Benton down the hallway towards the kitchen, we passed long lines of men, women, and children waiting with plates and tin cans.

"Chow line," said Mrs. Benton. "But I don't think they've started serving yet."

The Bentons' table was almost at the end of the corridor. It was next to a window that looked out directly on the patio. Above the table was a little cupboard where Mrs. Benton kept her dishes and silverware. It looked very trim and neat, and was even stocked with a few cans of meat and peanut butter and soup.

"We received a Canadian kit from the British government last Christmas," she said. "I still have a few cans left—hoard them for an emergency . . . in case Harry gets sick or something—Oh, here he comes now . . . recognize him?"

Professor Benton seemed to have aged ten years in the last year; his thin flesh hung in loose folds about his sunken cheeks. His face lit up when he saw us.

"The Johnstons—certainly good to see you—we'd given you up for lost. Let me look at you. Not too bad—proud of you for sticking out so long." He beamed, "We'd better eat now—you two must be starved. Come along with me," he said to Ron. "We'll get the chow and let the women do the dishes later."

"Does everybody have a table like this?" I asked Mrs. Benton.

"No, most of the people just eat on the tables and benches outside. The really lucky ones are those with the shanties—they eat there. But they can't sleep there—Jap rule—the women have to return to the main building in time for roll call at night."

"How come some have shanties and others don't?" I asked.

"Money and influence," she said indignantly. "Another thing that's been very bad—the morals of the young—the teenagers. In the beginning they used to lie around in the grass at night—didn't care about people seeing them or anything. Simply *disgraceful!* The Committee couldn't do a thing—the Japs had to issue all kinds of orders—about no unseemly displays of affection in public—that sort of thing."

"The Committee?"

"The Committee that represents us in dealing with the Japs. But they're so ineffectual . . ." She looked down the hall. "Here come the men with the chow. Now don't expect too much, but it'll be better than what the Japs fed you in the jail, I guess."

Ron had a tin can in each hand, while the Professor carried a tray. Two plates of rice, another of mungo beans with a sprinkling of tiny bits of meat, and a few *calamansi* (the Philippines lemon).

"Tea or coffee?" I asked Ron.

"Tea and *calamansi*—"

"What about sugar?" I turned to Mrs. Benton.

"We draw rations of brown sugar or *panocha* (sugar cakes) some-times—" She carefully divided the rice and beans on our four plates. As a special treat in our honor Mrs. Benton opened up a can of straw-berry jam she had been hoarding and some crackers in a tin. After-wards I helped her clear up and stack the things on the tray. We took them to washing troughs behind the kitchen, where people stood in line awaiting their turn to wash their dishes.

"I suppose there's a line for everything," I said.

"Yes," she sighed. "Everything. Even the toilets—that's the worst. Things are much better now though—in the beginning there were hundreds of women on one floor using the same few toilets. It was horrible!"

The Professor and Ron were waiting in the lobby, now jammed with people. The Professor took some folding chairs from a great pile stacked against the wall. They were painted with his name in big green letters. "I have an extra one somewhere," he said. "And maybe we can find a stool for Ron."

Outside on the grounds people were sitting in their chairs, read-ing or talking or knitting. Luxuriously I lay back in my chair and stared at the sky splashed with great streaks of pink and mauve and gold arch-ing over the camp and I thought of the mountains and the guerrillas still fighting. . . . The Professor was smoking a pipe and Mrs. Benton knitted. Ron gave me a cigarette from a new pack of Rositas. Sitting among these staid, comfortable people, I had a very pleasant feeling of safety and security. I heard the Professor's voice droning on:

"This camp was a wonderful opportunity for experimenting in cooperative living, in sharing alike, in planning. In the beginning many of us hoped that everything—money, food, clothes—would be pooled and shared equally." He sighed. "But unfortunately, it degenerated into the old dog-eat-dog philosophy. Those people with money can get almost anything—liquor, food, women—even bribe Jap guards—while the poor are starving to death on the chow line. If it hadn't been for the Filipinos, many of us would be dead by now—most of us have managed by living on what they bring through the gate. I'll never forget the first day when the Japs brought us here, how the Filipinos started throwing things over the wall to us—mattresses, *petates* (straw mats) chickens, fruits, cans of food, anything they could—until the Japs put a stop to it."

"What about money? Can you send notes and money out to Filipinos to buy things?"

"Yes—if you've got it. Some people haven't been so lucky—they were stuck without any funds at all."

"What did they do for money?" asked Ron.

"The Committee has arranged a system of loans that you guarantee to repay after the war," Professor Benton replied. "Some people have been making money in the camp—through concessions like laundries or shoe repairing or making candy or running restaurants."

Through the gathering darkness I heard music. I sat up. "What's that?" I asked.

"Concert over our amplifier," the Professor said.

Music . . . the light airy magic of a Chopin polonaise.

"You mean you lived in that prison thirteen days with ten men?" I saw several people turn to stare and Mrs. Benton lowered her voice to a whisper. "I'm sorry, I forgot where I was for a moment. . . . Those barbarians—some day they'll pay for it! How did you ever live through it?" she cried. "And now they put you in Room 54! My dear, it's a good thing you're used to almost anything . . . the scum of that room! There's that Viennese girl who tried to commit suicide by drinking iodine—the women caught her in time and got her to the hospital. She was estranged from her husband—a nice British boy, they say, right here in the camp too—and took to flirting with every man. The Monitor of the room next to yours—a room for men—caught her trying to climb into the bed of a Norwegian sailor in the middle of the night. There was a terrible scandal and I suppose she just couldn't take it."

"Did anyone ever try to escape?" I heard Ron ask.

"Three British men," replied the Professor. "The Japs tortured them right here—we could hear them screaming—then shot them. Another scare we had was when the Japs rounded up some Army men posing as civilians in the camp and took them out in trucks. Nobody knows where they went . . ."

His words were drowned out by the wild, stirring music of the Liszt Hungarian Rhapsody. Music . . . more than anything else during those long months in the mountains had I missed music.

"And I think one of the girls from that room was just taken to Hospicio San José," Mrs. Benton was saying, "to wait until her baby's born . . ."

I sat up startled.

"Baby? What do you mean?"

"Well—you know the Japs passed a rule recently that all pregnant women must go to the island—it's an Old Men's Home—until their babies are born. And the man is jailed for thirty days here in camp."

"Even husbands?"

"Doesn't matter—they're not exempt . . . thirty days in jail."

I learned later that one of the women affected by the Japs' fantastic ruling concerning pregnancies was my friend Grace Nash, who was well known as a violinist in Manila. She was the mother of two children and had been permitted by the Japs to live outside the camp for some months because of illness and her husband was allowed to visit her from time to time. When the Japs ordered all such privileged internees back into camp, Grace was pregnant with her third child and was sent to the Old Men's Home. During her confinement, she wrote a song (to be sung to the tune of *Solomon Levi*) commemorating the ordeal:

We are four pregnant women
And we come from Santo Tomas,
The Japanese are mad at us
Because we have done thus,
Our husbands have been put in jail,
Our children taken too,
And all because the Japs now say:
To propagate—no can do.

Chorus
We're with the old men
Living at San José,
We all eat together but
Three meager meals a day.
Here we get our liver shots
And iron cocktails too,
And in between some vitamin B
With all that it can do.

Second Verse
Now we must confess to you
Our duties here are nil
But sit and think and knit and sit

Of which we've had our fill.
But also we must say to you
That we have not lost face
Because we're doing all we can
To propagate the race.

Mrs. Benton continued: "We have our own jail. It's a barred room in the main building. The Committee sentences our lawbreakers. Of course that doesn't apply to women—they're usually just confined to their rooms."

The music split into a final frenzy of sound, like a great wave bursting against a rock, leaving the night suddenly empty and still.

The Professor rose. "That's the end of the concert."

The lobby of the main building was jammed with people moving slowly towards the stairs. Ron had left me at the entrance—he had to go in the opposite direction, across the camps to the gymnasium. It was the first night we had been separated since that terrible night in the dungeon and I felt rather forlorn, even among all these people, as I made my way through the crowds to the third floor.

In Room 54 the women were putting up their mosquito nets. Ruth Harris came up to me when I entered. "Better get your bed fixed before roll call. The lights go out soon afterwards. I'll help you." As we were tying up the net we heard the big gong announcing nine o'clock roll call and I had a sensation of being in a girl's dormitory.

Miss Kane stood in the center of the room and called out the names. I looked curiously at the woman who responded to the name of Ruby Heller (alias Shanghai Lil). With a cheap flowery kimono drawn tight around her slatternly figure, she did look like a prostitute. Her face was dead white against the curly black hair that fell loosely around her shoulders and her eyes had a nervous, rather frightened look.

When Miss Kane had finished, she looked through some papers in her hand and said:

"The only announcement tonight is from the Sanitation Committee which reports that the problem of flies is getting more and more serious with the spread of amoebic dysentery. They ask you all to cooperate and be very careful with your dishes and garbage disposal. That's all for tonight."

It was incredible: the problem of flies—I was thinking again of the filth and the degradation and the horror of the Cage—surely I must be dreaming now, to be in this world where flies were a serious "problem."

Some women were already retiring under their nets, while others were going out into the hall. Miss Kane stopped by my bed and asked whether I would like to sit outside for a while, until the lights went out. In the hall it was still very bright and lively. At the tables by the window, bridge players were absorbed in their games and others stood and looked on. Women in housecoats sat talking or reading or knitting. Miss Kane offered me a cigarette and we sat there smoking.

"I'm glad they sent you to our room," she said. "We need another American woman—we've got the melting pot of the Orient in there . . . Eurasians, both Jap and Chinese, and all kinds of mestiza combinations, plus the riffraff of the China coast. I've had my hands full—" she smiled grimly.

"Japanese Eurasians?" I asked.

"Yes—Japanese mother, American or British father—we've got two in this room. We've been worried about Jap informers and spies among us. It's been ghastly—the whole year. I've often wished I was in the hills myself . . . but that must have been even worse, I suppose. Take your time about getting assigned to a job—you need a rest."

"Job?"

"Yes—everybody has to work here—the women two or three hours a day; the men sometimes longer—it depends on the kind of work you do. But you'd better go to the hospital tomorrow for a physical check-up. And, by the way, if you need sanitary napkins or anything like that—and you probably do—I'll give you a slip and you can pick them up. Flannel cloths the Red Cross sent in to us. We have a special washing detail for that." She sighed. "I'm so weary of all these details . . . the same monotonous grind every day. Thank God I have my dancing—it makes me forget sometimes. I teach a class in ballet—also some modern dancing. I did it before the war in Manila."

The lights went out and Miss Kane rose. "Time for bed now. You must be tired after your long trip—and all the excitement."

I followed her into the room, now shadowy with the white blur of nets and moving figures, and undressed and crawled into bed. As I lay there staring at the walls of my net, I was seized by a terrible feeling of claustrophobia, shut in this room with all these people. . . . I wanted to get up and escape. My body was throbbing, my nerves were as taut as electric wires. I could not sleep. I jumped out of bed, put on my dress, and went out into the dark hall.

The hall was deserted now, except for an occasional woman in a bathrobe and slippers walking towards the toilet at the end of the corridor. I went to the window and stared out at the sky. It was a dark, starless night and no moon was visible, only whitish clouds scudding over the blackness. I thought of the city behind the concrete wall ringing the concentration camp, and the hills beyond, and the desperate struggle even now taking place in those hills, and the Jap jails filled with the men and women being tortured, the cries in the night . . . and suddenly I felt that I would never be able to sleep again. I had seen and suffered and lived through too much. I would never have peace again. I thought of the monotonous deadly waiting of these people, day after day and I was glad then of that year and a half in the mountains—at least it had been wild and free and we had seen the tide of resistance slowly rising against the Japs.

I began to pace up and down the silent deserted hall and I smoked cigarette after cigarette until I thought I would go mad in my nervous frenzy. Then I saw a man down the hall and as he came closer, I saw that he was wearing an armband. It was the night patrolman. He stopped when he saw me.

"What's the matter? Can't sleep?"

"No—"

"Would you like an aspirin?"

"Yes, thanks."

He took two pills from a small box in his pocket.

"Here you are. Always carry 'em for the women—" He disappeared down the hall.

I walked in the opposite direction to the water fountain and swallowed the aspirins. Then I lit another cigarette and smoked it to the end. I went back to my room and crawled under the net and fell asleep at last.

The next morning, after a breakfast of corn mush and bananas with the Professor and his wife, I went with Mrs. Benton to the clinic for a check-up. The hospital and main clinic were about a quarter of a kilometer down the road, to the right of which was shantytown, as it was called: a picturesque conglomeration of tiny shacks made of nipa or grass or cogon that the internees had built. Waiting for our turn outside the clinic, I saw Roy Bennett, editor of the *Manila Daily Bulletin,* and as he hobbled over to greet me, I was shocked at his terribly altered condition. Only about six months earlier he had come in from Fort Santiago, where the Japanese had held him prisoner for almost a year. He had never expected to come out alive and said he was more dead than alive when they finally brought him in. He had only just checked out of the hospital, where he had been recuperating for the past few months. We compared notes on our prison experiences, and I found that Fort Santiago was much like the Cage—both were under the dread Kempetai or Jap Gestapo. As we talked in low voices, a rather striking woman with a strong intelligent face and mannish haircut approached Bennett and greeted him. Roy introduced her:

"This is Mrs. Hornbustel—her husband was on Corregidor and now he's a prisoner somewhere."

Mrs. Hornbustel smiled and I remembered that smile two years later when I saw it again in newsreel films in America: She was the woman who contracted leprosy in Santo Tomas and was now at last with her husband, who had asked permission to join her.

We had expected to find that we had picked up all sorts of diseases in the Jap jails, but except for loss of weight and a low blood count, the doctor found nothing organically wrong with either of us.

"Amazing how you were able to come through it so well," he said. "Better get your teeth checked at the dentist's next door."

Again I was amazed at the efficiency the Americans had shown in organizing their medical facilities within the limitations the Japanese had imposed. Next door to the hospital, across the hall, was the dentist's office. The dentist commented on the good job the Filipino dentist had done. "You were very lucky—you would have had to have most of your front teeth out otherwise."

We spent the next week getting adjusted to the bewildering routine of the camp—endless waiting in lines until I thought sometimes I would prefer to walk twenty kilometers in the jungle than wait in another line . . .

The woman to whom I reported at the Work Committee suggested I take my time about working and find something in which I was really interested and would fit in with my professional background. I did not mention my newspaper or broadcasting work because I thought the less this was known in the camp the better, and the less chance of it leaking out to the Japs. I stressed only my educational work—teaching at the University and psychological work in the United States.

"You could always teach a class in our high school or college English," she said.

"You actually have a high school and college in the camp?"

"Everything from grade school for the children to college and the work will be credited for the students when they leave . . . that makes them take it all the more seriously."

"Don't the Japs interfere?"

"They put up certain restrictions as to subjects and subject matter, particularly in history, but otherwise we have a fairly free hand. I suggest you see the head of our Education Department, Dr. Engels and see where you can fit in."

Dr. René Engels was a short, white-haired little Frenchman, who had been a research scientist for the Benguet Mining People before the war. I was to find that he was also an accomplished musician. He was tremendously interested in psychology and suggested I try to work with the children in the camp.

"Of course, everyone—both adults and children—are problems in Santo Tomas," he said with a cynical smile. Then shrugging his shoulders, *"Mais, que faire?* We have a missionary who discusses problems with adults, but the children have been badly neglected."

So I became the child psychologist of the concentration camp and every morning from nine to twelve, worked with the problem children—bad boys who would not learn in class, little mestiza girls with deep-rooted inferiority complexes. I would take them out of school and bring them into the garden and work with them there—painting, drawing, reading, and teaching.

And so we became two of the 5,000 prisoners of Santo Tomas and after a few weeks Ron and I felt as if we had been there for years. We were treated for cuts and tropical ulcers that we had never dreamed of treating in the mountains and were given shots for cholera, typhoid, and dysentery, and "dewormed" regularly. This "deworming"—a ghastly procedure that necessitated taking an extremely bitter medicine after which one could not eat for twelve hours—was accepted as one of the necessary evils of Santo Tomas, and almost every internee had been dewormed at one time or another in the course of the year. To this day, when I think of Santo Tomas I think of worms—worms wriggling through the mush and rice. And also think of bedbugs—flagellated by the ever-vigilant

Sanitation Committee, we were always either looking for or killing
bedbugs.

In the ten months we remained in Santo Tomas, we saw conditions
in the camp grow more horrible every day as the Japanese, infuriated
by their military losses, vented their anger upon the civilian internees
and prisoners of war. One of the first retaliatory measures was to close
the "gate" to the Filipinos who had been supplying us with fresh food
and the few essentials to keep us alive. On a few occasions we had even
been able to see Fabian and his brothers, who brought us a basket of
food—chicken, adobo, papaya, chicos—and tobacco. Many of the
older internees, who had become dependent upon this extra food,
now had to exist solely on the chow line, which became worse and
worse. The hospital cases mounted by the hundreds, out of all pro-
portion to the medical supplies and facilities, which were dangerous-
ly low, and the death rate jumped alarmingly. The Japs forced the
American doctors to change the "starvation" on the death certificate to
"prolonged illness." Epidemics of children's diseases came in waves and
during one period the camp was in the grip of a terrible panic when
there were a few cases of polio. One of the victims was a young chap
of about twenty-five—a great, husky, strapping man who had been
doing some of the heaviest work in the camp on the garbage detail: He
died after one day of agony.

We were finally reduced to rice and fish, varying from the tiny little *tuyo* fish to just fish bones, and the camp began to stink of fish, fish,
fish, and squads of men were put on "fish details" to clean the fish. . . .
I believe the only thing that saved the internees from death at that time
and during the terrible year to come was the arrival of the comfort
kits from America around Christmas of that year (1943)—the first of
these kits to reach American prisoners since the outbreak of the war,
even though we heard later the United States had tried to negotiate for
the monthly shipment of such supplies via Vladivostok. Before we
came to Santo Tomas, the internees had received one small Canadian

kit, but nothing since then. To Ron and myself, the kit was a godsend; we had not had such food for years—Klim, corned beef and Spam, canned butter and jams; and cigarettes, tobacco, and pipes for the men and lipstick, cold cream, hairbrushes, dresses, and shoes for the women. For weeks the camp was in a frenzy of excitement and activity—eating, talking, and trading kit foods . . .

In the spring of that year, the Japanese already had seen the handwriting on the wall and had ordered all allied nationals who for one reason or another were still outside the camp to be interned, with the result that Santo Tomas became more and more crowded as the months went by. Apparently the Japs had foreseen this emergency, for some months before our arrival they had detailed a hundred of our able-bodied young men to build barracks for another camp at Los Banos, thirty miles south of Manila on the ground of the Agricultural College of the University of the Philippines. This camp, however, was to be mainly for younger people, and married couples without children. We were amazed also to hear that the Japs planned to allow couples to live together there instead of being separated as in Santo Tomas. The first group of internees left for Los Banos about Christmas 1943; Ron and myself were in the second group, assigned to go in May of 1944. We were glad to leave Santo Tomas, which was growing more fearful by the hour, with its disease and starvation and death—and if we had no great expectations of a change for the better, at least Los Banos would mean a trip beyond the hated "wall."

It was still dark as our fleet of Japanese trucks rumbled through the dim deserted streets of Manila, and I felt the tears blinding me as I remembered that more than two years had already passed since the day we had first left it, and we were still prisoners of the Japs and on our way to another concentration camp. The darkness merged into the blue light of the early dawn, and a few solitary Filipinos, roused by the rumbling of the trucks in the stillness, emerged to stare silently at us as we drove past.

At noon we arrived at Los Banos and the beauty of this spot immediately struck us. Against the background of the hills curving in the distance, the white buildings of the Agricultural College rose in the center, and beyond stretched the long rows of barracks. Made of swali and bamboo with nipa roofs, the barracks were neatly divided into cubicles partitioned by thin paper-wood walls. Each barrack was equipped with rough quarters for toilets and communal showers.

If we had hoped for any privacy at Los Banos we were disillusioned. Ron and I were assigned to Barrack No. 6, Cubicle 15, and soon discovered that our neighbors on our left were the Viennese girl who had attempted suicide in Santo Tomas and her husband, with whom she had become reconciled; and on our right was a Korean woman who had developed a case of hysterical paralysis and could not walk. And between the squeals of the over-sexed Viennese girl and the moaning of the Korean woman, I thought I would go mad. . . . But I was unusually lucky: I found two missionary women sharing a cubicle at the extreme end of our barracks with a full view of the hills beyond our camp and I persuaded them to change with us. And in the long months to come, as life became unbearably dependent upon the slightest sound, when you could hear even the breathing of the person beyond the wall, I was glad I had been able to make that change. There was only one disadvantage—when I ate my mush in the mornings and looked out at the hills, I often found myself staring at the immobile figure of a Jap sentry watching at his post near the barbed wire that surrounded the camp.

It was good to be away from the unhealthy diseased air of Manila and good to be out of Santo Tomas even though it had meant going from one prison to another, and it was good to see the hills again. Los Banos was much more alive than Santo Tomas, where one constantly had that sense of inevitable death, watching the old people slowly dying off day by day.

And as in Santo Tomas, schools were organized for the children of all age groups and I continued my work as child psychologist. Later I supplemented this with lectures on psychology and when Ron began to give lectures on philosophy, we became known as the "philosophy-psychology pair." We had a fairly good library, where I was able to do some research, and I could also get material from my friends, Ruth and Eric Fisher, who had managed somehow to bring many of their books into camp.

It was mainly due to my work in psychology that George Gray of the Committee staff asked me to act as the woman judge of Los Banos. I hesitated a long time for I knew that under the terrible conditions in the camp, it would be extremely difficult to judge any human being's action. In the beginning, the cases were mainly those girls or women charged with petty disorders—breaking siesta rules or refusing to report for work details. But as time went on and the situation grew really desperate, charges of stealing food or clothes from other internees began to come up more frequently. Shanghai Lil had somehow engineered a transfer to Los Banos and was living with some other character in a cubicle in our barracks, and she could be heard frequently commenting with raw gusto and in a sailor's vernacular on conditions in the camp. She was hauled up a few times for getting into brawls. Towards the end of our internment, she began to grow unusually patriotic and could be heard shouting about the "Jap bastards" and "what the Americans would do to them when they arrive," and it took considerable threatening to keep her quiet. Another girl who was repeatedly brought into court was a beautiful little tramp from the China coast, who was a prostitute, a kleptomaniac, and a lesbian all in one. She became somewhat chastened when the man with whom she was having a current affair refused to marry her and she was left pregnant and confined to her barracks for thirty days for stealing another woman's slip in the bathroom.

One of the most amazing cases of the Los Banos "court," which revealed the really incredible conditions at the time, was that of the young American, a big powerful fellow with curly blonde hair who was charged with "inhuman and barbarous conduct" in stealing and eating a dog—"the beloved pet" of the couple who made the accusations. The case was dismissed finally on the grounds that the charge of stealing was unfounded since dogs could not be considered "private property" in a concentration camp, where nominally there was no private property. The judges warned the accused, however, to refrain from eating the flesh of dogs or cats in the future, particularly if they happened to be domestic pets. Actually, the Committee knew that its hands were tied in this matter, for some internees were resorting to stalking any stray animals they could see around the camp and eating them.

By Thanksgiving, the conditions in the camp reached a shocking low; the Committee recorded that the Japs, under the sadistic command of the notorious Lt. Konishi, had set out on a deliberate policy of starving the internees. Konishi was reported to have said that the "Americans would eat dirt before we were through." And this prophecy came true during the months that followed, as many internees began to cook slugs, snails, and even worms with their rice, some even flowers and grass. Ron and I had a cactus plant in front of our cubicle, and one day he decided to taste it. He found that it had a fresh, apple-like flavor, even if it did lacerate his stomach. Some internees still had a few cans of food left from the comfort kits, and guarded them jealously, for they would be stolen almost from under their very noses. The diet for the camp now was a cupful of mush in the morning and a handful of rice at night, sometimes mixed with *camote* leaves or pigweed gathered from the "camp garden." Tobacco was another terrible problem in the camp, and everybody's nerves were reduced to the raw; men snapped at their wives and at each other as they took to smoking anything they could gather—papaya leaves, corn silk, and tomato leaves.

To climax this ghastly situation, Japanese soldiers, apparently with the illicit permission of their officers, suddenly began to appear in cubicles at any hour of the day or night with rice or sugar or tobacco, which they offered to trade to the internees for diamond rings, watches, or fountain pens. Groups of them would run through the barracks calling out *"watchee, watchee"* but the most ludicrous part of the whole thing was that they would often refuse to trade for anything less than a Parker pen or an Elgin watch—no other make would do— and for one of these precious objects they would offer a couple of kilos of rice or sugar or a bag of coconuts. Many women traded diamond or engagement rings they had sentimentally saved through the past three years.

The first sign of the end came to us one morning around Thanksgiving: A fleet of American planes, their stars gleaming in the sun, roared through the sky overhead in perfect formation. We were delirious with joy, and many internees shouted and waved frantically at the planes. Immediately afterwards the Japs issued a notice that anyone caught demonstrating in any way in the future at American planes would be punished severely. But we had had our first indication that the Americans were approaching the islands, and in the last desperate months until our final rescue it was actually only those planes roaring over our camp from time to time that kept our spirits alive.

By Christmas, the first signs of beriberi among internees were seen, as many found their faces and legs swelling. The life of the camp came to a standstill, as a sapping apathy born of starvation gripped people, and all activities, except the most essential, like cooking the rice, were suspended. Just at this time, the first batch of babies of the young couples was born when the starvation was most severe. It was heartrending to hear the cries of the babies whose mothers had no milk in their breasts to feed them. They were kept alive only by doses of the carefully rationed Klim issued by the hospital, which had saved these cans for just such an emergency.

About the first week in January, rumors came into camp that Santo Tomas had been liberated. Nobody knew exactly how these rumors had originated, since communication between the two camps had long since stopped, but George Gray said that it had come on very good authority and was probably true. It was not until much later, after the rescue, that we learned that George had been in touch with the guerrillas near Los Banos during these months and was waiting to give them the sign to "rescue" the camp, if and when the proper time came, and as the starvation in the camp became acute he was seriously considering the possibility of such action, until the news came about Santo Tomas and then we all knew it was just a matter of time before we too would be liberated. But how and when, nobody knew, and as the days crawled on, the tenseness became unbearable.

Then, during the first week of February, we were awakened in the middle of the night by shouting and the sound of people's voices in the barrack corridor. Still dazed with sleep, we rushed out of our cubicles to listen to a Committee courier who had come to tell us the astounding news that all the Japs had suddenly vanished at midnight, taking their guards and trucks with them, and that as far as the Committee knew we were free.

Free! The word "free" was the only word we could hear, but scarcely understand. It was so long since we had known its real meaning. In the strange half-darkness of that night we stared at each other uncomprehendingly, and then as we slowly realized the implications of this news, we went wild with joy. People rushed about madly crying: "The Japs are gone—we're free! We're *free!*"

Others celebrated by making roaring fires and internees who had saved any comfort kit cans now opened them to share with their neighbors: What was the use of saving now? In a day or so the Americans would arrive. The young boys of the camp immediately started to raid the barracks and quarters of the Japs and came back with kimonos and slippers and other clothes but the most important loot was a

Philco radio the Japs had left. They also reported that the Japs must have fled in a tremendous hurry, for they had left the remains of their dinner still cooking on the fire.

The Committee announced that the American flag would be raised over the camp that dawn to symbolize the beginning of our freedom. It was a dawn I shall never forget: Somewhere, somehow, an old patched American flag, hidden by some internee all these years and now unearthed, was slowly raised "by the dawn's early light" while we stood solemnly at attention with the tears streaming down our faces. . . . And that afternoon we listened to our first American broadcast from MacArthur's forces at Tacloban on Leyte and learned the actual position of our troops—instead of landing south of Luzon as had been expected, our forces had landed in the north, and now were fighting their way in our direction. It was in the expectation of the Americans approaching our camp in the very near future that the Japs had left us so suddenly. Now it was a question of waiting until they arrived, which would only be a matter of days or a week at most, we thought at that time.

A week. . . . it was a week of feasting and glorious anticipation and release. The Filipinos of the town of Los Banos and the surrounding countryside suddenly appeared at the gate as if by magic, bringing all kinds of food—pigs, chickens, fruits, coconuts, sugar, and cakes and we began to eat as we had never eaten before in three years. Some internees started going over the barbed wire to the surrounding countryside to visit the people living on the Agricultural College grounds, and a few even visited the guerrillas in the hills and decided not to come back but to stay with them. Actually, the Committee warned us against going too far into the hills because of the possibility of Japanese soldiers hiding or making camp there. Ron and I made a trip one afternoon to the house of a University professor living about a kilometer from the camp, and as I crawled through the barbed wire and found myself walking on a country road again, I felt as though I wanted to keep walking forever. At the house of the Filipino, we were welcomed with *lechon* and mangos and when we left to go they filled our arms with a basket of fruit and eggs and chicken and molasses syrup and bananas.

We were free . . .

During that week, and, for one week only, we wined and dined and literally killed the fatted calf as we waited for the Americans to arrive and rescue us "formally." And then in the night, exactly one week later, the Japs returned as mysteriously as they had disappeared. The same courier who had brought us the joyous news that we were free, now warned us to stay away from the barbed wire because the Japs had returned.

It was like a nightmare—utterly incredible and completely unreal. . . . What had happened? Why were the Japs back? And where were the American forces? It was not until weeks later that we actually knew what had happened. Anticipating the arrival of the Americans from the south, which would place them at a strategic point only about thirty or so miles from Los Banos, the Japs had decided to beat a hasty retreat and join their own forces somewhere in the vicinity. But reporting to General Yamashita, then Supreme Commander of the Imperial Japanese forces, for orders, they had been informed that the Americans had landed in the north by surprise and were still over 100 miles distant and would have to fight their way through the Jap lines. Konishi and his henchmen were ordered back to their posts at Los Banos, to stick it out there until further instructions. En route they must have engaged in a few skirmishes with the guerrilla forces, for some of their staff had bandages around their heads and looked badly battered.

It was obvious that they were in an ugly, vengeful mood. They had lost a tremendous amount of face, and the last straw was when they discovered that their barracks and quarters had been looted and their radio taken. We were immediately bombarded with a series of vindictive orders: All belongings must be returned by a certain time or various key people would be shot. Their offices were soon piled high with the returned loot; they even got back a radio, but it was not their Philco—that had been smuggled out to the guerrillas.

But the Japs kept their real vindictiveness and retaliatory measures for anyone attempting to leave the camp. At first they merely beat up any internee they found near the barbed wire; then they issued an ultimatum that anyone so caught would be shot on sight.

But even this did not stop many internees, who, after almost three years of starvation, had tasted food and freedom and now could not accept the ghastly fact that we were prisoners again. . . . And despite all warnings and ultimatums, some internees continued to go over the fence, with the result that the Japs redoubled their guards at various points along the barbed wire. Simultaneously they decided to punish the whole camp for this behavior by cutting our rice rations to one cup a day; but soon they stopped even this and instead distributed only *palay,* the hard shell of the rice which had to be ground by machine or pounded into rice meal as we had seen the mountain people do it. We were now reduced to the alternatives of spending a couple of hours a day pounding the *palay* or starving completely. It was a pitiful sight to see children barely able to lift their arms pounding away at the *palay* with bottles or stones or anything they had. And each day, at the morning and evening roll calls that the Japs subjected us to during this period, there was usually someone missing—another prisoner had escaped into the surrounding hills to join the guerrillas. . . . And so the days crawled on for us in an agony of suspense and starvation, until the morning of February the Twenty-third.

At dawn that day we were miserably huddled over a smudge fire, wondering what we were going to eat—the handful of *palay* the Japs had been issuing had given out. In a few moments we would have to line up for roll call in front of our barrack, and now we waited in silence, waiting for the familiar sound of planes overhead. For a whole week planes had been flying regularly over our camp, and we knew from the sound of the bombs falling and guns booming that a battle was raging somewhere.

The Americans came that dawn. There was something about this huge squadron of heavy black planes that was different from the others we had seen . . . a moment later we knew why as our parachute troops came floating down and we heard the *rat-a-tat* of machine guns and the barking of rifle shots. The guerrillas swarmed down from the surrounding hills and the battle between the Japs and our Filipino friends began. . . . We were in the crossfire of the battle, and some of the more cautious dropped to the floor to escape the flying bullets. But most of us crowded the doorways of our barracks watching the battle we had awaited for three years. Filipino guerrillas hiding behind banana trees or in the dugouts they had secretly built for themselves sprang upon the enemy.

It was over in about half an hour. Someone shouted: "They're here—the American soldiers are here!" Suddenly they were among us—tall, bronzed boys, familiar faces, smiling faces, the ones we knew so well in Brooklyn, in California, in Texas, from anywhere that brought America to us at that moment.

Water buffalo amphibian tanks manned by American soldiers appeared from nowhere, mammoth iron monsters plowing down the road where we stood waiting with our baggage to be taken out. What the paratroops, the planes, and now these amphibian tanks—it all reminded me of *The Shape of Things to Come*.

We climbed aboard the tanks. I shall never forget that journey into freedom. And as I watched the determined faces of our soldiers staring over the machine guns, for the first time in three years I felt a sense of security, a lack of fear—a feeling of being protected, defended by our own forces against any eventuality.

We rode to the water's edge. Jap machine guns blazed from the motionless grove of banana and coconut trees but at the same moment our P-38 planes appeared above us. They circled around and around trying to spot the guns that were spitting bullets at us. For a few anxious moments we crouched low in the tanks. . . . Later we learned that a few American civilians in the tank in front of us had been wounded.

Now it was all clear and we rode without delay across the bay. Once I looked back and saw a huge column of smoke rising where our camp had been. The rest of the trip to our new quarters behind the American lines was a victory parade. All along the road, Filipinos were cheering and waving, delirious with joy. From their nipa huts and the steps of their bamboo stairs, I saw women crying and lifting their children to wave to us. They raised their fingers to make the V sign—V for Victory—theirs as well as ours.

Across the bay on the strip of beachhead behind the Japanese lines where our "ducks" landed, American soldiers were waiting with great boilers of hot coffee and bread and butter . . . the first real bread we had tasted in three years. And to me that Bread was not only a symbol of victory, it was also my escape from the Japs to my own people at last, it was my coming home, my return to America.

American trucks and ambulances were waiting to take us to the base hospital at Muntilupa, about twenty miles inland, where they had temporarily established headquarters on the grounds of the New Bilibid Prison, recently taken from the Japanese. The old and the sick and the mothers with newborn babies were carried into ambulances and brought directly to the hospital; for the rest of us, everything had been arranged with the usual American efficiency and courtesy that was so miraculous to us after our three years of hell under the Japs. In our daze of happiness, it never occurred to us to regard as ironic that after our liberation we should now be housed in another prison, for nothing mattered except that we were with our own people.

Correspondents had already rigged up an office in one of the prison buildings and were sending out stories of our spectacular rescue by the Eleventh Airborne Division. The next morning I began working again with the United Press and one of the first queries I received was about W. H. Donald, the adviser of Chiang Kai-shek, and how he had managed to remain hidden in our internment camp without being suspected by the Japs. The story Donald himself told me was so simple as to seem almost incredible: During the early days of Santo Tomas, the Japanese had actually fine-combed the lists of prisoners to find him, looking for a man called W. Donald, aged thirty-five, whereas Chiang's adviser had been correctly listed as W. H. Donald, aged seventy. As usual, Jap intelligence had been singularly inefficient. The whole episode was even more amazing in the light of the fact that I myself had seen a book in the camp containing a picture of Donald with the Generalissimo and Madame Chiang.

The American executive commandant of our new camp was Lieutenant-Colonel John R. Jordan of Portland, Maine, and the American command could not have given us a more able man for the tremendously difficult and delicate job of nursing back to health over 2,000 physically and mentally sick internees. Possessed of unusual sympathy and understanding of our new psychological problems, Colonel Jordan was always ready and willing to listen and try to help the internees, for which he received innumerable letters of thanks from individuals and a formal vote of appreciation from our Committee. During the months we were kept at this base hospital, we were attacked several times by Jap snipers and suicide squads and Colonel Jordan once risked his life to help wipe out one of these patrols—for which he later received a citation.

It was Colonel Jordan who sent word one afternoon that a Filipino called Fabian San Juan was waiting to see us and our reunion with Fabian was like the happy ending of a fairy tale, the realization of the dream we had had those long months of bitter waiting in the mountains. . . . And even more miraculously, Fabian had brought us that precious leather portfolio with our writings which we had given him the night before we were captured by the Japs—he had kept it buried in his rice kaingin the entire year and a half and had managed to salvage it only just before the retreat by the remnants of the Jap army to those very hills where we had been hiding. Bitter fighting was even now raging in the Mariquina Valley where the Japs were making their last stand, and Fabian said that they had laid waste most of the town of Montalban and stolen the rice and carabaos to take with them into the hills. Nearly all the Filipinos had fled from the area and Fabian and his family had escaped to another town nearer Manila, where the Americans were in complete control. Fabian himself was destitute and jobless and now it was our turn to help him. One afternoon I rode in a jeep to Manila to Malacanan Palace to see my old friend President Osmena and I told him the story of Fabian and how he had saved our lives. Before the day was over, Fabian had been given work as a government employee.

That first sight of Manila in ruins was a traumatic shock to us who remembered only the gay graceful beauty of the pre-war tropical city. Staggering the imagination, it was like a phantasmagoria conjured up by some surrealist or dadaist artist—huge buildings tottering drunkenly, pillars of stone suspended crazily in midair, mountains of crumbling stone. But already the Filipinos were beginning their Herculean heartbreaking task of rebuilding their city. And it was this picture—the picture of a great and gallant people, who had fought and suffered with us against a common enemy, now struggling to bring order out of chaos and desperately needing our help—that I took back with me to America.

. . . Bread and Rice . . . Rice and Bread . . . from the seething chaos of the East from the burning jungle and the barren mountains the ironbarred jails of the Philippines I came home at last to the West to eat Bread again . . . the train sped through the blazing night and the golden day past the snowridged mountains of the West the fertile plains of the prairies the wheatfields bronzeburnished in the sun the farms of milk and fruit the yielding harvest on to the turbulent cities . . . and suddenly in this whirling dynamo of America I felt strangely lost and uprooted and I no longer knew where I belonged . . . to the East or the West . . . the West or the East . . . here in the feverish pulsations of her nervous cities with the towering buildings looming over the labyrinthine streets bursting with people I was bewildered and afraid . . . who were my people? were these hurrying frantic people my people? . . . I longed suddenly for the simple primitive ways of the mountain people the langorous indolent movements of the Malayan the exotic beauty of the Chinese . . . and when I saw a ship bound for the Orient her superstructure arched against the wide night sky something was born in me again and I wanted once more to ride the light waters of the Pacific and awake to white tropical heat and the strange beauty of the Oriental cities . . . to eat Rice again . . . and I knew then that for me there would never be peace never be roots for I had seen life and death in two worlds . . . to which do I now belong . . . the East or the West . . . Bread or Rice?